A MEMOIR

OF

THE REVEREND SYDNEY SMITH.

BY HIS DAUGHTER,

LADY HOLLAND.

WITH

A SELECTION FROM HIS LETTERS,

EDITED BY

MRS. AUSTIN.

IN TWO VOLUMES.
VOLUME I.

1855.

Copyright © 2011 Read Books Ltd.
This book is copyright and may not be
reproduced or copied in any way without
the express permission of the publisher in writing

British Library Cataloguing-in-Publication Data
A catalogue record for this book is available from
the British Library

Sydney Smith

Sydney Smith was born on 3rd June 1771 in Woodford, Essex, England.

Smith was educated at Winchester College, where he greatly distinguished himself, rising to the position of school captain. In fact, he and his brother were so recognised for thier all-round abilities that their school fellows signed a round-robin "refusing to try for the college prizes if the Smiths were allowed to contend for them anymore".

In 1789, upon leaving Winchester College, he became a scholar at New College, Oxford. He received a fellowship from the college and finally obtained his Master of Arts degree in 1796. Smith's intention was to go on to read for the bar, but his father refused and compelled him to join the clergy. He was ordained at Oxford in 1796 and became the curate of the village of Netheravon, near Amesbury in Salisbury Plain. The squire of the parish engaged Smith to tutor his son and the pair went to Edinburgh to study. While his pupil attended lectures, Smith studied moral philosophy, medicine, and chemistry.

Smith's first book 'Six Sermons, preached in Charlotte Street Chapel, Edinburgh' was published in 1800. He married Catharine Amelia Pybus in the same year and the couple settled in Edinburgh. While there, he helped set up the *Edinburgh Review* and became its first editor in 1802. He continued to write articles for the review for the next quarter of the century which were a key element to the publication's success.

Smith left Scotland in 1803 and relocated to London. He became well known as a preacher, lecturer, and society figure, and he often preached to huge crowds in Berkeley Chapel, Mayfair.. He lectured at the Royal Institution on moral philosophy and promoted progressive values such as the education of women and the abolition of slavery. He often destroyed paper copies of his lectures after they had served their purpose but his wife rescued some of the charred manuscripts and published them as 'Elementary Sketches of Moral Philosophy' in 1850.

His most famous work is *Peter Plymley's Letters* (1892) in

which he deals with the subject of Catholic emancipation, ridiculing the opposition of the country clergy.

Smith continued his career in the church, preaching in Yorkshire for twenty years and being appointed to a residentiary canonry at St Paul's Cathedral in 1831.

He is remembered as a fine wit and humourist, and is often quoted in English literary life. Smith died on 22nd February 1845.

THIS MEMOIR OF MY FATHER,

THE PREPARATION FOR WHICH WAS THE CONSTANT

OCCUPATION OF MY MOTHER'S LIFE,

AND THE COMPLETION OF WHICH WAS THE MOST EARNEST

OBJECT OF HER DESIRE,

BOTH IN HER LIFE AND AT HER DEATH,

WHICH NOTHING BUT HER EARNEST DESIRE COULD HAVE

GIVEN ME COURAGE TO ATTEMPT,

I NOW DEDICATE TO HER MEMORY,

BELIEVING IT

TO BE THE MOST GRATEFUL TRIBUTE I CAN OFFER

ON HER GRAVE.

AUTHOR'S PREFACE.

SYDNEY SMITH's Life: he who opens this book under the expectation of reading in it curious adventures, important transactions, or public events, had better close the volume, for none of these things will he find therein.

Nothing can be more thoroughly private and eventless than the narrative I am about to give; yet I feel myself, and I have reason to believe there are many who will feel with me, that this Life is not therefore uninteresting or unimportant: for, though circumstances over which my father had no control forbade his taking that active share in the affairs of his country, for which his talents and his character so eminently fitted him, yet neither circumstances nor power could suppress these talents, or subdue and enfeeble that character; and I believe I may assert, without danger of contradiction, that by them, and the use he has made of them, he has earned for himself a place amongst the great men of his time and country.

Such being the case, however, his talents, and the employment of them, are alone before the world. This is but half the picture, and I believe few who have known so much do not wish to know more.

The mode of life, the heart, the habits, the thoughts and feelings, the conversation, the home, the occupations of such a man,—all, in short, which can give life and reality to the picture,—are as yet wanting; and it is to endeavour to supply this want that I have ventured to undertake this task.

It is always more difficult to write the life of a private than of a public man. There are many things likewise which make that of my father a peculiarly difficult one to delineate; and I should shrink from the task I have undertaken, from the fear of not doing it justice, had not death made such fearful havoc amongst his early contemporaries, and those best fitted to do justice to his memory; and age, business, or health, placed insuperable obstacles in the way of all those abler pens which both my mother and I had once hoped might undertake it.

I therefore, from these causes, and in accordance with my mother's most earnest desire, repeated in her will, that some record of his virtues should be written, venture to give to the public these recollections of my father, which I had previously been collecting for some years solely for myself and my children, together with numerous contributions from various friends.

With these materials, illustrating the selection of his letters, which my friend Mrs. Austin has kindly undertaken to edit, I trust to lay before the public such a record of my father's character, as a son, a clergyman, a father, a husband, and a friend, as may be deemed by them not unworthy of the reputation he has already acquired for talent and honesty by his writings.

If I succeed, I shall have accomplished the object I have most at heart. If I fail, I trust that with many my motive will be some excuse; and that they will attribute it to the inability and inexperience of his advocate, and not to the weakness of the cause.

In giving these annals of my father's life, the object has been, as much as possible, to make him speak for himself, even where (as in some few instances) a portion of them have already appeared before the public; as these extracts serve to weave together the rest of the narrative, and are of course far better than anything I could put in their place.

The points which can alone justify the publication of these recollections and letters are, that they shall neither hurt the living, injure the dead, or impair the reputation of their author. These objects we have endeavoured most strenuously to keep in view. There is little in the whole work that could give pain, even if every particular were understood. Most of the persons alluded to have been long since dead, and the allusions forgotten. Yet, should there be, in either the letters or the narrative, any anecdote accidentally preserved which may meet the eye of those who, from intimacy with him, or from having been present at the scene described, could lift the veil that has been purposely thrown over it, let me here entreat them, if they loved my father in life, and honour his memory in death, never, by their explanations, to make the pen of Sydney Smith do in death what it never did in life,—inflict undeserved pain on any human being.

I must add, with respect to the letters collected from various sources, that it is a remarkable fact, as testifying the estimation in which my father was held by his contemporaries, that there are among them many small notes merely containing some trifling message or an invitation to dinner; things without the slightest merit or value in themselves, yet carefully folded up, dated, and preserved with the greatest care for years by those who had received them from him. This little trait speaks, I think, volumes. From these letters Mrs. Austin has selected those most calculated to interest the reader, or in any way to illustrate my father's feelings and character, without special reference to their talent only.

It will be seen in the narrative, and, in justice to my father, it ought not to be forgotten, that he entered the Church out of consideration for, and in obedience to, the wishes of his father; and like his friend, Dr. Stanley, Bishop of Norwich, with a strong natural bias towards another profession; so that, in his passage through life, he had often to exercise control over himself, and to make a struggle to do that which is comparatively easy to those who have embraced their profession from taste and inclination alone.

But having entered the Church from a sense of duty, I think the narrative will show that he made duty his guide through life;—that he honoured his profession, and was honoured in it by those who had the best opportunities of observing him;—that, ever ready to perform its humblest duties, he gathered (as he says) from the study of the Bible, that the highest duty of a clergyman was to calm religious hatreds, and spread religious peace and toleration;—that in this labour of love he exerted himself from the time of his entering the Church to the hour of his death;—and that he dreaded, as the greatest of all evils, that the "golden chain," which he describes as "reaching from earth to heaven," should be injured either by fanaticism or scepticism. Thus, lending himself to no extremes and no party in the Church, he endeavoured through life to guard religion simple and pure, as we received it from the hand of God, and as it is taught in that Church to which he belonged.

It now only remains for me to express my thanks to those who have aided my task by their contributions, which I should gladly have done by name, had they not been too numerous. But it has been deeply gratifying to my feelings, and has given me courage to proceed, to find that all my father's oldest friends have been eager to assist me in my task, and have all, with very few exceptions, contributed something towards it. I trust they may not think I have misused their gifts, and, for the sake of the father, will receive with indulgence the efforts of his daughter to do fresh honour to his memory by chronicling his virtues.

This slight sketch of my father's life has passed through the ordeal of his private friends, and has been pronounced by them to present a faithful picture of his habits and character. The subject of it is of course so deeply interesting to me, that I can form no estimate of what it may be to others; but I am encouraged by these friends to believe that the life of an honest man honestly told, can never be without some value and interest to every one. In deference therefore to their opinions I now offer this Memoir to the public, with some additions and such corrections as I have been able to make; though I fear there may still remain many errors as to time, inevitable in a narrative written (as this is chiefly) from memory, and with but few data to guide me.

I do not however, I confess, offer this Memoir to the public without some anxiety; not from the fear of any honest opposition to my father's opinions, or censure of the imperfect manner in which I may have performed my task: these are of course open to criticism, and are fair and honourable objects of attack. But I am aware how easily the frank and fearless, because innocent, expressions of my father's conversation may be misunderstood and misrepresented, or the private feelings of my friends wounded, should there be any one ungenerous enough to do so. I will however trust that, as this Memoir has been written with the most earnest desire to tell the truth, but in doing so to avoid giving just cause of pain to the feelings of any one, I shall meet with equal delicacy from the public; and shall find that any angry feelings which the bold, undisguised expression of my father's opinions during life may have formerly excited in the world, have been long since forgotten, or are buried in the grave of him whose loss I (may I not rather say, we all?) lament.

S. H.

London, May, 1855.

CONTENTS.

CHAPTER I.

Birth and Family.—Father.—Profession.—Marriage of Father.—Mother.—Sir Isaac Newton.—School.—Early Peculiarities.—Talleyrand.—College.—Goes to Normandy.—Profession.—Curate in Salisbury Plain.—Marries his Brother.—Becomes Tutor to Mr. Beach.—Goes to Edinburgh . 1

CHAPTER II.

Arrives at Edinburgh.—State of Society.—Manners of Scotch.—Anecdote of Mr. Jeffrey.—Acquaintance with Mr. Horner.—Marriage.—Early difficulties and poverty.—Generosity.—Birth of Daughter.—Introduces Mr. Allen to Lord Holland.—Originates Review.—State of Society.—State of Church.—Character of his writings in youth.—Sketch of opinions at the time.—Letter by Lord Monteagle.—Short sketch of Articles in Review 13

CHAPTER III.

Extracts from Lectures.—Preface to Sermons.—Analysis of Sermons.—Sermon for the Blind.—Returns to Edinburgh.—Takes Pupils.—Illness of Daughter.—Moral courage.—Studies Medicine and Moral Philosophy 38

CHAPTER IV.

Quits Edinburgh for London.—Settles in Doughty-street.—Makes legal and other friends.—Obtains Preachership of Foundling Hospital.—Refusal of Dr. —— to enable him to lease a Chapel.—Sermon to Volunteers.—Friendship with Lord Holland.—Introduction to Holland House.—Holland House, and Society there.—Obtains Preachership of St. John's Chapel, Bedford-square.—Gives Lectures at Royal Institution.—Descriptions of their effect.—Poverty.—Society at his House, and Suppers.—Anecdote of Sir J. Mackintosh and cousin.—Elected to the Johnson Literary Club.—The King reads his Review, and says he will never be a Bishop.—Preaches on Toleration at the Temple Church.—Increase of reputation and friends.—Natural Spirits; their effects.—Some anecdotes 64

CHAPTER V.

1806. Political changes.—Obtains preferment.—1807. Goes to Sunning in the Autumn.—Writes Peter Plymley.—Its effect.—Makes the acquaintance of Lord Stowell.—Revisits Edinburgh.—Goes to Howick.—No house on Living.—Non-residence permitted.—Residence Bill passed.—Goes down to see Living.—Difficulties.—Returns to London.—Publishes Sermons.—Removes Family to Yorkshire.—Tries to negotiate exchange of Living.—Difficulties of exchange.—Necessity of building.—Settles at Heslington . 99

CHAPTER VI.

Establishment in Yorkshire.—Habits; mode of life.—Reading.—Attention to children.—Power of abstracting thoughts.—Farmers' dinner.—Medical anecdotes.—Experiments.—Extracts from Diary.—Practical Essays.—Metaphysical Essays.—Hints for History.—Mr. Macaulay's letter.—Sir S. Romilly's visit.—Sermon on his death.—Anecdote of roasted Quaker.—Dining out in the country.—Brother and Sir J. Mackintosh's return from India.—Madame de Staël's visit to England.—Typhus fever.—Verses on Mr. Jeffrey . 110

CHAPTER VII.

Builds house.—Removes to Foston.—Description of establishment.—Visit of Sir James Mackintosh.—Becomes a Magistrate.—Visit to Newgate with Mrs. Fry, and Sermon.—Visit to Sir G. Philips in Immortal.—Forms the acquaintance of the Earl of Carlisle.—Death of only Sister.—Last Visit from Mr. Horner.—Bad harvest and fever.—Exertions amongst the poor.—Visit from Lord and Lady Holland.—Leaves off riding.—Description of Calamity.—Shopping and anecdotes.—Sends Son to school.—Visits Lord Grey.— Account of Travels. — Visit from Dr. Marcet.—Conversation, and Bunch.—Anecdote of Lord ——'s Son.—Assizes.—Hunt's Trial.—Danger of bad harvest.—Death of Grattan 156

CHAPTER VIII.

Legacy.—Visit to Edinburgh.—Visits London: popularity there.—Letters to home, and care of parish.—Takes Son to Charterhouse.—Visits Mr. Rogers.—Appointed Chaplain to High Sheriff.—Preaches in Cathedral.—Anecdote at Spencer House.—Meeting of Clergy, East Riding.—His Petition.—Speech.—Living of Londesborough.—Goes to Paris.—Letter on receiving irreligious book.—Death of Father.—Description of house by friend.—Love of chess and singing.—Marriage of youngest Daughter.—Becomes Canon of Bristol.—Effect produced at Bristol.—History of Apologue, by Mr. Everett 191

CHAPTER IX.

Happiness increased by his promotion.—Death of eldest Son.—Removal to Combe Florey.—Rebuilding of house.—Lord Jeffrey's last visit.—Increased popularity at Bristol.—Collects contributions to Review.—French Revolution.—Riots at Bristol.— Speech on Reform.— Letters on Preferment.—Appointed Canon of St. Paul's.—Death of Sir James Mackintosh in 1832.—Marriage of eldest Daughter in 1834.—Village anecdotes.—Christens Grandchild.—Buys house in Charles-street.—Rectitude of Stewardship at St. Paul's.—Tour to Holland in 1837.—Talleyrand.—Conversation in

London, and anecdotes.—Begins Controversy about Church.
—Petitions to House of Lords.—Inscription for Statue of
Lord Grey 223

CHAPTER X.

Visit to Combe Florey.—Kindness to Grandchildren.—Sudden
wealth.—Recollections of his Parishioners at Foston.—
Death of Lord Holland.—His Portrait.—Letter to Mr.
Webster.—Sketch of 'Revue des Deux Mondes.'—Letter
of Mr. Grenville.—Visit from Mr. Moore, and Verses.—
Bestows the Living of Edmonton on Mr. Tate's son.—Letter to Mrs. Sydney Smith.—Address of Parishioners, and
Answer.—Letter of Mrs. Marcet.—Receipt for making
every day happy.—Definition of happiness.—Petition to
the American Congress in 1843.—Effects.—Speech from
Mr. Ticknor.—Letter from Mr. Wainwright.—Abuse and
gifts from America.—Effect of preaching in old-age.—Letter of Miss Edgeworth.—Correspondence with Sir R. Peel.
—Extract from Journal, with anecdotes 279

CHAPTER XI.

Pamphlet on Ballot.—Fragment on Irish Church.—Letter from
Lord Murray.—Lines written on receiving garden-chair.—
Lines by Lady Carlisle.—Christens child.—Sketch of life
and conversation at Combe Florey.—Advice to Parishioners.
—Conversation.—Medicines for the poor.—Saves servant's
life.—Fallacies.—Studies.—Recipe for salad.—Letter of
Marion de Lorme.—Imitation of Sir James Mackintosh.—
Close of the day. 322

CHAPTER XII.

Extract from Lady ——'s Journal.—Last Illness.—Comes to
town.—Dr. Chambers called in.—Anxiety of friends for
his recovery.—Meeting of Brothers.—Living to poor clergyman.—Death of Sydney Smith.—Death of his eldest
Brother.—Lord Jeffrey's Letters.—Hints on Female Education 392

MEMOIR

OF

THE REV. SYDNEY SMITH.

CHAPTER I.

BIRTH AND FAMILY.—FATHER.—PROFESSION.—MARRIAGE OF FATHER.—MOTHER.—SIR ISAAC NEWTON.—SCHOOL.—EARLY PECULIARITIES.—TALLEYRAND.—COLLEGE.—GOES TO NORMANDY.—PROFESSION.—CURATE ON SALISBURY PLAIN.—MARRIES HIS BROTHER.—BECOMES TUTOR TO MR. BEACH.—GOES TO EDINBURGH.

My father, the Rev. Sydney Smith, was born at Woodford, in Essex, 1771, the second of four brothers and one sister, all remarkable for their talents; the two eldest eminently so. To these talents, as well as to his great animal spirits, he had an hereditary right; for my grandfather, Mr. Robert Smith, was a man of singular natural gifts; very clever, odd by nature, but still more odd by design, loving to astonish, and, fully aware that knowledge is power, he employed the activity of a very sagacious mind, through a long and varied life, in acquiring a minute acquaintance with the history of all he came in contact with. On becoming early his own master, by the death of his father, and possessed of some money, he employed all the early part of life (having first married a very beautiful girl, from whom he parted at the church-door, leaving her with her mother, Mrs. Olier, till his return from America) partly in wandering over the world for many years, and partly in diminishing his fortune by buying, altering, spoiling, and then selling about nineteen different places in England, till, in his old-age, he at last settled at Bishop's Lydiard, in Somersetshire, where he died.

My grandfather was a very handsome and picturesque old man when I knew him, his hair long, thin, and perfectly white. To add to the effect of his appearance and manner, he used to affect the drab-coloured dress of a Quaker, with a large flap hat, rather like those of our coal-heavers; this hat was so extraordinary in form, and had seen so many years' service, that when at last he offered its remains to his old factotum Charles, who was digging in his garden, the man, after twisting and twirling it round and round for some time, and examining its proportions, returned it to him with a broad grin, saying, "No, thank your honour, it's no use to I." I remember him sitting in his arm-chair basking in the sun, leaning forward on his crutch-stick, a fine study for Rembrandt, and telling this story of his favourite hat till the tears ran down his cheeks with laughter.

But though the sons inherited talent from their father, yet all the finer qualities of their mind they derived from their mother, Miss Olier, the youngest daughter of a French emigrant, from Languedoc, who was driven over to England for his religious principles at the Revocation of the Edict of Nantes, and was reduced to great poverty in consequence; but his eldest daughter, a woman of much sense and energy of character, established a school for young ladies in Bloomsbury-square, which acquired considerable celebrity under her direction, and thus enabled her to contribute to the support of her family. My father used to attribute a little of his constitutional gaiety to this infusion of French blood. His maternal grandfather, Mr. Olier, could not speak a word of English. He married a Miss Barton, who was a collateral descendant of Sir Isaac Newton's, through his mother's second marriage,—a very distinguished ancestor to possess, and one not to be lightly passed over.*

My grandmother, Mr. Olier's youngest daughter, had (I have been told, for I never saw her) a noble countenance, which two of her sons inherited, and as noble a mind. To her early care of them, and to the respect with which her virtues and high tone of feeling inspired their young hearts, may be ascribed much that was good and great in their characters. The charm of her mind and manner extended even to her correspondence. I heard a singular proof of

* At the moment of going to press, I learn from Sir David Brewster (now engaged on a Life of Sir Isaac Newton) that there is an error in the pedigree inserted in my first edition. In deference to his superior knowledge I therefore omit it; but I feel sure he will excuse me for still retaining a tradition so long preserved in our family, till I have had more time than I can command at present to investigate the subject.

this the other day, from a schoolfellow of my father's, who said that when he or his younger brother Courtenay received one of her letters at Winchester, the schoolboys would often gather round and beg to hear it read aloud. Her influence, however, did not remain to them very long in after-life. Delicate; with a husband who, though delightful from the charm of his manner to the world, was not very well suited to domestic life, from his wandering habits; and with the natural anxiety of a mother about four such sons, often left for long periods entirely to her care and guidance, she fell into ill-health while still young and beautiful, and, to the deep regret of all who knew her, died about two years after the marriage of my father.

This reminds me of an anecdote of Talleyrand, who, when living as an emigrant in this country, was on very intimate terms with her eldest son, Robert, more generally known by the name given him by his schoolfellows at Eton, of Bobus. The conversation turned on the beauty often transmitted from parents to their children. My uncle, who was singularly handsome (indeed I think I have seldom seen a finer specimen of manly beauty, or a countenance more expressive of the high moral qualities he possessed), perhaps with a little youthful vanity, spoke of the great beauty of his mother, on which Talleyrand, with a shrug and a sly disparaging look at his fine face, as if he saw nothing to admire, exclaimed, "Ah! mon ami, c'était donc apparemment monsieur votre père qui n'était pas bien."

The peculiarities and talents of the young Smiths were very early evinced; their mother describes them as neglecting games, seizing every hour of leisure for study, and often lying on the floor, stretched over their books, discussing with loud voice and most vehement gesticulation, every point that arose,—often subjects above their years, and arguing upon them with a warmth and fierceness as if life and death hung upon the issue;—a most interesting and curious spectacle, to a mother justly proud of her boys, and rejoicing in these signs of their future distinction.

They were like young athletes, constantly trying their intellectual strength against each other; "and the result," I have heard my father say, "was to make us the most intolerable and overbearing set of boys that can well be imagined, till later in life we found our level in the world."

As his sons were so nearly of an age, Mr. Smith deemed it advisable to separate them at school as much as possible, that there might not be too strong rivalry between them. Robert, the eldest, with Cecil, the third son, were therefore sent to Eton, where Robert distinguished himself greatly, and was one of the four boys (he was then only eighteen) who wrote the 'Microcosm;' Mr. Canning, Mr. Frere, and Mr. John Smith, being the other three.

From Eton he went to King's College, Cambridge, where (says a sketch of him written, I believe, by his friend Lord Carlisle, after his death,) "he added materially to the reputation for scholarship and classical composition which he had established at school; and if the most fastidious critics of our day would diligently peruse the three triposes which he composed in Lucretian rhythm, on the three systems of Plato, Descartes, and Newton, we believe that we should not run the least risk of incurring the charge of exaggeration, in declaring that these compositions in Latin verse have not been excelled since Latin was a living language. Be this said with the peace of Milton and Cowley, with the peace of his fellow-Etonians, Grey and Lord Wellesley."

My father was sent as early as six years of age to a school at Southampton, (kept by the Rev. Mr. Marsh, a scholar of some celebrity,) which he always spoke of with pleasure. Whilst there he received much kindness from the family of the present Lady Mildmay, whose friendship he retained from that time, and who still survives her old friend. From thence he was sent, with his youngest brother, Courtenay, to the foundation at Winchester;—a rough apprenticeship to the world for one so young, from which Courtenay ran away twice, unable to bear it. My father suffered here many years of misery and positive starvation; there never was enough provided, even of the coarsest food, for the whole school, and the little boys were of course left to fare as they could. Even in old-age he used to shudder at the recollections of Winchester, and I have heard him speak with horror of the misery of the years he spent there: the whole system was then, my father used to say, one of abuse, neglect, and vice. It has since, I believe, partaken of the general improvement of education. However, in spite of hunger and neglect, he rose in due time to be Captain of the school, and, whilst there, received, together with his brother Courtenay, a most flattering but involuntary compliment from his schoolfellows, who signed a round-robin,* " refusing to try for the College prizes if the Smiths were allowed to contend for them any more, as they always gained them." He used to say, " I believe, whilst a boy at school, I made above ten thousand Latin verses, and no man in his senses would dream in after-life of ever making another. So much for life and time wasted."

At school he was not only leader in learning, but in mischief, and was discovered inventing a catapult by lamp-light, and commended for his ingenuity by the master, who little dreamt it was intended to capture a neighbouring turkey, whose well-filled crop had long attracted the attention, and awakened the desires, of the hungry urchins. He was fond of telling an incident which happened to him when either at Winchester or Oxford, I am not sure which. A friend who was making a tour, wrote in great distress, asking him to lend him five guineas; he had but four, which he was conveying himself to the post, much lamenting he had not the sum wanted; when he suddenly saw shining on the high-road before him another guinea, and no owner being to be found to claim it, he with joy enclosed it in another cover to his friend.

* To Dr. Warton, then Head Master or Warden of Winchester.

I have heard my father speak of one of the first things that stimulated him in acquiring knowledge. A man of considerable eminence, whose name I cannot recall, found my father reading Virgil under a tree, when all his schoolfellows were at play. He took the book out of his hand, looked at it, patted the boy's head, gave him a shilling, and said, "Clever boy! clever boy! that is the way to conquer the world." This produced a strong impression on the young Sydney. Whilst at Winchester he had been one year Præpositor of the College, and another, Præpositor of the Hall. He left Winchester, as Captain, for New College, Oxford, where, as such, he was entitled to a Scholarship, and afterwards to a Fellowship. New College was chiefly then renowned for the quantity of port-wine consumed by the Fellows, but the very slender income allowed him by his father, perhaps luckily for his health, did not permit him to indulge in such habits. As my father was too proud to accept what he could not return, he lived much out of society, and thus lost one of the advantages of College to a poor man—that of making private friends.

Soon after quitting Winchester, and before he became a Fellow of New College, his father sent him to Mont Villiers, in Normandy, where he remained *en pension* for six months, to perfect his knowledge of French, which he always after spoke with great fluency. The fierceness of the French Revolution was then at its height, and for his safety it was thought necessary that he should enrol himself in one of the

Jacobin Clubs of the town, in which he was entered as " Le Citoyen Smit, Membre Affilié au Club des Jacobins de Mont Villiers." The only revolutionary peril he encountered, however, was in attending his two friends, Captain Drinkwater and his brother, to Cherbourg. These gentlemen, who were excellent draughtsmen, began sketching the works, in spite of my father's remonstrances, who said, " We shall all be infallibly hung on the next lantern-post, if you are seen;" and in truth, in a few minutes they had a gendarme upon them; and it required all my father's skill, address, and knowledge of the language, with a few good-humoured jokes, and boasts of his own citizenship, to extricate himself and his friends out of his hands. When clear off—" And now, my friends, no more sketching, if you please," said he.

I know little of his career at College, save that he obtained his Fellowship as soon as it was possible, and from that moment was cast upon his own resources by his father, who never afterwards gave him a farthing till his death. Yet with this small income, about £100 per annum, he not only preserved that honesty, so often disregarded by young men, of keeping out of debt; but undertook to pay a sum of £30 for a debt incurred when at Winchester School by his younger brother Courtenay, who had not had courage to confess it to his father before his departure for India. Courtenay became Supreme Judge of the Adawlut Court, subsequently made a very large fortune, acquired great reputation as a Judge and Oriental scholar, returned to this country in his old-age, and died suddenly a few years afterwards.

On leaving College it became necessary that my father should select a profession. His own inclinations would have led him to the Bar, in which profession he felt that his talents promised him success and distinction, and where a career was open to him that might gratify his ambition. But his father, who had been at considerable expense in bringing up his eldest brother Robert to that profession, and fitting out the other two for India, after giving up a project he once had of sending Sydney as supercargo to China, urged so strongly his going into the Church, that my father, after considering the subject deeply, felt it his duty to yield to my grandfather's wishes, and sacrifice his own, by entering the Church, and became a curate in a small village in the midst of Salisbury Plain. One of the first professional duties he was called upon to perform was to marry his eldest brother Robert to Miss Vernon, aunt to the present Lord Lansdowne. In a letter to his mother on the occasion he says, "The marriage took place in the library at Bowood, and all I can tell you of it is, that he cried, she cried, and I cried;" the only tears, I believe, this marriage ever produced, save those we shed on her grave.

Sydney Smith, a curate in the midst of Salisbury Plain! To those who knew him, and his cast of character, the mere statement of the fact will be enough to paint his feelings; but to those who knew him not, it would be difficult to express the famine of the mind that came over him when planted in that great waste of Nature. He has himself painted a curate as "the poor working-man of God—a learned man in a hovel, good and patient—a comforter and a teacher—the first and purest pauper of the hamlet; yet showing that, in the midst of worldly misery, he has the heart of a gentleman, the spirit of a Christian, and the kindness of a pastor."

This picture can hardly be heightened, as descriptive of a curate in the abstract; but here was a curate formed, by his wit and powers of conversation, for the society of his fellow-creatures, doomed to the most unbroken solitude; and, pauper as he was, with scarcely a hamlet to interest him, for the village consisted but of a few scattered cottages and farms, in the midst of Salisbury Plain. Once a week a butcher's cart came over from Salisbury; it was then only he could obtain any meat, and he often dined, he said, on a mess of potatoes, sprinkled with a little ketchup. Too poor to command books, his only resource was the Squire, during the few months he resided there; and his only relaxation, not being able to keep a horse, long walks over those interminable plains.

In one of these walks he narrowly escaped with his life, being overtaken in the midst of the Plain, far from any habitation, by a violent snow-storm; and, having lost all means of tracing his way, there being no trees or vestige of human habitation for miles round, it was by mere chance that he arrived, late at night, and fearfully exhausted, at his own home.

The Squire, after the good old orthodox fashion of squires, asked his curate to dinner on Sunday, and, to his surprise, found the tedium of a Sunday evening in the country so much beguiled by the society of his young friend, that the invitations became more and more frequent. This acquaintance soon ripened into friendship, and ended by the Squire requesting my father to resign the curacy at the termination of the two years, and accompany his eldest son abroad. Here my father best paints what happened.

"When first I went into the Church, I had a curacy in the middle of Salisbury Plain; the parish was Netherhaven, near Amesbury. The Squire of the parish, Mr. Beach, took a fancy to me, and after I had served it two years, he engaged me as tutor to his eldest son, and it was arranged that I and his son should proceed to the University of Weimar, in Saxony. We set out; but before reaching our destination, Germany was disturbed by war, and, in stress of politics, we put into Edinburgh, where I remained five years. The principles of the French Revolution were then fully afloat, and it is impossible to conceive a more violent and agitated state of society."

CHAPTER II.

ARRIVES AT EDINBURGH.—STATE OF SOCIETY.—MANNERS OF SCOTCH.
—ANECDOTE OF MR. JEFFREY.—ACQUAINTANCE WITH MR. HORNER.
—MARRIAGE.—EARLY DIFFICULTIES AND POVERTY.—GENEROSITY.
—BIRTH OF DAUGHTER.—INTRODUCES MR. ALLEN TO LORD HOLLAND.—ORIGINATES REVIEW.—STATE OF SOCIETY.—STATE OF CHURCH.—CHARACTER OF HIS WRITINGS IN YOUTH.—SKETCH OF OPINIONS AT THE TIME.—LETTER BY LORD MONTEAGLE.—SHORT SKETCH OF ARTICLES IN REVIEW.

In the year 1797, the period, I believe, at which my father arrived in Edinburgh with his pupil, Mr. Beach, that city was rich in talent, full of men who have acted important parts whilst they lived, and many of whom have left names that will live after them:—Jeffrey, Horner, Playfair, Walter Scott, Dugald Stewart, Brougham, Allen, Brown, Murray, Leyden, Lord Webb Seymour, Lord Woodhouselee,* Alison, Sir James Hall, and many others.

Society at that time in Edinburgh was upon the most easy and agreeable footing; the Scotch were neither rich nor ashamed of being poor, and there was not that struggle for display which so much diminishes the charm of London society, and has, with the increase of wealth, now crept into that of Edinburgh.

* Father of the historian Mr. Peter Tytler.

Few days passed without the meeting of some of these friends, either in each other's houses, or (in what was then very common) oyster-cellars, where, I am told, the most delightful little suppers used to be given, in which every subject was discussed, with a freedom impossible in larger societies, and with a candour which is only found where men fight for truth and not for victory.

Into this soil, then, so congenial to his mind and tastes, my father was transplanted; and, though a perfect stranger, the kindness with which he was received is best shown by the strong attachment he ever retained for his Scotch friends, though far removed from them in after life, and by the pleasure with which he always looked back to this period, which he often refers to in his letters. In one of them he exclaims, "When shall I see Scotland again? Never shall I forget the happy days passed there, amidst odious smells, barbarous sounds, bad suppers, excellent hearts, and most enlightened and cultivated understandings!" I believe he kept up, with hardly any exception, the friendships then formed, and I heard an incident yesterday which, trifle as it was, showed such affection for my father's memory that it quite touched me. One evening my father was at his old friend Lord Woodhouselee's country-house, near Edinburgh, when a violent storm of wind arose, and shook the windows so as to annoy everybody present and prevent conversation. "Why do you not stop them?" said my father; "give me a knife, a screw, and a bit of wood, and I will cure it in a moment;" he soon effected his purpose, fixed up his little bit of wood, and it was christened *Sydney's button.* Fifty years after, one of the family finding Mr. Tytler papering and painting this room, exclaimed, " Oh ! James, you are surely not touching Sydney's button?" but on running to examine the old place at the window, she found Sydney's button was there, preserved and respected amidst all the changes of masters, time, and taste.

Though truly loving them, his quick sense of the ludicrous made him derive great amusement from the little foibles and peculiarities of the Scotch; and often has he made them laugh by his descriptions of things which struck his English eye. " It requires," he used to say, " a surgical operation to get a joke well into a Scotch understanding. Their only idea of wit, or rather that inferior variety of this electric talent which prevails occasionally in the North, and which, under the name of WUT, is so infinitely distressing to people of good taste, is laughing immoderately at stated intervals. They are so imbued with metaphysics that they even make love metaphysically; I overheard a young lady of my acquaintance, at a dance in Edinburgh, exclaim, in a sudden pause of the music, ' What you say, my Lord, is very true of love in the *aibstract,* but—' here the fiddlers began fiddling furiously, and the rest was lost. No nation has so large a stock of benevolence of heart: if you meet with an accident, half Edinburgh immediately flocks to your door to inquire after your *pure* hand or your *pure* foot, and with a degree of interest that convinces you their whole hearts are in the inquiry. You find they usually arrange their dishes at dinner by the points of the compass; 'Sandy, put the gigot of mutton to the south, and move the singet sheep's head a wee bit to the nor-wast.' If you knock at the door, you hear a shrill female voice from the fifth flat shriek out, 'Wha's chapping at the door?' which is presently opened by a lassie with short petticoats, bare legs, and thick ankles. My Scotch servants bargained they were not to have salmon more than three times a week, and always pulled off their stockings, in spite of my repeated objurgations, the moment my back was turned." "Their temper stands anything but an attack on their climate; even the enlightened mind of Jeffrey cannot shake off the illusion that myrtles flourish at Craig Crook. In vain I have represented to him that they are of the genus *Carduus*, and pointed out their prickly peculiarities. In vain I have reminded him that I have seen hackney-coaches drawn by four horses in the winter, on account of the snow; that I had rescued a man blown flat against my door by the violence of the winds, and black in the face; that even the experienced Scotch fowls did not venture to cross the streets, but sidled along, tails aloft, without venturing to encounter the gale. Jeffrey sticks to his myrtle illusions, and treats my attacks with as much contempt as if I had been a wild visionary, who had never breathed his caller air, nor lived and suffered under the rigour of his climate, nor spent five years in discussing metaphysics and medicine in that garret of the earth—that knuckle-end of England—that land of Calvin, oat-cakes, and sulphur."

The reigning bore at this time in Edinburgh was ——; his favourite subject, the North Pole. It mattered not how far south you began, you found yourself transported to the north pole before you could take breath; no one escaped him. My father declared he should invent a slip button. Jeffrey fled from him as from the plague, when possible; but one day his arch-tormentor met him in a narrow lane, and began instantly on the north pole. Jeffrey, in despair and out of all patience, darted past him, exclaiming, "D— the north pole!"* My father met him shortly after, boiling with indignation at Jeffrey's contempt of the north pole. "Oh, my dear fellow," said my father, "never mind; no one minds what Jeffrey says, you know; he is a privileged person; he respects nothing, absolutely nothing. Why, you will scarcely believe it, but it is not more than a week ago that I heard him speak disrespectfully of the equator!"

My father tells of his first acquaintance with Horner, who was at that time among the most conspicuous young men in "that energetic and unfragrant city." "My desire to know him proceeded first of all from being cautioned against him by some excellent and

---

* I see this anecdote in Mr. Moore's Memoirs attributed to Leslie, but I have so often heard it told as applying to a very different person, that I think he was mistaken.

feeble people to whom I brought letters of introduction, and who represented him as a person of violent political opinions. I interpreted this to mean a person who thought for himself, who had firmness enough to take his own line in life, and who loved truth better than he loved Dundas, at that time the tyrant of Scotland. I found my interpretation just, and from then till the period of his death we lived in constant society and friendship with each other." In speaking of him after his death, in a letter to his brother, he says, "Horner loved truth so much that he never could bear any jesting upon important subjects. I remember one evening the late Lord Dudley and myself pretended to justify the conduct of the Government in stealing the Danish fleet. We carried on the argument with some wickedness against our graver friend; he could not stand it, but bolted indignantly out of the room. We flung up the sash, and, with a loud peal of laughter, professed ourselves decided Scandinavians; we offered him not only the ships, but all the shot, powder, cordage, and even the biscuit, if he would come back; but nothing could turn him; he went home, and it took us a fortnight of serious behaviour before we were forgiven." I wish his pen had left us any account of the other distinguished men whose friendship he obtained in Edinburgh; but it has left but one other, and that, I believe, was written at a later period of life.

After two years' residence in Edinburgh he returned to England, to marry Miss Pybus, to whom he had long been engaged, and whom he had known from a very early period of his life, as she was the intimate friend and schoolfellow of his only sister, Maria. This marriage took place with the entire consent of her mother, Mrs. Pybus; but with so vehement an opposition on the part of her brother, Mr. Charles Pybus, (who was a strong politician, and one of the Lords of the Admiralty under Mr. Pitt,) as produced a complete breach between them, and deprived them of the assistance and protection he might have given them on their entrance into life.

Thus deprived of the only relation capable of affording her protection and assistance, it was lucky that Miss Pybus had some fortune, for my father's only contribution towards their future *ménage* (save his own talents and character) were six small silver teaspoons, which, from much wear, had become the ghosts of their former selves. One day, in the madness of his joy, he came running into the room and flung these into her lap, saying, "There, Kate, you lucky girl, I give you all my fortune!"

Upon this small portion (which my father's first step was to secure in the strictest manner to his wife and children, though Mrs. Pybus, who had perfect confidence in him, had thought it would have been better to leave a portion of it unsettled in case of need,) and the six silver spoons, they determined to return to Edinburgh and set up housekeeping.

"One of our early difficulties," said my mother, "was, how we should buy the necessary plate and linen for our new household; but my dear mother's liberality had furnished me with the means, by bestowing on me, when I entered the world, my sister, Lady Fletcher's, necklace, consisting of a double row of pearls, which were said to be the finest, except Mrs. Hastings', that had been brought to this country. I took them to ———, and sold them for £500, and all we most wanted was thus obtained. Several years after, when visiting the shop with Miss Fox and Miss Vernon, I saw in one of the glass cases my own necklace, every pearl of which I knew, and had often strung. I had the curiosity to ask the price; 'Fifteen hundred pounds,' was the answer."

Mr. Beach presented my father, soon after, with a thousand pounds for his care of his eldest son, which he put into the Stocks, and in which consisted his whole worldly wealth. And here I must introduce a little trait, which, though trifling in itself, yet, considering his circumstances, deserves to be mentioned.

He had made the acquaintance, during his residence in Edinburgh, of a family consisting of a lady (one of the most beautiful specimens of old-age I have ever met) and four daughters, who seemed to live for no other object than this mother. He accidentally discovered that this interesting old lady was suddenly involved in pecuniary difficulties. Regretting how little he had to offer, he entreated she would not refuse the loan of a hundred pounds out of his little store; it was accepted with the same kind feeling with which it was offered. I never heard the circumstance till after his death, and I only mention it now because she who received it is no more, and those few who survive her would, I know, gladly contribute anything that would honour the memory of their old friend. What added to the generosity of this little offering was, that he was then about to become a father, and had but little prospect of increasing his means.

Another instance of his generosity at that time was in behalf of Mr. Leyden, who, born a poor shepherd-boy in Teviotdale, had become so remarkable by his learning, that an effort was made by subscription to enable him to attend the College classes in Edinburgh, where he made the most astonishing progress in almost every branch of knowledge taught there. Having obtained, through Mr. Dundas, an appointment to India, he was quite unable to accomplish his outfit. Sir Walter Scott and my father, and a few others, were chiefly instrumental in effecting it, the latter contributing £40 out of his very small means. Mr. Leyden afterwards died in India.

About this period Lord Holland, with whom my father had been slightly acquainted, wrote to ask if he could recommend any clever young medical man to accompany him to Spain, where he was going. My father had the pleasure of recommending his friend Mr. Allen, whose high character and talents were so valued at Holland House, that he never after left it, but remained there even after Lord Holland's death, and died loved, honoured, and respected by the whole of Lord Holland's family.

As the time approached for the birth of his child, he constantly expressed his wish, first, that it might be a daughter, and secondly, that she might be born with one eye, that he might never lose her. The daughter came in due time, according to his wish, but, unfortunately, with two eyes; however, in spite of this unpropitious circumstance, she was very graciously received, and the nurse, to her horror, during five minutes' absence, found he had stolen her from the nursery a few hours after she was born, to introduce her in triumph to Jeffrey and the future Edinburgh Reviewers.

Being now in possession of a daughter with two eyes, it became necessary to give her a name; and nobody would believe the meditations, the consultations, and the discussions he held on this important point. At last he determined to invent one, and Saba was the result.

About the period in which he was engaged in settling this important domestic point, he was likewise employed in arranging with Messrs. Jeffrey, Brougham, Murray, and his other friends, the preliminaries of that periodical which, under the name of the 'Edinburgh Review,' has grown into such importance, has produced such useful results, and has bestowed on its chief contributors a European reputation.

He must state its origin and results:—" Towards the end of my residence in Edinburgh, Brougham, Jeffrey, and myself happened to meet in the eighth or ninth story or flat in Buccleugh Place, the then elevated residence of Mr. Jeffrey. I proposed that we should set up a Review; this was acceded to with acclamation; I was appointed editor, and remained long enough in Edinburgh to edit the first number of the Review. The motto I proposed for the Review was, 'Tenui Musam meditamur avenâ'—'We cultivate literature on a little oatmeal;' but this was too near the truth to be admitted, so we took our present grave motto from Publius Syrus, of whom none of us had, I am sure, read a single line; and so began what has since turned out to be a very important and able journal. When I left Edinburgh it fell into the stronger hands of Lords Jeffrey and Brougham, and reached the highest point of popularity and success."*

"To appreciate the value of the Edinburgh Review, the state of England at the period when that journal began should be had in remembrance. The Catholics were not emancipated. The Corporation and Test Acts were unrepealed. The Game-laws were horribly oppressive; steel-traps and spring-guns were set all over the country; prisoners tried for their lives could have no counsel. Lord Eldon and the Court of

---

* A distinguished periodical, speaking of the Edinburgh Review, says:—"The world will long look to this as to the opening of an important era in English literary history, for then, so to say, was founded an empire of criticism, wider in its objects, more vigorous in its provisions, more perfect in its administrative machinery, than any of the dynasty which had flourished in the eighteenth century. The cause of tolerance without licentiousness, and philanthropy without cant, was substantially aided by its exertions and the attention they commanded. If the good done thereby should be apportioned out, a large share would fall to the Rev. Sydney Smith."

Chancery pressed heavily on mankind. Libel was punished by the most cruel and vindictive imprisonments. The principles of political economy were little understood.* The laws of debt and conspiracy were upon the worst footing. The enormous wickedness of the slave-trade was tolerated. A thousand evils were in existence, which the talents of good and able men have since lessened or removed; and these efforts have been not a little assisted by the honest boldness of the Edinburgh Review."

To estimate justly my father's moral courage in projecting and contributing to such a Review, not only the personal risk to which those who expressed liberal opinions were exposed (of which nothing gives a more vivid impression than the third volume of Mr. Fox's letters, just published), should be taken into consideration, but his profession, and the corrupt state of that profession at this period. As this is a subject of which I am quite incompetent to speak, I shall quote a short passage from a remarkable article on Church Parties in the Edinburgh Review, which gives a very striking description of it. "The thermometer of the Church of England sank to its lowest point in the first thirty years of George III. Unbelieving bishops, and a slothful clergy, had succeeded in driving from the Church the faith and zeal of Methodism which Wesley had

* "In a scarcity which occurred little more than twenty years ago, every judge (except the Chancellor and Sergeant Runnington), when they charged the Grand Jury, attributed the scarcity to the combinations of the farmers. Such doctrines would not now be tolerated in the mouth of a school-boy."

organized within her pale. The spirit was expelled, and the dregs remained. That was the age when jobbery and corruption, long supreme in the State, had triumphed over the virtue of the Church; when the money-changers not only entered the temple, but drove out the worshipers; when ecclesiastical revenues were monopolized by wealthy pluralists; when the name of curate lost its legal meaning, and, instead of denoting the incumbent of a living, came to signify the deputy of an absentee."

The Dean of St. Paul's and others have spoken of the remarkable increase in vigour of style and boldness of illustration in my father's writings as he advanced in years; but I have seldom seen it noticed, except in a very clever sketch of him written by some friend soon after his death, that he had *no youth* in his writings; no period of those crude, extravagant theoretical opinions, with which the French Revolution had infected society to a degree of which we can hardly now form any estimate; though it is alluded to in almost every publication of the times.

A letter from Mr. Montagu to Mr. Mackintosh, given in the Life of his father Sir James Mackintosh, describes this vividly. "At this time, the wild opinions which prevailed at the commencement of the French Revolution misled most of us who were not as wise as your father, and he did not wholly escape their fascinating influence. The prevalent doctrines were, that man was so benevolent as to wish only the happiness of his fellow-creatures, so intellectual as to be able readily to discover what was best, and so far above the power of temptation as never to be drawn by any allurements from the paths of virtue. Gratitude was said to be a vice, marriage an improper restraint, law an imposition, and lawyers aiders of fraud. It is scarcely possible to conceive the extensive influence which these visions had on society."

"Yet in the midst of this" (continues the writer to whom I have alluded) "Sydney Smith showed, from the outset, a singular union of courage and good sense, without a tincture of the extravagance by which, in so many young men of ability, they were at that time accompanied. He did not hesitate to embrace and avow a sound principle, however obnoxious; but neither enthusiasm or party spirit could carry him a hair's-breadth beyond what his judgment approved."

He seems to have discerned, in the first blush of youth, that true liberty was never in such danger of destruction as when seized by the rude hands of her intemperate and unenlightened worshipers; and that true religion was never in such peril of being brought into ridicule and contempt, as when disfigured by the indiscreet zeal of ignorance and fanaticism. These convictions will, I think, be seen to pervade all his works, and even his correspondence,—to have been the great incentives under which he laboured to open the eyes of our rulers, under which he endeavoured to promote reforms at their legitimate source, and to ward off those horrors which the long neglect of reform had so recently produced in France. Speaking of reforms, in one of his early letters, he says: "What I want to see the State do, is to listen in these sad times to some of its numerous enemies. Why not do something for the Catholics, and scratch them off the list? then the Dissenters, a mitigation of the Game-laws, etc., anything that would show the Government to the people in some other attitude than that of taxing, punishing, and restraining." It is curious, in going through his writings, to observe that there is scarcely any one principle he has advocated, with the exception of the payment of the Catholic clergy, that has not been granted bit by bit; and, as my father says, after many throes and struggles, and hard-fought battles, that justice has been reluctantly conceded in the midst of fear and degradation, often when it was too late, which, had it been yielded in times of peace and strength, would have prevented many of the miseries the last forty years have witnessed in Ireland, and the many turmoils that have at various times agitated this country, and placed it on the verge of revolution. "In this way peace was concluded with America, and emancipation granted to the Catholics; and in this way the war of complexion will be finished in the West Indies." And again, he says: "Most of the concessions which have been given to Ireland, have been given in fear. Ireland would have been lost to this country, if the British Legislature had not, with all the rapidity and precipitation of the truest panic, passed those Acts which Ireland did not ask, but demanded, in the times of her armed association." Yet now these measures are so confirmed by the general sanction of society, that it seems almost trite and commonplace to allude to them.

I shall leave my father to paint the fate of those who ventured to maintain such opinions at the period of which I am speaking.

"From the beginning of the century (about which time the Review began), to the death of Lord Liverpool, was an awful period for those who ventured to maintain liberal opinions; and who were too honest to sell them for the ermine of the judge, or the lawn of the prelate. A long and hopeless career in your profession, the chuckling grin of noodles, the sarcastic leer of the genuine political rogue; prebendaries, deans, bishops made over your head; reverend renegades advanced to the highest dignities of the Church, for helping to rivet the fetters of Catholic and Protestant Dissenters; and no more chance of a Whig administration than of a thaw in Zembla. These were the penalties exacted for liberality of opinion at that period, and not only was there no pay, but there were many stripes."

"It is always considered a piece of impertinence in England if a man of less than two or three thousand a year has any opinions at all on important subjects; and in addition he was sure to be assailed with all the Billingsgate of the French Revolution,—Jacobin, leveller, atheist, Socinian, incendiary, regicide, were the gentlest appellations used; and any man who breathed a syllable against the senseless bigotry of the two

Georges, or hinted at the abominable tyranny and persecution exercised against Catholic Ireland, was shunned as unfit for the relations of social life. Not a murmur against any abuse was permitted; to say a word against the suitorcide delays of the Court of Chancery,* or the cruel punishments of the game-laws, or against any abuse which a rich man inflicted and a poor man suffered, was treason against the plousiocracy, and was bitterly and steadily resented. Lord Grey had not then taken off the bearing-rein from the English people, as Sir Francis Head has now done from horses."

My father speaks of himself as having a passionate love of common justice and common sense. He says, speaking of justice, "Truth is its handmaid, freedom is its child, peace is its companion, safety walks in its steps, victory follows in its train; it is the brightest emanation from the Gospel, it is the greatest attribute of God. It is that centre round which human motives and passions turn; and justice, sitting on high, sees genius, and power, and wealth, and birth revolving round her throne, and teaches their paths, and marks

---

* He says, on this subject, in his speech on the Reform Bill: "Look at the gigantic Brougham, sworn in at twelve, and before six o'clock has a bill on the table abolishing the abuses of a court which has been the curse of England for centuries. For twenty-five long years did Lord Eldon sit in the court, surrounded with misery and sorrow, which he never held up a finger to alleviate. The widow and the orphan cried to him as vainly as the town-crier cries when he offers a small reward for a full purse; the bankrupt of the court became the lunatic of the court; estates mouldered away and mansions fell down, but the fees came in and all was well; but in an instant the iron mace of Brougham shivered to atoms this house of fraud and of delay."

out their orbits, and warns with a loud voice, and rules with a strong hand, and carries order and discipline into a world which but for her would be a wild waste of passions."

Entering life then with these feelings, we shall, I think, best find their fruits by following the efforts of his pen through the greater part of his life in the Edinburgh Review. I have been told that I ought to give some analysis of them here; but they are now before the public in such various forms, are so well known, and, after various trials, I find them so much injured by any attempt to condense them, that I shall make his friend, Lord Monteagle, speak for me (as he states in a few lines what it would have cost me many pages to tell), and shall merely content myself with shortly enumerating what were the subjects that occupied my father's thoughts and employed his pen during so large a portion of his life; a pen which, I think I may venture to assert, was never sullied by private passion or private interest, never degraded by an impure or unworthy motive, and, with all its unexampled powers of sarcasm, never wounding but for the public good.

Lord Monteagle says: "Looking at all he did, and the way in which he did it, it must be an inexpressible pleasure to all who knew, valued, and loved him, to observe that there was scarcely one question in which the moral, the intellectual, social, or even physical well-being of his fellow-men were concerned, to the advancement of which he has not endeavoured to contribute."

Some of his earliest efforts seem to have been directed to subjects more immediately belonging to his profession, such as the use and abuse of the pulpit for political subjects, and the very inefficient state of pulpit eloquence. He touches on clerical reforms; he endeavours to protect the curates and inferior clergy, and to restrain the increasing power of the bishops, or rather to define those powers by laws, not leaving them dependent on the caprice of individual character or prejudice, as they then were. Toleration, from every motive, private, political, and religious, he inculcates on all occasions and in every form; and, as connected with and mainly depending on this, no subject more earnestly or frequently occupied his thoughts than the state of Ireland.

Education, as existing in this country in every class and in both sexes, claimed his attention. The injurious effects of Methodism and fanaticism on true religion in this country; the infinite importance of correcting vice in such a manner as should not produce hatred to virtue; the danger of religious wars, or of the total loss of our Indian possessions from the injudicious attempts at conversion by men totally unfitted for so important a work; the injuries we were inflicting on some of our finest colonies by bad governors and worse laws,—all these he describes and deprecates. He found in the cell of the lunatic chains, darkness, terror, cruelty, everything that unrestrained power and human passions could add of horror to that heaviest of God's afflictions, and he brought into public notice the mild and humane treatment of the Quakers and its beneficial effects. He examined the state of our gaols; he read the reports of good and laborious men who had dedicated much time and attention to the subject, "but men whom the fat and sleek people, the enjoyers, the mumpsimus, the well-as-we-are people of the world," had contrived to keep down and hide from the public eye; and he endeavoured to convince the unsuspecting world that we were paying and nourishing in every county of England a public school for the instruction and encouragement of profligacy and vice: no order, no division, no public eye; the innocent with the guilty; youth just tottering on the threshold of sin, living with and learning from the most hardened profligates; punishments inflicted before trial at the caprice of the magistrate or governor; and many other evils, moral as well as physical, which it only wanted the public eye and public attention to correct and improve.

At a time when the greater part of the Bench, as well as the Bar, with some noble exceptions, were opposed strongly to any change in our criminal procedure, he looked with horror at the scenes he witnessed in our courts of law, and the judicial murders that he felt must often occur under such a system; and he pleaded the cause of the poor unprotected prisoner in language so earnest and so forcible, that it may, I hope, entitle him to share with his great friends, Sir S. Romilly and Sir J. Mackintosh, the merit of having aided in that great work of mercy they fought for so long and so ably, and the prisoner yet unborn may live to bless their names.

Though living in the midst of large landed proprietors, all zealous in the preservation of their game, the cruelty, injustice, and increasing severity of the Game-laws,* and their oppressive and demoralizing effects on the poor, frequently occupied his attention and excited his most earnest opposition. The perplexing, but, as he says, most trite of subjects, the Poor-laws, occupied his thoughts; though, I fear, with as little result as has generally been produced by all the thought that has been expended on this most difficult question.

"Thinking (as he says) the United States the most magnificent picture of human happiness," and feeling the importance of the great political experiments that were going on there, he endeavoured to bring forward and attract public attention to both their merits and defects, urging America not to abuse the advantages she possessed, inciting Europe to profit by the example she set, and concluding by warning her, in a well-known passage, against a taste for military glory.

These, I think, were amongst the most important subjects he treated of; but there were many others of a lighter character, which he handled always with the same objects in view—to promote truth and expose evil. He leads us amusingly through the wanderings of Waterton; he unmasks the mischievous sophistry

---

* In the course of the preceding year no fewer than 12,000 persons were committed for offences against the Game-laws.

of Madame de Staël's 'Delphine;' he shows the comparatively innocuous effects which the plain, unvarnished exposure of vice in 'Anastasius' was calculated to produce; he points out the truth of the social picture given in 'Granby;' he acts as middle-man to Bentham; he brings out to public notice, from the mass of blue-books under which they were buried, all the cruelties to which the poor climbing-boys were exposed in sweeping chimneys; he points out the utility of the Hamiltonian system in diminishing the long and valuable period of time sacrificed in our places of education to acquiring a knowledge of the learned languages. There are some few others which he has not republished, no longer thinking them of any general interest.

I am anxious, in this sketch, not to be thought to attribute an undue share of influence to my father's efforts for the public good. It is often difficult to say who gave the death-blow to an abuse; and my father's blows, all will admit, were no light ones where they fell; yet he was but one of the many wise men who have used their talents for the benefit of their fellow-creatures, and many of them have devoted more time and attention to these objects than my father was enabled to do. But I think he has one peculiarity above almost any writer of his day,—that of *attracting public attention;* he was born for a *teacher* of the people, and, as Lord Ashburton says in his striking address to schoolmasters, "I wish to familiarize to the youngest amongst you this important truth, that no knowledge, however profound, can constitute a teacher. A teacher must have knowledge, as an orator must have knowledge, as a builder must have materials; but as, in choosing the builder of my house, I do not select the man who has the most materials in his yard, but I proceed to select him by reference to his skill, ingenuity, and taste; so also, in testing an orator or a teacher, I satisfy myself that they fulfil the comparatively easy condition of possessing sufficient materials of knowledge with which to work; I look then to those high and noble qualities which are the characteristics of their peculiar calling. There were hundreds at Athens who knew more than Demosthenes, many more that knew more at Rome than Cicero, but there was but one Demosthenes and one Cicero." So I think, though there are hundreds who have known more, laboured more, thought more, in England, yet in our day there was but one Sydney Smith.

He was a sort of rough-rider of a subject; sometimes originating, but more frequently taking up what others had for years been stating humbly, or timidly, or obscurely, or lengthily, or imperfectly, or dully, to the world; extracting at once its essence, unveiling the motives of his opponents, and placing his case clearly, concisely, simply, eloquently, boldly, brightly before the public eye. Thus the subject became read, thought of, discussed, and often acted upon by thousands of persons, dispersed over various parts of the world. This cannot have been without powerful influence on the opinions and conduct of society.

The peculiar talent possessed by my father is well described in a sketch by a personal friend of considerable talent, printed at the time of his death.

"In fact, he had read much, and always with the sincerest desire to arrive at truth; and if he lacked that quality of intellect which is capable of imparting original views on profound subjects, no man was ever more successful in possessing himself of the results of other men's thoughts, and in diffusing them in a form suited to the apprehension of ordinary readers. A distinguished scholar now living, writing of Sydney Smith to a friend in 1840, observes:—'Ridicule seems to me to be admirably fitted to confound fools and to destroy their prejudices. It is not needed in order to recommend truth to wise men, and indeed, from its generally dealing in exaggeration and slight misrepresentation, is likely to offend them. It is his mastery of ridicule which renders Sydney Smith so powerful as a diffuser of ideas, for in order to diffuse widely it is necessary to be able to address *fools*. His powers as a *diffuser*, as compared with the powers of a great *inventor*, who was latterly altogether wanting in the diffusing power, are well shown in his article on Bentham's Book of Fallacies; indeed, as a diffuser of the good ideas of other men, I do not know whether he ever had an equal.'

"When the imaginative faculty was in question, however, Sydney Smith was creative and original enough, God knows. When in good spirits, the exuberance of his fancy showed itself in the most fantastic images and most ingenious absurdities, till his hearers and himself were at times fatigued with the merriment they excited. He had the art, too, of divesting personalities of vulgarity, and not unfrequently was the object of his wit seen to enjoy the exercise of it quite as much as others; in fact, many persons rather felt it as a compliment when Sydney singled them out for sport."

In another sketch of my father's writings I have met with this passage, which I think so just that I shall insert it.

"Few men could write with his disregard of common forms, and his perfect expression of individual peculiarities, without falling into coarseness or buffoonery; the writings of Sydney are free from all vulgarities usual to the familiar writer. The great peculiarity of his works is their singular blending of the beautiful with the ludicrous, and this is the source of his refinement; he is keen and personal, almost fierce and merciless, in his attacks on public abuses; he has no check on his humour from authority or conventional forms, and yet he very rarely violates good taste; there is much good-humour in him in spite of his severity: it would be difficult to point out the source of this power of fascination, but it strikes us as being different from anything else we have ever seen."

CHAPTER III.

EXTRACTS FROM LECTURES.—PREFACE TO SERMONS.—ANALYSIS OF SERMONS.—SERMON FOR THE BLIND.—RETURNS TO EDINBURGH.—TAKES PUPILS.—ILLNESS OF DAUGHTER.—MORAL COURAGE.—STUDIES MEDICINE AND MORAL PHILOSOPHY.

I HAVE endeavoured in the last Chapter (with as little commentary as possible) to give a short sketch of the most important subjects that occupied my father's thoughts, and employed his pen, during twenty-eight years of his life, in the Edinburgh Review.

But to perform my task properly, I ought perhaps to add some account of the subject-matter of his lectures and sermons. The former of these, if done at all, must be done by an abler pen than mine; I shall therefore content myself with only two extracts. The first has often been quoted, not only for its beauty, but as affording a specimen of the high moral tone which pervades these lectures; the second was extracted by one of his earliest college associates (and, I believe, now oldest friend alive), Mr. Duncan, and sent to my mother, as giving what he thought the best description of my father that has ever been written. The first is from the Lecture " On the Conduct of the Understanding;" the second is from that on "Wit and Humour."

"Therefore, when I say, in conducting the understanding, love knowledge with a great love, with a vehement love, with a love coeval with life, what do I say but love innocence, love virtue, love purity of conduct, love that which, if you are rich and powerful, will sanctify the blind fortune which has made you so, and make men call it justice? Love that which, if you are poor, will render your poverty respectable, and make the proudest feel it unjust to laugh at the meanness of your fortunes. Love that which will comfort and adorn you, and never quit you, which will open to you the kingdom of thought, and all the boundless regions of conception, as an asylum against the cruelty, the injustice, and the pain that may be your lot in this outward world; that which will make your motives habitually great and honourable, and light up in an instant a thousand noble disdains at the very thought of meanness and of fraud.

"Therefore, if any young man has embarked his life in the pursuit of knowledge, let him go on without doubting or fearing the event; let him not be intimidated by the cheerless beginnings of knowledge, by the darkness from which she springs, by the difficulties which hover around her, by the wretched habitation in which she dwells, by the want and sorrow which sometimes journey in her train. But let him ever follow her as an angel that guards him, and as the genius of his life. She will bring him out at last into the light of day, and exhibit him to the world, comprehensive in acquirements, fertile in resources, rich in imagination, strong in reasoning, prudent and powerful above his fellows in all the relations and in all the offices of life."

"The meaning of an extraordinary man is, that he is eight men, not one man; that he has as much wit as if he had no sense, and as much sense as if he had no wit; that his conduct is as judicious as if he were the dullest of human beings, and his imagination as brilliant as if he were irretrievably ruined. But when wit is combined with sense and information; when it is softened by benevolence and restrained by principle; when it is in the hands of a man who can use it and despise it; who can be witty and something more than witty; who loves honour, justice, decency, good-nature, morality, and religion ten thousand times better than wit, wit is then a beautiful and delightful part of our nature.

"Genuine and innocent wit like this is surely the flavour of the mind. Man could direct his ways by plain reason, and support his life by tasteless food; but God has given us wit, and flavour, and brightness, and laughter, and perfumes, to enliven the days of men's pilgrimage, and to charm his pained steps over the burning marle."

The character and design of his Sermons will perhaps be best explained by a short preface he published as early as the year 1801, but never reprinted, explaining his reasons for the course he has taken; then showing what that course has been, and giving a few extracts from his sermons.

"He who publishes sermons should explain whether he publishes speeches, or essays, or what it is he does publish; for metaphysical dissertations, theological polemics, Scripture criticism, historical disquisition, and moral and religious doctrine, and exhortation, are all included under the appellation of sermons. Now every work should be tried by the intentions with which it was written. A moral sermon, delivered before a mixed audience of both sexes, would be very bad, if it contained a profound analysis of human motives and actions; and such an analysis should never be attempted before a mixed audience, because a continued attention to a difficult subject is a very rare quality, which the habits of the mass of mankind can never lead them to acquire. Before such an audience all these sermons were delivered, and whoever does me the honour of judging of them at all, will, I hope, do me the justice of judging them with a relation to this circumstance.

"The clergy have at all times complained of the decay of piety, in language similar to that which they now hold from the pulpit. The best way of bringing this declamation to proof is to look into the inside of our churches, and to remark how they are attended.

In London, I daresay, there are full seven-tenths of the whole population who hardly ever enter a place of worship from one end of the year to the other. At the fashionable end of the town the congregations are almost wholly made up of ladies, and there is an appearance of listlessness, indifference, and impatience, very little congenial to our theoretical ideas of a place of worship. In the country villages half of the parishioners do not go to church at all, and almost all, with the exception of the sick and old, are in a state of wretched ignorance and indifference with regard to all religious opinions whatever.

"The clergy of a district in the diocese of Lincoln associated lately for the purpose of forming an estimate of the state of religion within their own limits. The amount of the population, where the inquiry was set on foot, was 15,042. It was found that the average number of the ordinary congregations was 4933, and of communicants at each sacrament 1808; so that not one in three attended divine service, nor one in six of the adults (who amounted to 11,282) partook of the Sacrament.

"Though other grave and important causes have unquestionably contributed very largely to produce this indifference, which is by no means necessarily connected with infidelity, still, I am afraid, it must in some little degree be attributed to our form of worship, and to the clergy themselves.

"That the attention of the greater part of an audience can be kept up, through many repetitions, in a service that lasts an hour and a half, or an hour and three-quarters, is as much to be wished as it is to be little expected. Piety, stretched beyond a certain point, is the parent of impiety. By attempting to keep up the fervour of devotion for so long a time, we have thinned our churches, and driven away those fluctuating, lukewarm Christians who will always outnumber the zealous and devout, and whom it should be our first object to animate, allure, and fix.

"The English clergy, though upon the whole a very learned, pious, moral, and decent body of men, are not very remarkable for professional activity; and when they have discharged the formal and exacted duties of religion, are not very forward, by gratuitous inspection and remonstrance, to keep alive and diffuse a due sense of religion in their parishioners.

"To these causes may be added the low state of pulpit eloquence.

"Preaching has become a bye-word for long and dull conversation of any kind; and whoever wishes to imply, in any piece of writing, the absence of everything agreeable and inviting, calls it a sermon.

"One reason for this is the bad choice of subjects for the pulpit. The clergy are allowed about twenty-six hours every year for the instruction of their fellow-creatures; and I cannot help thinking this short time had better be employed on practical subjects, in explaining and enforcing that conduct which the spirit of Christianity requires, and which mere worldly happiness commonly coincides to recommend. These are the topics nearest the heart, which make us more fit for this and a better world, and do all the good that sermons ever will do. Critical explanations of difficult passages of Scripture, dissertations on the doctrinal and mysterious points of religion, learned investigations of the meaning and accomplishment of prophecies, do well for publication, but are ungenial to the habits and taste of a general audience. Of the highest importance they are to those who can defend the faith and study it profoundly; but, God forbid it should be necessary to be a scholar, or a critic, in order to be a Christian. To the multitude, whether elegant or vulgar, the result only of erudition, employed for the defence of Christianity, can be of any consequence: with the erudition itself they cannot meddle, and must be fatigued if they are doomed to hear it. In every congregation there are a certain number whom principle, old-age, or sickness, has rendered truly devout; but in preaching, as in everything else, the greater number of instances constitute the rule, and the lesser the exception.

"A distinction is set up, with the usual inattention to the meaning of words, between moral and religious subjects of discourse; as if every moral subject must not necessarily be a Christian subject. If Christianity concern itself with our present, as well as our future happiness, how can any virtue, or the doctrine which inculcates it, be considered as foreign to our sacred religion? Has our Saviour forbidden justice,—proscribed mercy, benevolence, and good faith? or, when we state the more sublime motives for their cultivation, which we derive from revelation, why are we not to display the temporal motives also, and to give solidity to elevation by fixing piety upon interest?

"There is a bad taste in the language of sermons evinced by a constant repetition of the same scriptural phrases, which perhaps were used with great judgment two hundred years ago, but are now become so trite that they may, without any great detriment, be exchanged for others. 'Putting off the old man—and putting on the new man,' 'The one thing needful,' 'The Lord hath set up his candlestick,' 'The armour of righteousness,' etc. etc. etc. etc. The sacred Scriptures are surely abundant enough to afford us the same idea with some novelty of language: we can never be driven, from the penury of these writings, to wear and fritter their holy language into a perfect cant, which passes through the ear without leaving any impression.

"To this cause of the unpopularity of sermons may be added the extremely ungraceful manner in which they are delivered. The English, generally remarkable for doing very good things in a very bad manner, seem to have reserved the maturity and plenitude of their awkwardness for the pulpit. A clergyman clings to his velvet cushion with either hand, keeps his eye riveted upon his book, speaks of the ecstasies of joy and fear with a voice and a face which indicate neither, and pinions his body and soul into the same attitude of limb and thought, for fear of being called theatrical and affected. The most intrepid veteran of us all dares no more than wipe his face with his cambric sudarium; if, by mischance, his hand slip from its orthodox gripe of the velvet, he draws it back as from liquid brimstone, or the caustic iron of the law, and atones for this indecorum by fresh inflexibility and more rigorous sameness. Is it wonder, then, that every semi-delirious sectary who pours forth his animated nonsense with the genuine look and voice of passion should gesticulate away the congregation of the most profound and learned divine of the Established Church, and in two Sundays preach him bare to the very sexton? Why are we natural everywhere but in the pulpit? No man expresses warm and animated feelings anywhere else, with his mouth alone, but with his whole body; he articulates with every limb, and talks from head to foot with a thousand voices. Why this holoplexia on sacred occasions alone? Why call in the aid of paralysis to piety? Is it a rule of oratory to balance the style against the subject, and to handle the most sublime truths in the dullest language and the driest manner? Is sin to be taken from men, as Eve was from Adam, by casting them into a deep slumber? Or from what possible perversion of common sense are we all to look like field-preachers in Zembla, holy lumps of ice, numbed into quiescence, and stagnation, and mumbling?

"It is theatrical to use action, and it is Methodistical to use action.

"But we have cherished contempt for sectaries, and

persevered in dignified tameness so long, that while we are freezing common sense for large salaries in stately churches, amidst whole acres and furlongs of empty pews, the crowd are feasting on ungrammatical fervour and illiterate animation in the crumbling hovels of Methodists. If influence over the imagination can produce these powerful effects; if this be the chain by which the people are dragged captive at the wheel of enthusiasm, why are we, who are rocked in the cradle of ancient genius, who hold in one hand the book of the wisdom of God, and in the other grasp that eloquence which ruled the Pagan world, why are we never to rouse, to appeal, to inflame, to break through every barrier, up to the very haunts and chambers of the soul? If the vilest interest upon earth can daily call forth all the powers of the mind, are we to harangue on public order, and public happiness, to picture a re-uniting world, a resurrection of souls, a rekindling of ancient affections, the dying day of heaven and of earth, and to unveil the throne of God, with a wretched apathy which we neither feel nor show in the most trifling concerns of life? This surely can be neither decency nor piety, but ignorant shame, boyish bashfulness, luxurious indolence, or anything but propriety and sense. There is, I grant, something discouraging at present to a man of sense in the sarcastical phrase of popular preacher; but I am not entirely without hope that the time may come when energy in the pulpit will be no longer considered as a mark of superficial understanding; when animation and affectation will be separated; when churches will cease (as Swift says) to be public dormitories; and sleep be no longer looked upon as the most convenient vehicle of good sense.

"I know well that out of ten thousand orators by far the greater number must be bad, or none could be good; but by becoming sensible of the mischief we have done, and are doing, we may all advance a proportional step; the worst may become what the best are, and the best better.

"There is always a want of grandeur in attributing great events to little causes; but this is in some small degree compensated for by truth. I am convinced we should do no great injury to the cause of religion if we remembered the old combination of *aræ et foci*, and kept our churches a little warmer. An experienced clergyman can pretty well estimate the number of his audience by the indications of a sensible thermometer. The same blighting wind chills piety which is fatal to vegetable life; yet our power of encountering weather varies with the object of our hardihood; we are very Scythians when pleasure is concerned, and Sybarites when the bell summons us to church.

"No reflecting man can ever wish to adulterate manly piety (the parent of all that is good in the world) with mummery and parade. But we are strange, very strange creatures, and it is better perhaps not to place too much confidence in our reason alone. If anything, there is, perhaps, too little pomp and ceremony in our worship, instead of too much.

We quarrelled with the Roman Catholic church, in a great hurry and a great passion, and furious with spleen; clothed ourselves with sackcloth, because she was habited in brocade; rushing, like children, from one extreme to another, and blind to all medium between complication and barrenness, formality and neglect. I am very glad to find we are calling in more and more the aid of music to our service. In London, where it can be commanded, good music has a prodigious effect in filling a church; organs have been put up in various churches in the country, and, as I have been informed, with the best possible effect. Of what value, it may be asked, are auditors who come there from such motives? But our first business seems to be, to bring them there from any motive which is not undignified and ridiculous, and then to keep them there from a good one: those who come for pleasure may remain for prayer.

"Pious and worthy clergymen are ever apt to imagine that mankind are what they ought to be; to mistake the duty for the fact; to suppose that religion can never weary its votaries; that the same novelty and ornament which are necessary to enforce every temporal doctrine are wholly superfluous in religious admonition; and that the world at large consider religion as the most important of all concerns, merely because it is so: whereas, if we refer to facts, the very reverse appears to be the case. Every consideration influences the mind in a compound ratio of the importance of the effects which it involves and their proximity. A man who was sure to die a death of torture in ten years would think more of the most trifling gratification or calamity of the day than of his torn flesh and twisted nerves years hence. If we were to read the gazette of a naval victory from the pulpit, we should be dazzled with the eager eyes of our audience; they would sit through an earthquake to hear us. The cry of a child, the fall of a book, the most trifling occurrence, is sufficient to dissipate religious thought, and to introduce a more willing train of ideas: a sparrow fluttering about the church is an antagonist which the most profound theologian in Europe is wholly unable to overcome. A clergyman has so little previous disposition to attention in his favour, that, without the utmost efforts, he can neither excite it or preserve it when excited. It is his business to awaken mankind by every means in his power, and to show them their true interest. If he despise energy of manner and labour of composition, from a conviction that his audience are willing, and that his subject alone will support him, he will only add lethargy to languor, and confirm the drowsiness of his hearers by becoming a great example of sleep himself.

"That many greater causes are at work to undermine religion I seriously believe; but I shall probably be laughed at when I say that warm churches, solemn music, animated preaching upon practical subjects, and a service some little abridged, would be no contemptible seconds to the just, necessary, and innumerable invectives which have been levelled against Rousseau, Voltaire, D'Alembert, and the whole pandemonium of those martyrs to atheism who toiled with such laborious malice, and suffered odium with such inflexible profligacy, for the wretchedness and despair of their fellow-creatures.

"I have merely expressed what appears to me to be the truth in these remarks. I hope I shall not give offence; I am sure I do not mean to do it. Some allowance should be made for the severity of censure when the provident satirist furnishes the raw material for his own art, and commits every fault which he blames."

Entering on his ministry, then, with these views, we shall, I think, find that my father's religion is tinctured in great measure by his character—it has nothing intolerant, repulsive, or morose in his hands. He first seeks to inspire the love of God, by painting the world overflowing with beauties of form, colour, sight, taste, smell, feeling; the mind of man filled with genius, fancy, wit, imagination, eloquence,—properties and feelings totally unnecessary to the mere bare cold existence that might have been the lot of man, but bestowed upon him in such variety and profusion as almost baffles the comprehension, and shows the boundless love of the Creator in placing such happiness within the reach of his creatures.

This feeling is evinced in the following passage, taken from a sermon on 'The Immortality of the Soul;' and will be seen to pervade not only his sermons, but his lectures, and even his reviews, wherever the subject admits of any allusion to religion.

He says, speaking of the faculties of animals: "If man, like these, had only talents to gather his support, and defeat the hostile animals which surround him, no hope of immortality could be gathered from a condition like this; man would be of the earth, earthy; destined to live in the world with qualities fitted for this world, and to all appearance limited to it. But in speaking of the mind of man, we forget and we pass over all those faculties which are sufficient for the preservation of life. We do not wonder at man because he is cunning in procuring food, but we are amazed with the variety, the superfluity, the immensity of human talents. We are astonished that he should have found his way over the seas, and numbered the stars, and called by its name every earth, and stone, and plant, and creeping reptile that the Almighty has made. We see him gathered together in great cities, guided by laws, disciplined by instruction, softened by fine arts, and sanctified by solemn worship. We count over the pious spirits of the world, the beautiful writers, the great statesmen, all who have invented subtlely, who have thought deeply, who have executed wisely:—all these are proofs that we are destined for a second life; and it is not possible to believe that this redundant vigour, this lavish and excessive power, was given for the mere gathering of meat and drink. If the only object is present existence, such faculties are cruel, are misplaced, are useless. They all show us that there is something great awaiting us, —that the soul is now young and infantine, springing up into a more perfect life when the body falls into dust."

On various occasions he dwells on the evidences of the authenticity of the Christian religion. He says: "I have selected this train of reasoning with some care from the best writers in defence of Christianity, because it is always right that a man should be able to render a reason for the faith that is within him."

In discoursing on these evidences, he enforces them with all the powers with which he was endowed. Having shown the authenticity of the religion he teaches, he proceeds to inculcate in a variety of forms the most important duties that religion enjoined: amongst these he has dwelt on none more frequently than "the *purity and government of the heart*," which, he says, "is God's, and to God it will return;" "it is the ark of God." "Is the passport to heaven written anywhere else than in a pure heart?" He shows how in this respect the Christian differs from all spurious religions, not contenting itself with ceremonies and outward forms, but requiring thought, word, and deed.

"The beauty of the Christian religion is, that it carries the order and discipline of heaven into our very fancies and conceptions, and, by hallowing the first shadowy notions of our minds from which actions spring, makes our actions themselves good and holy."

Toleration, long-suffering, and charity, he gathers

from every page of the Gospel. "The Church," he says, "must be distinguished from religion itself; we might be Christians without any Established Church at all, as some countries of the world are at this day. A church establishment is only an instrument for teaching religion, but an instrument of admirable contrivance and of vast utility. The Church of England is the wisest and most enlightened sect of Christians; I think so, or I would not belong to it another hour. But is it possible for me to believe that every Christian out of the pale of that Church will be consigned after this life to the never-ending wrath of God? If I were to preach such doctrines, who would hear me? Can I paint God as the protector of one Christian creed, dead to all prayers, blind to all woes but ours? —God, whom the Indian Christian, whom the Armenian Christian, whom the Greek Christian, whom the Catholic, whom the Protestant, adore in a varied manner, in another climate, with a fresh priest and a changed creed. Are you and I to live again, and are these Christians as well as us not to live again? Foolish, arrogant man has said this, but God has never said this. He calls for the just in Christ. He tells us that through that name He will reward every good man, and accept every just action; that if you take up the cross of Christ he will reward you for every kind deed, repay you sevenfold for every example of charity, carefully note and everlastingly recompense the justice, the honour, the integrity, the benevolence of your present life. And yet, though God is the God of all Christians, each says to the other, He is not your God, but my God; not the God of the just in Christ, but the God of Calvin, the God of Luther, or the God of the Papal Crown."

"The true Christian, amid all the diversities of opinion, searches for the holy in desire, for the good in council, for the just in works; and he loves the good, under whatever temple, at whatever altar he may find them."

"If I have *read well my Gospel*, it is in such wise we should imitate the patient forbearance of our common Father, who pities the frailties we do not pity, who forgives the error we do not forgive, who maketh His sun to rise on the evil and on the good, and sendeth rain on the just and the unjust."

He insists strongly on the vital importance of the religious education of youth :—" When you see a child brought up in the way he should go, you see a good of which you cannot measure the quantity, nor perceive the end; it may be communicated to the children's children of that child. It may last for centuries; it may be communicated to innumerable individuals. It may be planting a plant, and sowing a seed, which may fill the land with the glorious increase of righteousness, and bring upon us the blessings of the Almighty."

He then points out the true pleasures, the use and the abuse, of youth; the preparations for age; the warnings sent by a merciful God; the utility of meditation on death; the worthlessness of this world but as a stepping-stone to a better. And thus, whilst raising the mind from earth to heaven, and urging, as he says, "nothing foolish, nothing romantic, nothing bordering on ridicule or enthusiasm," he inculcates a recollection that there are really and truly things above this world, and coming after this world, and better than this world. He exhorts us to live as others live, and do as others do, but at the same time to live to higher purposes than others live, and do greater and better actions than others do. He then enters into the detail of those virtues, and the attack of those vices, which the wisdom of God has either commanded or forbidden for the happiness of man.

This, I believe, will be found to be an accurate analysis of the use he made of his ministry. Few extracts have been made, from the difficulty of selection; but I may venture to say that those who will seek, and select for themselves, will not be unrewarded.

As however my opinion can hardly be considered an impartial one, I may be allowed to quote two or three extracts from publications, after his death, in confirmation of it. "In a literary point of view," says one writer, "these sermons stand alone among modern pulpit discourses; they have not the theological learning which distinguishes some, or the mystical eloquence that gives character to the outpourings of the present Bishop of Oxford; but how full of freshness and life they are! There is nothing of compilation or imitation in them; the writer has not consulted other divines for topics and ideas, but, selecting his text, he has treated it from the stores of his own mind, exhibiting his own view on questions of doctrine, and illustrating matters of practice from his own observation and experience of mankind, and it bears the strong impress which vigorous life always imparts."

Another says :—" Christianity was not a dogma with Sydney Smith, it was a practical and most beneficent creed; it was the rule of action to his life. The volume contains not a thought or opinion at war with Christian charity."

And again, one says:—" But how beautiful were the serious moods of Sydney Smith! What a fine fulness and solidity they had; drawn from the strength and justice which we believe to have been the ruling sense of his mind, and tempered with the warmth of character, of which no man had a larger share. What a picture is that in one of his sermons where he describes the village school, and the tattered scholars, and the aged, poverty-stricken master, teaching the mechanical art of reading or writing, and thinking he was teaching that alone, while in truth he was protecting life, insuring property, fencing the altar, guarding the throne, giving space and liberty to all the fine powers of man, and lifting him up to his own place in the order of creation!"

I shall content myself with but one more extract, from his Charity Sermon in behalf of the Blind, as it was the one which elicited the splendid eulogium from

Mr. Dugald Stewart, to which I have alluded elsewhere.

"The author of the book of Ecclesiastes has told us 'that the light is sweet, that it is a pleasant thing for the eyes to behold the sun.' The sense of sight is indeed the highest bodily privilege, the purest physical pleasure, which man has derived from his Creator. To see that wandering fire, after he has finished his journey through the nations, coming back to his eastern heavens, the mountains painted with light, the floating splendour of the sea, the earth waking from deep slumber, the day flowing down the sides of the hills till it reaches the secret valleys, the little insect recalled to life, the bird trying her wings, man going forth to his labour,—each created being moving, thinking, acting, contriving, according to the scheme and compass of its nature, by force, by cunning, by reason, by necessity. Is it possible to joy in this animated scene, and feel no pity for the sons of darkness? for the eyes that will never see light? for the poor clouded in everlasting gloom? If you ask me why they are miserable and dejected, I turn you to the plentiful valleys; to the fields now bringing forth their increase; to the freshness and the flowers of the earth; to the endless variety of its colours; to the grace, the symmetry, the shape of all it cherishes and all it bears; these you have forgotten, because you have always enjoyed them; but these are the means by which God Almighty makes man what he is—cheerful, lively, erect, full of enterprise, mutable, glancing from heaven to earth, prone to labour and to act. Why was not the earth left without form and void? Why was not darkness suffered to remain on the face of the deep? Why did God place lights in the firmament, for days, for seasons, for signs, and for years? That He might make man the happiest of created beings; that He might give to this his favourite creation a wider scope, a more permanent duration, a richer diversity of joy. This is the reason why the blind are miserable and dejected—because their soul is mutilated, and dismembered of its best sense,—because they are a laughter and a ruin, and the boys of the streets mock at their stumbling feet.

"Therefore I implore you, by the Son of David, have mercy on the blind. If there is not pity for all sorrows, turn the full and perfect man to meet the inclemency of fate; let not those who have never tasted the pleasures of existence be assailed by any of its sorrows; the eyes which are never gladdened by light should never stream with tears.

"How merciful our blessed Saviour was wont to show himself to their afflictions! Blind Bartimeus sat by the wayside begging; and as the crowd passed by, he cried with a loud voice, 'Thou Son of David, have mercy upon me!' Jesus stopped the multitude, and before them all restored to him his sight. The first thing that he saw, who never saw before, was the Son of his God! These blind people, like Bartimeus, will never see, till they behold their Redeemer on the last day: not as He then was, in his earthly shape, but girded by all the host of heaven,—the Judge of nations, the everlasting Counsellor, the Prince of peace. At that hour this heaven and earth will pass away, and all things melt with fervent heat: but in the wreck of worlds no tittle of mercy shall perish, and the deeds of the just shall be recorded in the mind of God."

In giving this little sketch of his writings, I have somewhat anticipated in my narrative, and must return to my father's residence in Edinburgh. Mr. Beach had requested him to receive his second son under his charge, and at the same time Mr. Gordon, of Ellon Castle, was entrusted to his care by his guardians.

For the care of each of these young men, he received £400, the highest sum which had been then given to any one but Mr. Dugald Stewart. He fully justified the trust reposed in him; he lived with them as a father and a friend: they are both still alive, and both, I believe, retain warm feelings of love and respect for the memory of their former Mentor; indeed, one of them always evinced a truly filial affection towards him.

On one occasion he was much amused by the complaints made by his young friends of the difficulty of finding conversation for their partners in the two balls a week which he allowed them during the season. "Oh," said he, "I'll fit you up in five minutes: I'll write you some conversations, and you will be considered the two most agreeable young men in Edinburgh." Pen and ink were brought, the conversations—numbers one, two, and three—written down amidst fits of laughter; each youth chose his conversation; and it would be difficult to say who was the most amused, the writer, the speaker, or the hearer, by this novel expedient.

During his residence in Edinburgh, though without any clerical duties of his own, my father not unfrequently preached in the Episcopal church, then served by Bishop Sandford; and I believe the earliest of the charity sermons he has preached (of which there are several very touching ones amongst those which have been published) was for the Lying-in Hospital. The singular custom which was then always observed, of delivering these sermons at night, seems to have given occasion to a striking passage in it.

A few months after the birth of his daughter, he went in the summer for a short time to Burnt Island, a small sea-bathing place at no great distance from Edinburgh, for the recovery of my mother's health; and here, but for his courage and firmness, he would have lost his long-wished-for daughter, in a way he had not at all anticipated. When only six months old she fell ill of the croup, with such fearful violence, that it defied all the remedies employed by the best medical man there. The danger increased with every hour. Dr. Hamilton, then one of the most eminent medical men in Edinburgh, was sent for, could not come, but said, "Persevere in giving two grains of calomel every hour; I never knew it fail." It was given for eleven hours; the child grew worse and worse; the medical man in attendance then said, "I dare give no more; I can do no more, the child must die, but at this age I would not venture to give more to my own child." "You," said my father, "can do no more; Hamilton says, Persevere; I will take the responsibility, I will give it to her myself." He gave it, and the child was saved.

Another instance of his moral courage and presence of mind occurred in after-life, when, accidentally in the house of a near relation soon after her confinement, who was suddenly seized by a most alarming attack, her husband from home, a very eminent medical man who attended her absent; all the others sent to in this moment of distress, out also. At last, a young medical man was brought, who declared the danger to be imminent; that if the patient were a pauper, he would bleed her instantly, and probably save her life: he feared, however, to interfere in a case attended by so eminent a man, as, if he failed, he should be ruined. My father's medical knowledge confirming this opinion, he determined to take the whole responsibility on himself, and insisted upon its being done before he left the house. Relief was immediate, and, by the time the husband returned, the patient was safe.

At the end of the autumn he returned again to Edinburgh for the winter, and his time there was divided between his pupils, the Edinburgh Review (to which he was at that period not only contributor, but editor), the enjoyment of the choicest society that was to be found anywhere out of London, and the study of medicine, anatomy, and moral philosophy. He was a constant attendant on the beautiful lectures of Mr. Dugald Stewart, in the University of Edinburgh, with whom he lived in habits of almost daily communication; as also with that remarkable man, Dr. Thomas Brown, who succeeded Mr. Stewart in the Professor's chair of Moral Philosophy, from whom he imbibed a keen love of the subjects connected with that science. Medicine and anatomy had always been favourite pursuits of my father's even when at Oxford, where he bestowed so much attention on the study of the former under Sir Christopher Pegge, that the Professor much wished him to become a physician. Feeling now that such knowledge might be of the greatest use in his future destination, the Church, he pursued it with the more ardour, and attended the Clinical Lectures in the hospitals in Edinburgh, given by Dr. Gregory.

He thus obtained a degree of knowledge that enabled him afterwards to be of the greatest service to the poor of his parish, who entirely depended on him for assistance, and to become the favourite doctor of his own family, who rarely summoned any other medical man to their aid: and I have the authority of my husband, Sir Henry Holland (who had frequent opportunities of observing his practice, and ascertaining his knowledge of medicine), for saying, that both his judgment and knowledge were very remarkable, and used with the same prudence and good sense which he exercised on all other subjects.

CHAPTER IV.

QUITS EDINBURGH FOR LONDON.—SETTLES IN DOUGHTY STREET.—MAKES LEGAL AND OTHER FRIENDS.—OBTAINS PREACHERSHIP OF FOUNDLING HOSPITAL.—REFUSAL OF DR. —— TO ENABLE HIM TO LEASE A CHAPEL.—SERMON TO VOLUNTEERS.—FRIENDSHIP WITH LORD HOLLAND.—INTRODUCTION TO HOLLAND HOUSE.—HOLLAND HOUSE, AND SOCIETY THERE.—OBTAINS PREACHERSHIP OF ST. JOHN'S CHAPEL, BEDFORD SQUARE.—GIVES LECTURES AT ROYAL INSTITUTION.—DESCRIPTIONS OF THEIR EFFECT.—POVERTY.—SOCIETY AT HIS HOUSE, AND SUPPERS.—ANECDOTE OF SIR J. MACKINTOSH AND COUSIN.—ELECTED TO THE JOHNSON LITERARY CLUB.—THE KING READS HIS REVIEW, AND SAYS HE WILL NEVER BE A BISHOP.—PREACHES ON TOLERATION AT THE TEMPLE CHURCH.—INCREASE OF REPUTATION AND FRIENDS.—NATURAL SPIRITS, THEIR EFFECTS.—SOME ANECDOTES.

In 1803, the education of Mr. Sydney Smith's pupils being finished, and his income in consequence much reduced, it became necessary for him to resolve upon some course of life which might secure to him a permanent independence.

He was most reluctant to quit Edinburgh, where he had many valuable friends and was much sought after; and where his name would have probably continued to procure him pupils.

My mother however was more ambitious for him than he was for himself; and feeling that he was meant for better and higher things, and that his talents were worthy of a more extensive sphere, she used all her influence to induce him to seek it where alone it was to be found. After much deliberation he determined to yield to her wishes, plunge at once into London, and endeavour to make known, where they were most likely to be appreciated, such talents as he possessed. He therefore broke up his camp in Edinburgh, much to his own and his friends' regret, and established himself in London in the year 1804.

On his first arrival there, he took a small house in Doughty-street, Russell-square, attracted thither by the legal society which then resided in that part of London, and of which he was always very fond.

This resolution to settle in London turned out the wisest he could have taken; yet, friendless as my father then was, and obnoxious to Government as he had become by his principles and writings, and without any obvious means of increasing his income, it was not carried through without considerable anxiety and a severe and courageous struggle with poverty; and, to add to his difficulties and anxieties, soon after his arrival in town his family was increased by the birth of his eldest son, Douglas.

My grandmother, Mrs. Pybus, whose death had taken place shortly before my father quitted Edinburgh, had left my mother her own and her eldest daughter's (Lady Fletcher's) jewels, which were of some value. My mother, feeling that such ornaments were most unbecoming in her present position, insisted upon their being sold as soon as they came to London, and she describes my father's "comical anxiety lest mankind should recover from their illusion, and cease to value such glittering baubles before they could be sold. The negotiation begun with the jeweller, Sydney was not easy till it was accomplished; and even then, she says, she does not think he was quite easy in his mind at having helped to continue the illusion by accepting so large a price for them.

Of the early part of his career in London I of course know nothing, and recollect hearing but little. He early formed the acquaintance, and obtained the friendship, of several eminent lawyers then living in that neighbourhood. The most distinguished of these were Sir S. Romilly, Mr. Scarlett (afterwards Lord Abinger), and Sir J. Mackintosh. To these may be added Dr. Marcet, M. Dumont, Mr. Whishaw, Lord Dudley (then Mr. Ward), Mr. Sharpe, Mr. Rogers, Mr. Luttrell, and Mr. Tenant—who, under the most uncouth appearance, combined such simplicity, warmth of heart, and varied knowledge, as made him a general favourite in the little circle, and the mysteries of whose *ménage* often afforded amusement to his friends. He lived in a small lodging, and his establishment consisted solely of an old black servant, who tyrannized over him in no small degree, called Dominique. He was overheard one morning calling from his bed, "Dominique! Dominique!" but no Dominique appeared. "Why don't you bring me my stockings, Dominique?" "Can't come, massa." "Why can't you come, Dominique?" "Can't come, massa, I am dronke." Mr. Tenant, who probably thought it a law of nature that Dominique should be drunk, for he was seldom otherwise, submitted with the greatest meekness.

My father also became acquainted with some of the French emigrants, of whom there were many at this time resident in London and its neighbourhood; amongst these, some, from their cultivation and the refinement of their manners, became very agreeable additions to his society. Of these, I remember a M. Dutens,* and a charming old Abbé, who became quite one of the family. I can recall his pale, mild face, his thin figure, smart shoe-buckles, cane, and snuff-box, though I forget his name. He was bent on inventing a *universal language;* and used in his simplicity constantly to come and consult my father, who, much amused, suggested a few grammatical difficulties from time to time. The poor old Abbé, out of all patience, at last exclaimed, " Oh non, monsieur, ce sont là des bagatelles! La seule difficulté que je trouve c'est de faire agir tous les rois d'Europe au même instant." My father admitted that this was a slight difficulty; but we left London, or the old Abbé left England, before he had solved it.

In the summer of 1804 the alarm occasioned by the idea of French invasion was rapidly increasing, and volunteers were pouring in from all ranks and classes. One of the earliest sermons my father seems to have been called upon to preach was on this subject, before a large body of volunteers collected in the Metropolis;

* Author of ' Mémoires d'un Voyageur qui se repose.'

he closes it by saying, "I have a boundless confidence in the English character; I believe that they have more real religion, more probity, more knowledge, and more genuine worth, than exists in the whole world besides; they are the guardians of pure Christianity, and from this prostituted nation of merchants (as they are in derision called) I believe more heroes will spring up in the hour of danger than all the military nations of ancient and modern Europe have ever produced. Into the hands of God, then, and his ever-merciful Son, we cast ourselves, and wait in humble patience the result. First we ask for victory; but, if that cannot be, we have only one other prayer—we implore for death."

A year or two after, he preached another sermon for the suffering Swiss.

About this time he made the acquaintance of Sir Thomas Barnard, who was so much struck with his sense and originality that he recommended him to the preachership of the Foundling Hospital, at £50 per annum, which employment, small as was the remuneration, was gladly accepted. Slight as this service was, and probably suggested more for the benefit of the Hospital than for that of my father, I must still feel grateful to one who thus held out a helping hand to a clever and friendless young man struggling with the difficulties of the world and eager to perform the duties of his profession; a kindness which was the more felt from the contrast it afforded to the impediments most unexpectedly thrown in his way about the same time by others.

A chapel, then occupied by a sect of Dissenters calling themselves the New Jerusalem, and belonging to Mr. D——, was most kindly offered by him on lease to my father, if he could obtain the necessary license from the rector of the parish. His earnest and touching appeal to one he believed to be his friend, to grant this, and thus enable him to support his family and benefit the parish by his exertions in his profession, will be seen in the following letters; and with what result, and for what reasons rejected. I mention no names, as I wish to excite no angry feelings, and both men are now gone to a higher tribunal; but I cannot refrain from stating one of the many difficulties my father had to contend with.

To Dr. ——.

"*London.*

"Dear Sir,

"I am about to address myself to you upon a subject which very materially concerns my happiness and interest, and on which therefore I am sure you will consider, with as much disposition to befriend a brother clergyman as you can entertain consistently with your duty. Messrs. —— and Co. have agreed to let me a lease of the chapel in —— street: will you, *under any restrictions, and upon any conditions, allow me to preach there?*

"In the first place, I cannot doubt that where a place of worship is to exist in your parish, you would rather that the worship of the Church of England were carried on there, than that it should belong to such sectaries as the Christians of the New Jerusalem (as they entitle themselves). I should have greater reluctance in making this request if the places of worship in your parish were thinly attended, or if they were more than sufficient for the population of the parish; but, on the contrary, numbers are sent away every Sunday from your church, for want of room. Many families have in vain waited for years to obtain seats there; and the other chapels-of-ease I understand to be quite filled, though they cannot be said to be so overflowing. This chapel does not hold above three hundred and fifty persons, exclusive of servants; the mere overflowings of your church would fill it.

"It is, I admit, of great importance for you to consider whether I am, or am not, such a person as you would wish to perform the duties of a minister in your parish. This you can easily enough ascertain. I have officiated nearly two years in Berkeley Chapel, where the Primate of Ireland, the Bishop of Lichfield, and Dr. Dutens have seats: of the two former gentlemen I know nothing; with Dr. Dutens I am well acquainted. If these three dignified and respectable clergymen have any objection to make to my doctrines, I do not wish that the request I make to you should be successful, and I am the first to withdraw it. But if they say of me that my preaching commands attention, that I have any talent for enforcing moral and religious truth, and that I may be beneficially entrusted with such an office in any situation,—such testimony,

I am sure, will have its due weight with you, and if you can let me preach, you will. It has often been said of the proprietors of chapels, that they are rather apt to tell such truths as are pleasant, than such as are useful. I appeal to the same gentlemen, whether the fear of offending any one, let his rank and situation be what it may, has ever prevented me from enforcing duties on which I thought myself bound to animadvert; and you will excuse me if I say that you yourself, who have nothing to gain by pleasing or to lose by offending, have not attacked the vices of the rich and the great with more honest freedom than I have done, though your superior years, station, and understanding have of course enabled you to do it with much greater effect.

"My pretensions however of this nature must of course be judged by others. But of my situation in life (as I am the only judge of it) I hope you will allow me to say a few words. I am a married man, with two children, and as I am young my family may increase; I have a very small fortune, no preferment, nor any friends who are likely to give me any. The chapel where I preach at present will, I fancy, soon be sold; and it is not impossible that the clergyman who can afford to purchase it may choose to preach himself. It is not for want of exertion, my situation in the Church is not better, for I have not been idle in the narrow and obscure field which is open to the inferior clergy. I hope you will have the kindness to consider these circumstances, before you refuse me the opportunity of supporting my family and bettering my situation by my own exertions.

"A few years ago, my dear Sir, when your situation was what mine is, such considerations would have touched you, and you would have acknowledged their force. You know well the difficulties and the miseries of a curate's life; and I am sure you are the last man in the world to forget them, merely because you have overcome them with so much honour and distinction. I am aware it will be necessary to apply to the patron of the living if your answer should be favourable to me, but I fancy it is regular to make the first application to you; and I rather write than call upon you, because I think it unfair, on such subjects, to take gentlemen by surprise, where sufficient leisure ought to be given for deliberation. In a week's time I will call upon you for an answer; if you grant my request, I shall feel very grateful to you. I shall receive your answer with great anxiety, and am,

"My dear Sir, with great respect,
"Your obedient servant,
"Sydney Smith."

From the Rev. Sydney Smith to Dr. ——.

"Dear Sir,

"If I do not hear from you to the contrary, I will call upon you after morning service on Sunday. I forgot to mention in my letter to you, that Mr. Barnard* gave me leave to make any use I please of his

* Afterwards Sir T. Barnard.

name in the way of reference. I beg you to recollect that the question before you for your decision, is a choice between fanaticism and the worship of the Church of England in your parish; one or the other must exist. If I doubted of any of the doctrines of the Church of England, if I were possessed of any foolish and absurd tenets of my own, I should be immediately qualified by law to open the chapel: I hope you will not disqualify me merely because I am a firm and zealous advocate in the same cause with yourself, for this would be to give a bounty on dissent and heresy. It would be a very different question if I asked you to let me open a new place of worship; but I merely ask you to change that worship from the present method, which you completely disapprove, to that which you completely approve and eminently practise.

"Excuse the trouble I give you; but when a poor clergyman sees an honest and respectable method of improving his situation in life, you cannot wonder at his anxiety. You will make me a very happy man, if you consent to my request.

"With great respect, etc. etc.,

"Sydney Smith."

Dr. ——'s first answer is not given, as Mr. Smith's next letter states its contents.

From the Rev. Sydney Smith to Dr. ——.

"Dear Sir,

"The principal objection which your letter contained against the permission I requested, is the reluctance you state yourself to feel to imposing an obligation on your successors. Would you then object to give me leave to preach during your life, leaving it entirely open, by such limited concession, to those who succeed you, to continue or suspend the permission? Let me place myself entirely out of the question, and put the argument to you:—if any new person whom you may allow to preach in your parish, is a man very little calculated for such an office, it is not probable that people will quit the Established places of worship to resort to him; if he is, it is probable he will draw many to church, who would not otherwise go, and that the mass of people who attend public worship in that parish will be materially increased; which, I presume, is a consequence that every parish minister sincerely wishes for and would make some effort to obtain. I beg you to reflect, as I said in my last note (which crossed your letter), that I am not asking you to let me open a place of worship in your parish,—it is already open,—but I ask you to let me change the absurd and disgraceful devotion which is going on there at present (and will go on there still), for the devotion of the Church of England. I ask you to give me the preference over a low and contemptible fanatic; and will you allow me, without the slightest intention of offending you, to lay before you the seeming inconsistency of your answer?

"You say, 'I allow you have considerable talents for preaching. I know you have been well educated, I am sure you will be of great use, but I give a decided preference over you to a very foolish and a very ignorant Methodist, whose extravagance is debauching the minds of the lower class of my parishioners, and whom I should be heartily glad to see driven out of my parish.' Excuse my freedom, but such are inevitably to be the consequences deduced from your answer.

"I appeal to you again, whether anything can be so enormous and unjust, as that that privilege should be denied to the ministers of the Church of England which every man who has folly and presumption enough to differ from it can immediately enjoy? I hope you will give these observations some consideration, and, as soon as you have, return me your answer upon them.

"You observe that what I ask is unnecessary, and that it is an innovation; but I sincerely hope you would not refuse me so great an advantage, unless it was pernicious as well as unnecessary; and that if the plan I suggest is an improvement, you will not reject it merely because it is an innovation.

"I thank you very kindly for all the good you say of me: I will endeavour to deserve it.

"I am, my dear Sir, truly yours,
"SYDNEY SMITH."

From Dr. ―― to the Rev. Sydney Smith.

"Dear Sir,

"I was in hopes I had so expressed myself in my letter of Wednesday, that you would have immediately seen my unwillingness to admit the arrangement you propose respecting this chapel; although at the same time I am sorry to be an obstacle in the way of your interest, I can only add, that the expediency of the measure having been considered by my predecessors, I mean to abide by their decision. I hope never to be offended, Sir, at the freedom of any who are so kind as to teach me to know myself; and the inconsistency of my letter to you, which you are so good as to point out, is, alas! an addition to the many inconsistencies of which I fear I have been too often guilty through life.

"You will, I daresay, be glad to hear that there exists a hope that, ere long, the dissenters from the Establishment will not enjoy greater privileges than the ministers of the Establishment themselves.

"I have the honour to be,
"Dear Sir,
"Your obliged servant,
"———."

Thus, in spite of his most earnest endeavours to obtain employment, he remained poor for many years; indeed it has often been an enigma to me how, in these early days, my father contrived to meet the necessary expenses of settling in London; but I have lately discovered, from an old memorandum, that during this early period his eldest brother Robert kindly contributed £100 per annum for a few years; and that in 1809, when all the expenses of his removal into Yorkshire took place, he lent my father about

£500; an assistance which must have been of the greatest importance to him at this particular time.

I believe he had not been long in London before he became known, and his society sought after in various quarters. One of the earliest friendships he formed on coming there was that of Lord Holland, whose acquaintance he had previously made when on a visit to his eldest brother Robert, at college; and the subsequent marriage of this brother with Miss Vernon, Lord Holland's aunt, perhaps the more inclined Lord Holland to cultivate one with whose merits he was then but slightly acquainted.

I have often heard my father speak of his first introduction to Holland House,—the most formidable ordeal, considering the talents of its host and hostess and the society always to be found there, that a young and obscure man could well go through. He was shy too then; but I believe, in spite of the shyness, they soon discovered and acknowledged his merits, and deemed him no unmeet company for their world—and what a world it was!

I can hardly write of my father, and not pause a moment to speak of that society of which he afterwards so frequently formed a part, and to which he was bound through life by every tie of social enjoyment, gratitude, and friendship. The world has rarely seen, and will rarely, if ever, see again, all that was to be found within the walls of Holland House. Genius and merit, in whatever rank of life, became a passport there, and all that was choicest and rarest in Europe seemed attracted to that spot as to their natural soil.

Then the house itself,—a beautiful specimen of the olden times; with its ancient banqueting-hall, recalling traditions of past grandeur; and its noble library, full of the wisdom of ages, and hung round with the portraits of those who so often animated it with their presence, ought not to be forgotten.

How melancholy to feel that so many of those who, together with their much-loved host, acted so great a part in our own times, and have left names that will live long after them, are now gone.

My father found in Lord Holland one able and willing to appreciate him, and whose society it was impossible to enjoy without loving as well as admiring him; and they formed together one of those true friendships, so rare in human life, "which, like the shadows of evening, increase even till the setting of the sun." I do not of course presume to speak of Lord Holland but in reference to the charm of his intercourse with my father, which I had such frequent opportunities of witnessing; and it always seemed to me on such occasions that there never were two men who, from the constitution of their minds, were more calculated to enjoy and understand each other's character than Lord Holland and Sydney Smith. The same intense love of public liberty and public happiness, the same exquisite enjoyment of wit and humour, the same clearness and conciseness of understanding, with great constitutional gaiety of spirits, made their con-

versation more charming to listen to than it is well
possible to conceive without having done so, and evidently productive of the purest enjoyment to themselves. It was short, varied, interspersed with wit, illustration, and anecdote on both sides; in short, it was
the perfection of social intercourse, a sort of *mental
dram-drinking*, rare as it was delightful.

From the opportunities thus afforded my father of
meeting at Holland House all the best Whig society,
his acquaintance in London increased rapidly; and as
he became generally known there, his company was
eagerly sought for.

Meantime his reputation was spreading in other
and better ways than by the powers of his conversation alone. His negotiation to obtain a license from
the clergyman of the parish, to preach in the chapel
then occupied by the sect of the New Jerusalem,
failed, as we have seen; but in addition to the evening
preachership of the Foundling Hospital, he had for two
years, at the request of Mr. Bowerbank, the proprietor
of Berkeley Chapel, in John-street, Berkeley-square,
officiated as the morning preacher there. The chapel
had been so deserted (though the position was very
advantageous), that Mr. Bowerbank had been for some
time endeavouring to dispose of it. In a few weeks
after my father accepted it, not a seat was to be had:
gentlemen and ladies frequently stood in the aisles
throughout the whole service. All idea was then given
up of disposing of it by the proprietor; and till my
father left London, in 1809, he continued morning

preacher there, alternately with Fitzroy Chapel. The concise, bold raciness of his style was singularly calculated to stir up a lazy London congregation, accustomed to slumber over their weekly sermon; and the earnestness of his manner, I have reason to believe, caused many to think who never thought before.* Of the effect his preaching produced at different periods of his life I have the most flattering evidence. When such a man as Mr. Dugald Stewart exclaimed, after hearing him preach, "Those original and unexpected ideas gave me a thrilling sensation of sublimity never before awakened by any other oratory;" when his virtuous friend Horner expresses his admiration of his eloquence, and of the effect it produced on his congregation; when the Bishop of Norwich writes, on hearing him in the country, "He plainly showed he felt what he said, and meant that others should feel too;" when another very distinguished writer, on reading his sermons, says, "I opened on the Sermon on Toleration, and could not lay it down; the wisdom, truth, and beauty of it, and the true Christian spirit shining through every sentence, and illuminating the whole piece as with a celestial light, perfectly enchanted me: as he was one of the wisest of men, so I am sure he was one of the best;" when one as true as he is distinguished in his profession reminded me the other day how he had both seen and

* My father had the satisfaction more than once of receiving letters of gratitude, assuring him that his preaching had not been in vain, and had stopped the writer in a course of guilt and dissipation.

heard my father's emotion in the pulpit;—when such testimony is given by such men, united to that of many others which will appear in the course of the narrative, we are surely justified in affirming that, though originally entering into the Church reluctantly, yet having done so, he devoted all the powers of his heart and mind to the profession to which he had before devoted his life.

In addition to his fame as a clergyman, he obtained considerable increase of reputation by a course of lectures on Moral Philosophy, which Sir Thomas Barnard, who interested himself much about the Royal Institution, proposed to him to give; and which, though my father speaks of them as without merit in one of his letters to his friend Dr. Whewell, afford, as I am told, the strongest evidence of the clearness of his intellect and the justness of his opinions. They gained so much at the time from the charm of his voice and manner of delivery, that the sensation they created in London is perhaps unexampled.

" You would be amused," says his friend Mr. Horner, in his Letters, " to hear the account he gives of his own qualifications for the task, and his mode of manufacturing philosophy; he will do the thing very cleverly, I have little doubt."*

" I was," says Mrs. Marcet, " a perfect enthusiast

* An eye-witness says: "All Albemarle-street, and a part of Grafton-street, were rendered impassable by the concourse of carriages assembled there during the time of their delivery. There was not sufficient room for the persons assembling: the lobbies were filled, and the doors into them from the lecture-room were left open;

during the delivery of those lectures. They remain, but he who gave a very soul to them by his inimitable manner is gone! He who at one moment inspired his hearers with such awe and reverence by the solemn piety of his manner, that his discourse seemed converted into a sermon, at others, by the brilliancy of his wit, made us die of laughing. The impression made on me by these lectures, though so long ago, is still sufficiently strong to recall his manner in many of the most striking passages."

"I was present at the lectures forty years ago," says the late Sir Robert Peel, "and was a very young man at the time; but I have not forgotten the effect which was given to the speech of Logan, the Indian Chief, by the tone and spirit in which it was recited." ... "I do not find," he adds, "some verses I recollect to have been quoted by Mr. Sydney Smith, to which equal effect was given."

These verses alluded to were a beautiful little song of Mrs. Opie's, 'Go, youth beloved, in distant glades:' and she gives an amusing account, in a letter to my mother, of my father suddenly telling her, as she met him at the entrance of the lecture-room, that he was going to quote it. She describes the struggle between her timidity and her vanity, whether she should enter; and the new light in which both she and her poem

the steps leading into its area were all occupied; many persons, to obtain seats, came an hour before the time. The next year galleries were erected, which had never before been required, and the success was complete. He continued to lecture there for three consecutive years."

seemed to shine in the eyes of her friends, after this notice of its beauty in his lecture.

Mr. Horner, in his Life, speaks of these Lectures, calling my father by the *nom de guerre* he had in their circle, of the Bishop of Mickleham,—the name of his friend Mr. Sharpe's cottage in Surrey, where they often assembled.

"His Lordship's success has been beyond all possible conjecture;—from six to eight hundred hearers, not a seat to be procured, even if you go there an hour before the time. Nobody else, to be sure, could have executed such an undertaking with the least chance of success. For who could make such a mixture of odd paradox, quaint fun, manly sense, liberal opinions, and striking language?"

They have, since my father's death, thanks to my mother (who luckily preserved a considerable portion of them from the flames, to which he had as usual condemned them), been given to the public, which has confirmed this opinion of his friend Horner. Lord Jeffrey, to whom they were submitted in manuscript, had at first dissuaded their publication; but, on receiving a printed copy, with his usual candour and sweetness of disposition, he wrote to my mother, only three days before the fatal illness which terminated his noble life, the following letter:—

"I am now satisfied that, in what I then said, I did great and grievous injustice to the merit of these lectures, and was quite wrong in dissuading their publication, or concluding they would add nothing to the reputation of the author; on the contrary, my firm impression is, that, with few exceptions, they will do him as much credit as anything he ever wrote, and produce on the whole a stronger impression of the force and vivacity of his intellect, as well as a truer and more engaging view of his character, than most of what the world has yet seen of his writings."

The following lines have been kindly sent me by Miss Berry's executor, Sir Frankland Lewis, as found amongst her papers; and as Miss Berry, from her talents, beauty, high character, her friendship with Horace Walpole, her ninety years of life (thus as it were connecting two centuries), and the distinguished society always to be found in her house, almost belongs to history, she gives to these lines a value independent of their intrinsic merits.

ODE BY MISS BERRY

ON BUYING A NEW BONNET TO GO TO ONE OF MR. SYDNEY SMITH'S LECTURES—"ON THE SUBLIME."

Lo! where the gaily-vestured throng,
   Fair Learning's train, are seen,
Wedged in close ranks her walls along,
   And up her benches green!
Unfolded to their mental eye
Thy awful form, Sublimity,
The moral teacher shows;
   Sublimity! of silence born,
   And solitude, 'mid "caves forlorn,"
And dimly-vision'd woes,
Or steadfast worth that, inly great,
Mocks the malignity of fate.

Whisper'd Pleasure's dulcet sound
Murmurs the crowded room around,
And Wisdom, borne on Fashion's pinion,
Exulting hails her new dominion.
Oh! both on me your influence shed;
Dwell in my heart, and deck my head!

Where'er a broader, browner shade
　The shaggy beaver throws,
And with the ample feather's aid,
　O'er-canopies the nose;
Where'er, with smooth and silken pile,
Lingering in solemn pause awhile,
　The crimson velvet glows;
From some high bench's giddy brink,
With me, my friend begins to think,
　As bolt upright we sit,
That dress, like dogs, should have its day,
That beavers are too hot for May,
　And velvets quite unfit.
Then Taste, in maxims sweet, I draw
　From her unerring lip—
"How light! how simple are the straw!
　How delicate the chip!"

Hush'd is the speaker's powerful voice,
　The audience melt away;
I fly to fix my final choice,
　And bless the instructive day.

The milliner officious pours
Of hats and caps her ready stores,
　The unbought elegance of spring;
Some, wide, disclose the full round face,
Some, shadowy, lend a modest grace,
　And stretch their sheltering wing.
Here clustering grapes appear to shed
Their luscious juices on the head,
　And cheat the longing eye:
So round the Phrygian monarch hung
Fair fruits, that from his parched tongue

For ever seemed to fly.
Here early blooms the summer rose,
Here ribbons wreathe fantastic bows;
There plays gay plumage of a thousand dyes.—
Visions of beauty, spare my aching eyes!

Ye cumbrous fashions, crowd not on my head!
  Mine be the chip of purest white,
  Swan-like, and as her feathers light
When on the still wave spread;
  And let it wear the graceful dress
  Of unadorned simpleness!

Ah, frugal wish! Ah, pleasing thought!
  Ah, hope indulged in vain!
Of modest fancy cheaply bought,
  A stranger yet to Payne!
With undissembled grief I tell,
  (For sorrow never comes too late,)
The simplest bonnet in Pall Mall
  Is sold for one pound eight.

To calculation's sober view,
  That searches every plan,
Who keep the old, or buy the new,
  Shall end where they began.
Alike the shabby and the gay
Must meet the sun's meridian ray,
  The air—the dust—the damp:
This, shall the sudden shower despoil,
That, slow decay by gradual soil,
  Those, envious boxes cramp.

Who will, their squander'd gold may pay,
  Who will, our taste deride;
We 'll scorn the fashion of the day
  With philosophic pride.

Methinks we thus, in accents low,
  Might Sydney Smith address:—

"Poor moralist! and what art thou,
　Who never spoke of dress?
Thy mental hero never hung
Suspended on a tailor's tongue,
　In agonizing doubt!
Thy tale no fluttering female show'd,
Who languish'd for the newest mode,
　Yet dares to live without!"

The proceeds of these lectures,—for which, after the first series, he was allowed to name his own terms,—enabled him to furnish his new house in Orchard-street, where he continued to live during the remainder of his residence in London, and where two more children were born to him;—a son who died in infancy, and his youngest daughter, Emily.

In this house, though from the various sources mentioned his means were slightly increased, yet he still remained poor. But it was poverty in its most pleasing form; not that struggle with wealth, not that false shame, the outward show, the constant seeming, which we so often witness in the world, and which is the real sting of poverty; but the poverty of a man of sense who respected himself.

All was consistent about him: the comfort and happiness of home he considered the "grammar of life;" and his house, though plain, often in every sense of the word, was all his life the perfection of comfort. Considering domestic comfort so important, he thought no trouble too great, no detail too small, to merit his attention; and, though brought up in wealth and luxury, affection soon taught his wife to second him. He never affected to be what he was not; he never concealed the thought, labour, and struggle it often was to him to obtain the simple comforts of life for those he loved; as to its luxuries, he exercised the most rigid self-denial. His favourite motto, which through life he inculcated on his family, on such matters was, "Avoid shame, but do not seek glory,—nothing so expensive as glory;" and this he applied to every detail of his establishment. Nothing could be plainer than his table, yet his society often attracted the wealthy to share his single dish.

But the pleasantest society at his house was to be found in the little suppers which he established once a week; giving a general invitation to about twenty or thirty persons, who used to come as they pleased; and occasionally adding to, and varying them by accidental and invited guests. At these suppers there was no attempt at display, nothing to tempt the palate; but they were most eagerly sought after; and were I to begin enumerating the guests usually to be found there, no one would wonder that they were so. There are still a few living who can look back to them, and I have always found them do so with a sigh of regret. There was no restraint but that of good taste,—no formality,—a happy mixture of men and women,—the foolish and the wise,—the grave and the gay,—and sometimes conversation was varied by music. I see it stated in the Life of Sir James Mackintosh, that a great part of this choice little society used to meet likewise every week at Sir James's house; and one present says, "These social meetings left so delightful an impression on the minds of all those who composed them, that many plans were formed, even some years after, to renew them on Sir James's return to England; but, alas! no pleasure is renewed."

To these suppers occasionally came a country cousin of my father's,—a simple, warm-hearted rustic; and she used to come up to him and whisper, "Now, Sydney, I know these are all very remarkable men; do tell me who they are." "Oh yes," said Sydney, laughing, "that is Hannibal," pointing to Mr. Whishaw, "he lost his leg in the Carthaginian War; and that is Socrates," pointing to Luttrell; "and that is Solon," pointing to Horner,—"you have heard of Solon?" The girl opened her ears, eyes, and mouth with admiration, half doubting, half believing that Sydney was making fun of her: but perfectly convinced that if they were not the individuals in question, they were something quite as great.

It was on occasion of one of these suppers that Sir James Mackintosh happened to bring with him a raw Scotch cousin, an ensign in a Highland regiment. On hearing the name of his host he suddenly turned round, and, nudging Sir James, said in an audible whisper, "Is that the great Sir Sudney?" "Yes, yes," said Sir James, much amused; and giving my father the hint, on the instant he assumed the military character, performed the part of the hero of Acre to perfection, fought all his battles over again, and showed how he had charged the Turks, to the infinite delight of the young Scotchman, who was quite enchanted with the kindness and condescension of "the great Sir Sudney," as he called him, and to the absolute torture of the other guests, who were bursting with suppressed laughter at the scene before them. At last, after an evening of the most inimitable acting on the part both of my father and Sir James, nothing would serve the young Highlander but setting off, at twelve o'clock at night, to fetch the piper of his regiment to pipe to "the great Sir Sudney," who said he had never heard the bagpipes; upon which the whole party broke up and dispersed instantly, for Sir James said his Scotch cousin would infallibly cut his throat if he discovered his mistake. A few days afterwards, when Sir James Mackintosh and his Scotch cousin were walking in the streets, they met my father with my mother on his arm. He introduced her as his wife, upon which the Scotch cousin said in a low voice to Sir James, and looking at my mother, "I did na ken the great Sir Sudney was married." "Why, no," said Sir James, a little embarrassed and winking at him, "not ex-act-ly married,—only an Egyptian slave he brought over with him; Fatima—you know—you understand." My mother was long known in the little circle as Fatima.

By this time many of his Scotch friends had likewise come to England, which offered a wider field for the exercise of their talents,—Horner, Lord Webb Seymour, Mr. Brougham, and others, with whom he lived on terms of the greatest intimacy, and who contributed much to the charm of his little suppers.

He was very early elected a member of a very agreeable dining club, calling itself by the modest title of *The King of Clubs*, which he often alludes to with pleasure in his letters; but it was not till the year 1838 that he was admitted into that very remarkable literary Club established by Dr. Johnson and his friends, and calling itself *The Club*, of which Dr. Johnson says, "There is no club like our club." On its books may be seen the names, not only of Johnson, Goldsmith, Sir Joshua Reynolds, Burke, Gibbon, etc.; but a list of all the most eminent men that England has produced in every class and rank of society since its foundation. Mr. Van de Weyer, the Belgian Minister, is, I believe, the only foreigner that has ever been admitted since its first establishment; and, as was observed to him by a distinguished member of the Club, on being so admitted, he has received the highest title of naturalization that it is in the power of this country to bestow.

My father was now, with many of his early friends, contributing largely to the Edinburgh Review; and as his powers and principles became more known, he of course became more and more obnoxious to the party in power, and was the object of much abuse and much misrepresentation. One of the earliest recollections I have, is, that of being stopped at our door, when returning from my walk, by Mr. ——, and desired to tell my father that the King had been reading his reviews, and said, "He was a very clever fellow, but that he would never be a bishop." He felt this abuse and misrepresentation; and the hopelessness of his situation, where, in his profession, no merit or exertion of his own could advance him a single step, and where his only alternative was poverty or baseness; but he seldom allowed it to depress him; for he thought, with his sensible friend Sharpe, "if you cannot be happy in one way, be happy in another. Many in this world run after felicity like an absent man hunting for his hat, while all the time it is on his head or in his hand." And he used to say, "One must look downwards as well as upwards in human life. Though many have passed you in the race, there are many you have left behind. Better a dinner of herbs and a pure conscience, than the stalled ox and infamy, is my version."

An anecdote has lately reached me from a very early friend, which is an epitome of what I have observed of my father through life, and has quite delighted me;— that having once made up his mind as to what he ought to do, he did it, be the consequences what they might to himself. It was on this principle he entered the Church, on this he acted in it, and on every important occasion of private life. He was going to preach at the Foundling Hospital, and had selected a sermon containing a strong attack upon opinions which he thought were rapidly increasing, and producing most injurious effects on religion. My mother saw and knew the sermon, and exclaimed, "Oh, Sydney, do change that sermon; I know it will give such offence to our friends the F—s, should they be there this evening." "I fear it will," said my father, "and am sorry for it; but, Kate, do you think, if I feel it my duty to preach such a sermon at all, that I can refrain from doing so from the fear of giving offence?" The sermon was preached, the offence was given, and he felt the loss of his friends deeply, for he loved and valued those he offended. Time however produced its usual effects on really good men: my father lived to regain their friendship, and I have reason to believe there are few who love or honour his memory more than the only survivor now left.

In the year 1807 he preached a sermon on Toleration, in the Temple Church, and was requested to publish it. He did so, and added the following preface:—

"This sermon is not published from a belief that it has any merit in composition, or any claim to originality of thinking, but to bear my share of testimony against a religious clamour, which is very foolish in all those in whom it is not very wicked.

"I am sorry to write what I know it has been extremely disagreeable to many of those before whom I am in the habit of preaching to hear, but I should be infinitely more sorry that this or any other apprehension should prevent me from doing what I believe to be my duty.

"Charity towards those who dissent from us on religious opinions is always a proper subject for the pulpit. If such discussions militate against the views of any particular party, the fault is not in him who is thus erroneously said to introduce politics into the Church, but in those who have really brought the Church into politics. It does not cease to be our duty to guard men against religious animosities, because it suits the purpose of others to inflame them; nor are we to consider the great question of religious toleration as a theme fit only for the factions of Parliament, because intolerance has lately been made the road to power. It is no part of the duty of a clergyman to preach upon subjects purely political, but it is not therefore his duty to avoid religious subjects which have been distorted into political subjects, especially when the consequence of that distortion is a general state of error and of passion."

Meantime he had the satisfaction of feeling that he was not leading a useless life. He writes: "It pleases me sometimes to think of the very great number of important subjects which have been discussed in the Edinburgh Review in so enlightened a manner; it is a sort of magazine of liberal sentiments, which I hope will be read by the rising generation, and infuse into them a proper contempt for their parents' stupid and unphilosophical prejudices." He had also the consolation, as his character displayed itself, of obtaining what he said was the one "earthly good worth struggling for, the love and esteem of many good and great men." Amongst these, the two most intimately associated with his career in after-life were Lord Grey and Lord Carlisle (then Lord Morpeth). To the constant affection and unvarying kindness of Lord Holland and these two friends, he was indebted for most of the pleasures that were shed upon a path which, to any man of less energy of character and buoyancy of spirits, would have been for many years a very dark and dreary one. But there was within himself a natural source of happiness—a perpetual flow of spirits—a cheerfulness of disposition, for which he often thanked God, as one of the greatest benefits conferred upon him.

At this period of his life, indeed, his spirits were often such that they were more like the joyousness and playfulness of a clever school-boy than the sobriety and gravity of the father of a family; and his gaiety was so irresistible and so infectious, that it carried everything before it. Nothing could withstand the contagion of that ringing, joy-inspiring laugh, which seemed to spring from the fresh, genuine enjoyment he felt at the multitude of unexpected images which sprang up in his mind, and succeeded each other with a rapidity that hardly allowed his hearers to follow him, but left them panting and exhausted with laughter, to cry out for mercy.

An amusing instance of this occurred once, when he met that Queen of Tragedy, Mrs. Siddons, for the first time. She seemed determined to resist him, and preserve her tragic dignity; but after a vain struggle yielded to the general infection, and flung herself back in her chair, in such a fearful paroxysm of laughter, and of such long continuance, that it made quite a scene, and all the company were alarmed.

He contrived to make the most commonplace subjects amusing, and carried everybody along with him, in his wildest flights of drollery. One evening, the subject of conversation was the meteorological turn of mind of the English nation. "What would become of us had it pleased Providence to make the weather unchangeable? Think of the state of destitution of the morning callers. Now, I will give you a specimen of their conversation: Mrs. Jackson and Mrs. Jones, two respectable ancient females, shall be calling upon Mrs. Green, and Mrs. Brown shall join their party, and return by moonlight; Mrs. Brown shall catch cold and expire in the arms of her friend, calling for peppermint water, and exclaiming, The moon! the moon!" And taking up his pen, partly from the comical delight he had in what he was doing, partly from the exquisite commonplaces he strung together, and the faithful picture he drew of a morning visit in England, he kept us all in such roars of laughter, and he laughed so heartily himself as he wrote, that we all went quite exhausted to bed; the very recollection of that scene, even at this distance of time, makes me laugh again as I write.

Another day he came home, with two hackney-coach loads of pictures, which he had met with at an auction; having found it impossible to resist so many yards of brown-looking figures and faded landscapes going "for absolutely nothing,—unheard of sacrifices." Kate hardly knew whether to laugh or to cry, when she saw these horribly dingy objects enter her pretty little drawing-room, and looked at him as if she thought him half mad; and half mad he was, but with delight at his purchase. He kept walking up and down the room, waving his arms, putting them in fresh lights, declaring they were exquisite specimens of art, and, if not by the very best masters, merited to be so.

He invited all his friends, displayed them at his suppers, insisted upon their being looked at and admired in every point of view, discovered fresh beauties for each new comer; and, for three or four days, under the magic influence of his wit and imagination, these gloomy old pictures were a perpetual source of amusement and fun.

At last, finding he was considered no authority in the fine arts, and that his pictures made no progress in public opinion, off they went, to my mother's great relief, as suddenly as they came, to another auction; but all rechristened first by himself, amidst his laughing friends, with names never before heard of. One, I remember, was "a beautiful landscape, by Nicholas de Falda, a pupil of Valdeggio, the only painting by that eminent artist." The pictures sold, I believe, for rather less than he gave for them under their original names, which were probably as real as their assumed ones.

On another occasion he took it into his head to make a crusade against an unfortunate Mrs. Dumplin, who was filled with the ambition of giving a rout.

He found everybody going away from his house, and all to Mrs. Dumplin's rout; upon which he reasoned, he laughed, he persuaded, he quizzed, he entreated, he painted and described in such glowing colours the horrors of a Dumplin rout—the heat, the crowd, the bad lemonade, the ignominy of appearing next day in the 'Morning Post,'—that at last, with one accord, all turned back, finding it impossible to leave him. He shouted victory, and Mrs. Dumplin was heard of no more. Yet in the midst of all this wild mirth and genuine enjoyment of youth and health, a pretty domestic trait occurs to my mind, which, from such a man, then the idol of the London world, deserves to be told. One of his little children, then in delicate health, had for some time been in the habit of waking suddenly every evening; sobbing, anticipating the death of parents, and all the sorrows of life, almost before life had begun. He could not bear this unnatural union of childhood and sorrow, and for a long period, I have heard my mother say, each evening found him, at the waking of his child, with a toy, a picture-book, a bunch of grapes, or a joyous tale, mixed with a little strengthening advice and the tenderest caresses, till the habit was broken, and the child woke to joy and not to sorrow.

These are some of the little nothings which he had the art to turn into somethings, but which, I fear, resume their original insignificance under my pen; for I feel it impossible to give to them the life and raciness they had in reality, and which constituted their chief charm.

CHAPTER V.

1806. POLITICAL CHANGES.—OBTAINS PREFERMENT.—1807. GOES TO SONNING IN THE AUTUMN.—WRITES PETER PLYMLEY.—ITS EFFECT.—MAKES THE ACQUAINTANCE OF LORD STOWELL.—REVISITS EDINBURGH.—GOES TO HOWICK.—NO HOUSE ON THE LIVING.—NON-RESIDENCE PERMITTED. — THE RESIDENCE BILL PASSED.—GOES DOWN TO SEE THE LIVING.—DIFFICULTIES.—RETURNS TO LONDON.—PUBLISHES SERMONS.—REMOVES FAMILY TO YORKSHIRE. — TRIES TO NEGOTIATE EXCHANGE OF LIVING. — DIFFICULTIES OF EXCHANGE.—NECESSITY OF BUILDING.—SETTLES AT HESLINGTON.

In 1806 those political changes took place which so unexpectedly, and for so short a period, brought the Whigs into power.

To one who, as he says, "had lived so long on the north side of the wall, this ray of sunshine was very cheering, and gave some hopes that he who had so well and so honestly fought the good fight, would now have some opportunity afforded him of exerting himself in his profession." But as he had no connections and little political interest, I do not know what might have been the result, had it not been for the indefatigable exertions of his friends at Holland House, who never rested till they saw justice done to him, and had obtained from the Chancellor, Lord

Erskine, the living of Foston-le-Clay, in Yorkshire, for him.

For this he always felt that he owed Lord and Lady Holland a deep debt of gratitude; as, in addition to the immediate increase of his income, being a permanent provision, it gave him the first feeling of independence and security that he had enjoyed after a life of anxiety and uncertainty. An old friend of my father's told me the other day, "I was present at Bishopthorpe when your father first came down to be inducted to the living of Foston (now nearly fifty years ago), under the reign of old Archbishop Markham; I was then so young as to be placed at the side-table in that large dining-room; but I well remember the unwonted animation and the brilliant conversation that constantly attracted all our attention to the great table, and which we were told proceeded from a young clergyman of the name of Sydney Smith, just come down to take possession of a living in Yorkshire. When he went away, the old Archbishop, I could see, though struck with his extraordinary abilities, did not half like, or understand, how one of the inferior clergy should be so much in possession of his faculties in the presence of his diocesan. On my return home the next day I found my family in a state of great excitement. They had just, they said, had a long visit from the most delightful person they had ever met, a Mr. S. Smith, who had brought letters of introduction from Lord Abinger, then Mr. Scarlett, saying that the bearer was one of the most distinguished young men then in London, and congratulating my mother on the probability of having such a man established in her neighbourhood,—a piece of good fortune which, when it did happen shortly after, she fully appreciated, and was not inclined to neglect. From this time we saw more and more of him; and though I have enjoyed now all that is best in life, I think if I were to select the day of my life that has left the most agreeable impression on my mind, it would be a long summer afternoon we all spent with your father at Heslington. We walked over with Lord —— and several of the lawyers of the Northern Circuit, and found a Mrs. Hamilton in the house, who had just come from Edinburgh. The weather was lovely, everything looked bright, your father and Lord —— were in the highest spirits; the conversation turned on Edinburgh, the mode of life there, the remarkable men it contained or had produced; it was most brilliant and interesting,—the first taste I had had of what I must still think the perfection of society. After dinner we all walked back by moonlight. 'I have never forgot that day; I think it was one of the happiest of my life, and this has not been an unhappy one, as you know.'"

In the summer of 1807 he took his family for a short time to a little cottage in the village of Sunning, near Reading, to give them their first taste of the country; and even now I recollect with delight "each rural sight, each rural sound,"—this first breath of air, free from carpet-shakings, that we had inhaled.

I believe it was about this period that a letter from Peter Plymley to his brother Abraham, on the subject of the Irish Catholics, appeared suddenly in the London world. Its effect, I have been told, was like a spark on a heap of gunpowder. It was instantly dispersed all over London, was to be found on every table, spread in every direction over the country, and was the topic of general conversation and conjecture. It was quickly followed by another and another; each fresh letter increased the eagerness and curiosity of the public. Every effort was made on the part of the existing Government to find out the author,—in vain: the secret was well kept. It is true, strong suspicion pointed towards the little village in which my father then was, and a few of those best acquainted with his style felt convinced there was but one man in England who could so write,—who could make the most irresistible wit and pleasantry the vehicle of the soundest and most unanswerable argument; but no proof could be obtained. The editions were bought up as fast as they could be printed, and I am afraid from memory to state the numbers that were sold.

At the request of the Catholics, cheaper editions were made for dispersion in Ireland; and few works, I have heard, ever did more to open men's minds to the absurdity and danger of the system then pursued by England,* and there are, or rather were, few Catholics

* Lord Holland, I see, bears witness to the powerful effect this work and the Edinburgh Review had on this question, in his Reminiscences of that period; and Lord Murray, in writing of it. says, "After Pascal's Letters, it is the most instructive piece of

who did not venerate the name of Sydney Smith, as one who, though an honest servant of another church, felt that the strongest tenet of that church was charity and mercy; and in this feeling laboured incessantly to remove the heavy burdens and disqualifications imposed on them by the actual state of the laws.

And let no man say that he laboured in vain; that the seeds he sowed have not brought forth fruit, though not all the fruit they would have produced had they been sown when they were offered.

All admit, much has still to be done, and much time must elapse before such sufferings can be forgotten: but look what Ireland was when my father first entered life, in the midst of the tumult and violence of the French Revolution, and look at what it has been of late; look at what he advised, and how he advised it; look at what has been done; and who will then say that the efforts of such a man were unavailing, that his honest labours were in vain, that he who dedicated the fine talents God had given him from early youth to the hour of his death, to spread religious toleration, has not done good in his generation? I believe that his memory will live with the good men of every land, and that his best monument will be the love and respect of his countrymen.

Referring, some time after my father had left London for Yorkshire, to Peter Plymley, Lord Holland writes to him from Dropmore:—

wisdom in the form of irony ever written, and had the most important and lasting effects."

"My dear Sydney,

"I wish you could have heard my conversation with Lord Grenville the other day, and the warm and enthusiastic way in which he spoke of Peter Plymley. I did not fail to remind him that the only author to whom we both thought it could be compared in English, lost a bishopric for his wittiest performance; and I hoped that, if we could discover the author, and had ever a bishopric in our gift, we should prove that Whigs were both more grateful and more liberal than Tories.

"He rallied me upon the affectation of concealing who it was, but added that he hoped Peter would not always live in Yorkshire; for, among other reasons, we felt the want of him just now in the state of the press, and that he wished to God Abraham would do something to provoke him to take up the pen again."

In this little village of Sunning he first made the acquaintance of Sir William Scott, afterwards Lord Stowell, then our nearest neighbour, whose society he found most agreeable; and by whom, though differing on almost every point of politics, he was fully appreciated, and his acquaintance eagerly sought after by him, not only then, but during the remainder of my father's life, whenever opportunity offered in London; and during the period of this intercourse he not unfrequently said to my father, "Ah, Mr. Smith, you would have been in a different situation, and a far richer man, if you would have belonged to us." These observations, from one so cautious, so sagacious, and so strong a politician as Lord Stowell, were, of course, gratifying to my father, as they showed that his powers and talents were fully felt and appreciated by his political opponents.

On his return to town, receiving an invitation, I believe from his friend Mr. Sharp, to dine with him at Fishmongers' Hall, he sent the following playful answer, which, trifling as it is, as my tale is made up of trifles, I shall give.

> " Much do I love, at civic treat,
> The monsters of the deep to eat;
> To see the rosy salmon lying,
> By smelts encircled, born for frying;
> And from the china boat to pour,
> On flaky cod, the flavour'd shower.
> Thee, above all, I much regard,
> Flatter than Longman's flattest bard,
> Much honour'd turbot!—sore I grieve
> Thee and thy dainty friends to leave.
> Far from ye all, in snuggest corner,
> I go to dine with little Horner:
> He who, with philosophic eye,
> Sat brooding o'er his Christmas pie:
> Then, firm resolved, with either thumb,
> Tore forth the crust-enveloped plum,
> And, mad with youthful dreams of future fame,
> Proclaim'd the deathless glories of his name."

In the autumn of this year, 1808, he paid a short visit to his old haunts in Edinburgh, and on his return visited for the first time Lord Roslyn and Lord Grey;—saw the latter (where he was ever best seen) in the midst of his family, at Howick; and laid the foundation of that friendship which was a constant source of pleasure and gratification to him in after-life, and ended only with his death.

As there was no house on his living, and no means of procuring one in the neighbourhood, and the population of the parish was small, Dr. Markham, the then Archbishop of York, permitted his continued residence in town, on condition of his appointing an efficient curate; till the passing of the Residence Bill by Mr. Percival in 1808 (a bill the most just in its intentions, and the most unjust in its effects) compelled him to resign or build.

From the blamable negligence on the subject of residence of the clergy, which had existed for so long a period in the Church, one-third of the parsonage-houses in England had gone to decay; and thus, by the effects of this bill, one generation of clergymen was compelled suddenly to atone for the accumulated sins of their predecessors, and to benefit their successors, by building parsonage-houses out of their own private fortunes; unaided, save by a sum (I think a two or three years' income of the living) which they were allowed to borrow from Queen Anne's Bounty. Of this sum they were to repay a portion each year, with interest upon the rest; and thus, if they retained the living a few years, they were obliged to refund the whole sum, and it was utterly lost to them and their families.

On receiving the startling summons from the Archbishop, my father went down immediately into Yorkshire, to see what his fate was to be. He found his living well deserved its name of Foston-le-Clay; consisting as it did of three hundred acres of glebe-land of the stiffest clay, in a remote village of Yorkshire, where there had not been a resident clergyman for a hundred and fifty years, owing to the wretched state of the hovel which had once been a parsonage-house. This consisted of one brick-floored kitchen, with a room above it, which was in so dangerous a condition that the farmer, who had occupied it hitherto, declined living any longer in it, and which opened on one side into a foal-yard, and on the other into the churchyard; and placed in a village where there was no society above the rank of a farmer.

His parishioners were so unaccustomed to the sights of civilized life, that they could hardly recover from their surprise at the sight of a gentleman from London in a superfine coat and a four-wheeled carriage.

The prospect, it must be allowed, was not cheering, either morally or physically; for the country was as unpromising as the house. The clerk, the most important man in the village, was summoned; a man who had numbered eighty years, looking, with his long grey hair, his threadbare coat, deep wrinkles, stooping gait, and crutch-stick, more ancient than the parsonage-house. He looked at my father for some time from under his grey shaggy eyebrows, and held a long conversation with him, in which the old clerk showed that age had not quenched the natural shrewdness of the Yorkshireman. At last, after a pause, he said, striking his crutch-stick on the ground, "Muster Smith, it often stroikes moy moind, that people as comes frae London is such *fools*. . . . But you," he said (giving him a nudge with his stick), "I see you are no fool." Having thus gained the respect of the old, prejudiced clerk, he endeavoured to prove himself no fool. He examined carefully and understood thoroughly all the difficulties of his position, viz. a house to be built without experience or money; a family and furniture to be moved into the heart of Yorkshire,—a process, in the year 1808, as difficult as a journey to the back settlements of America now, to a man of small means; the absolute necessity of becoming a farmer, the living consisting of land and no tithe, there being no farm-buildings on it to enable him to let it, and the profound ignorance of all agricultural pursuits inevitable in a man who had passed life hitherto in towns, and whose time and attention had been divided between preaching, literature, and society.

Add to these, the moral difficulty of breaking through all the habits of his life, and tearing himself from the many valuable friends he had by this time formed, and who delighted in his society. But he felt it a duty, both to his profession and family, that the effort should be made.

He returned immediately to London, and obtained the means of transporting his family and furniture, by the publication of two volumes of the sermons he had preached during his residence there with so much success. The means obtained, and the order of march arranged, he set about breaking up his little establishment in London, which was not effected without great opposition from his friends there, and many kind attempts and schemes to detain him amongst them.

We all left town in the summer of 1809. He preceded the party, and hired for their reception a small but cheerful house in a village about two miles from York; from whence, not having been able to procure one nearer, he proposed to do the duties of his living for the present, whilst he endeavoured, with Dr. Vernon Harcourt's (the present Archbishop of York's) consent, to negotiate some exchange of living, and thus to avoid the necessity of building.

Lord Eldon required that a chancery living should only be exchanged for another chancery living, and that the parties so exchanging should be exactly of the same age. These conditions rendered exchange almost impossible; but to one with such slender means, it was worth any effort to avoid the ruinous expense of building. He therefore exerted himself in every possible way, and began several negotiations, but from these reasons they all failed.

CHAPTER VI.

ESTABLISHMENT IN YORKSHIRE.—HABITS.—MODE OF LIFE.—READING. — ATTENTION TO CHILDREN. — POWER OF ABSTRACTING THOUGHTS.— FARMER'S DINNER.— MEDICAL ANECDOTES.— EXPERIMENTS.—EXTRACTS FROM DIARY.—PRACTICAL ESSAYS.—METAPHYSICAL ESSAYS.—HINTS FOR HISTORY.—MR. MACAULAY'S LETTER.—SIR S. ROMILLY'S VISIT.—SERMON ON HIS DEATH.—ANECDOTE OF ROASTED QUAKER.—DINING OUT IN THE COUNTRY.— BROTHER AND SIR J. MACKINTOSH'S RETURN FROM INDIA. — MADAME DE STAEL'S VISIT TO ENGLAND.— TYPHUS FEVER.— VERSES ON MR. JEFFREY.

OUR first establishment at Heslington was a great source of enjoyment to the younger part of the family, glad to escape from the confinement of London; and our happiness contributed not a little to reconcile my father to the change.

He now began to arrange his mode of life and establishment. He bought a little second-hand carriage, and a horse, called Peter; and the groom once exclaiming he had a "cruel face," he went ever after by the name of Peter the Cruel: in this little carriage he used to drive himself and my mother every Sunday, summer and winter (for she always accompanied him), to serve his church at Foston, and returned late in the evening.

At first it was not without fear that she entrusted herself to so inexperienced a coachman; "but she soon," he said, "raised my wages, and considered me an excellent Jehu." The streets of York required some skill in this art. My father once exclaiming to one of the principal tradesmen there, "Why, Mr. Brown, your streets are the narrowest in Europe; there is not actually room for two carriages to pass." "Not room!" said the indignant Yorkist, "there's plenty of room, Sir, and above an inch and a half to spare!" He used to dig vigorously an hour or two each day in his garden, as he said, "to avoid sudden death," for he was even then inclined to *embonpoint*, and perhaps, as a young man, may have been considered somewhat clumsy in figure (though I never thought so), for I have often heard from my father that a college friend used to say to him, "Sydney, your sense, wit, and clumsiness, always give me the idea of an *Athenian carter*." He spent much time in reading and composition; his activity was unceasing; I hardly remember seeing him unoccupied, but when engaged in conversation. He never considered his education as finished; he had always some object in hand to investigate. He read with great rapidity. I think it was said of Johnson, "Look at Johnson, tearing out the bowels of his book." It might be said of my father, that he was running off with their contents, for he galloped through the pages so rapidly, that we often laughed at him when he shut up a thick quarto as his morning's work, and said he meant he had looked at it, not read it. "Cross-examine me, then," said he; and we generally found he knew all that was worth knowing in it; though I do not think he had a very retentive memory. The same peculiarity characterized his compositions;—when he had any subject in hand, he was indefatigable in reading, searching, inquiring, seeking every source of information, and discussing it with any man of sense or cultivation who crossed his path. But having once mastered it, he would sit down, and you might see him committing his ideas to paper with the same rapidity that they flowed out in his conversation,—no hesitation, no erasions, no stopping to consider and round his periods, no writing for effect, but a pouring out of the fulness of his mind and feelings, for he was heart and soul in whatever he undertook. One could see by his countenance how much he was interested or amused as fresh images came clustering round his pen; he hardly ever altered or corrected what he had written (as I find by many manuscripts I have of his); indeed, he was so impatient of this, that he could hardly bear the trouble of even looking over what he had written, but would not unfrequently throw the manuscript down on the table as soon as finished, and say, "*There*, it is done; now, Kate, do look it over, and put in dots to the *i*'s and strokes to the *t*'s"—and he would sally forth to his morning's walk.

He used frequently to lay out his plans of study for the year. I find the following have accidentally been preserved in one of his commonplace books, and shall give them, though not strictly belonging to this period:—

"*Plan of Study for* 1820.

"Translate every day ten lines of the 'De Officiis,' and re-translate into Latin. Five chapters of Greek Testament. Theological studies. Plato's 'Apology for Socrates;' Horace's Epodes, Epistles, Satires, and Ars Poetica.

"*Plan of Study for* 1821.

"Write sermons and reviews, Monday, Wednesday, and Friday. Read, Tuesday, Thursday, Saturday. Write ten lines of Latin on writing days. Read five chapters of Greek Testament on reading days. For morning reading, either Polybius, or Diodorus Siculus, or some tracts of Xenophon or Plato; and for Latin, Catullus, Tibullus, and Propertius.

"Monday: write, morning; read Tasso, evening. Tuesday: Latin or Greek, morning; evening, theology. Wednesday, same as Monday. Friday, ditto. Thursday and Saturday, same as Tuesday. Read every day a chapter in Greek Testament, and translate ten lines of Latin. Good books to read :—Terrasson's 'History of Roman Jurisprudence;' Bishop of Chester's 'Records of the Creation.'"

He was very fond of children,—liked to have them with him; indeed, in looking back, it often fills me with regret to think of the many advantages that ought to have been turned to better account, in passing a life with such a man.

He took a lively interest in all our pursuits and

happiness (a happiness which, he often touchingly said, he had never known in childhood); he never lost an opportunity of showing us whatever could instruct or amuse, that came within his reach; he loved to exercise our minds; and I remember, often in childhood, gave my elder brother and myself subjects on which to write essays for him. He encouraged the ceaseless questions of childhood; he was never too busy to explain or assist; as we grew older, he endeavoured to stimulate us to exertion by shame at ignorance. He loved to discuss with us, met us as his equals, and I look back with wonder at his patient refutation of our crude and foolish opinions.

As we grew up we became his companions; we were called in to all family councils; his letters were common property; the tenderest mother could not have been more anxious and careful as to the religious tendency of any books we read, and often he has taken books out of my hands which I had ignorantly begun, with strict injunctions to consult him about my studies. He regarded it as the greatest of all evils to produce doubt or confusion in a youthful mind on such subjects; indeed he has said, in his sermons, that he "would a thousand times prefer that his child should die in the bloom of youth, rather than it should live to disbelieve."

After his evening walk he would sit down to his singular writing establishment, which I shall describe hereafter, placed by the servant always in the same place; and here, after looking through business papers and bills with as much plodding method as an attorney's clerk, he would suddenly push them all aside, and, as if to refresh his mind, take up his pen. His power of abstraction was so great that he would begin to compose, with as much rapidity and ease as another man would write a letter, those essays which are before the world, or some of those sermons of which my mother has given a few to the public since his death; often reading what he had written, listening to our criticisms (as Molière did to his old woman), and this in the midst of all the conversation and interruptions of a family party, with talking or music going on.

"A clergyman complaining of want of society in the country, saying, 'They talk of *runts*' (young cows), Johnson expressed himself much flattered by the reply of Mrs. Thrale's mother: 'Sir, Dr. Johnson would learn to talk of *runts;*' meaning that I was a man that would make the most of my situation, whatever it was."* This was most strikingly the case with my father; he always endeavoured to see the bright side of things, and to adapt himself to the circumstances in which he was placed, however uncongenial to his former tastes and habits. He could talk of *runts* with those who talked only of runts, and he not only talked, but entered so eagerly into the subject before him that he ended by generally finding sources of interest in them; affording, in this respect, a striking contrast to a brother clergyman, who about the same time (having been a popular preacher in London) received

* Boswell's Life of Johnson.

a valuable living in Yorkshire, and came down to a good house and a more populous neighbourhood than my father's. But alas! he could not talk of runts; he sighed after Piccadilly; his face grew thinner and longer every time we met; he used often to call, and lament over his hard fate, and wonder how my father could endure it with so much cheerfulness; and I believe he would have died of green fields and runts, if he had not succeeded in effecting an exchange, which restored him again to London.

Talking of runts reminds me of a practice my father established as soon as he was settled at Foston, of inviting some of the most respectable farmers in his neighbourhood to dine with him once a year. On these occasions he did not make it a mere man's dinner, but the ladies of his family were always present; and, without lowering his own dignity or appearing to descend to the level of his more humble guests, it was interesting to observe how he drew out the real sense and knowledge they possessed, how he discussed their opinions, and with what tact he gave a tone of general interest to the conversation. Trifling as this was, it was evidently of great utility: it gave him more knowledge of them and influence amongst them than he could otherwise have obtained; each man went away better pleased with himself and less of a grumbler than he came; and, I suspect, with a greater value for character, which was the only passport to his table.

My father employed himself much in acquiring a

knowledge of all rural arts and details of farming, such as baking, brewing, fattening poultry, churning, etc.; talking much to the working people, whose shrewdness and blunt sense delighted him. He always acquired some information from them, often kindly taking up some old woman returning from market into his gig and learning her history. He said he never found anything well done in a small household, if the master and mistress were ignorant of the mode in which it ought to be done.

He began too on a small scale to exercise his skill in medicine, doing much good amongst his poor neighbours, though there were often ludicrous circumstances connected with his early medical career. On one occasion, wishing to administer a ball to Peter the Cruel, the groom, by mistake, gave him two boxes of opium pills in his bran mash, which Peter composedly munched, boxes and all. My father, in dismay, when he heard what had happened, went to look, as he thought, for the last time on his beloved Peter; but soon found, to his great relief, that neither boxes nor pills had produced any visible effects on him. Another time he found all his pigs intoxicated, and, as he declared, "grunting God save the King about the stye," from having eaten some fermented grains which he had ordered for them. Once he administered castor-oil to the red cow, in quantities sufficient to have killed a regiment of Christians; but the red cow laughed alike at his skill and his oil, and went on her way rejoicing.

He never sat a moment after dinner when alone with his family, having contracted a horror of it from the long sittings inflicted on him in early life by his father; who, dining at three, used to sit till dark, and expect his family to do the same. My father rushed into the opposite extreme; and the cloth was scarcely removed ere he called for his hat and stick, and sallied forth for his evening stroll, in which we always accompanied him. Each cow, and calf, and horse, and pig, were in turn visited, and fed and patted, and all seemed to welcome him: he cared for their comforts as he cared for the comforts of every living being around him. He used to say, "I am all for cheap luxuries, even for animals; now all animals have a passion for scratching their backbones; they break down your gates and palings to effect this. Look! There is my universal scratcher, a sharp-edged pole, resting on a high and a low post, adapted to every height, from a horse to a lamb. Even the Edinburgh Reviewer can take his turn; you have no idea how popular it is; I have not had a gate broken since I put it up; I have it in all my fields."

He always had some experiment going on. At one time he was bent on inventing a method of burning the fat of his own sheep, instead of candles; and numerous were the little tin lamps, of various forms and sizes, produced; great the illuminations and greater the smells, the house being redolent of mutton-fat whilst this fancy lasted.

Then he took smoking chimneys in hand, and invented patent iron backs, to throw out the heat of the fire by contracting the chimney, and facilitate sweeping them by the ease of removal; and, I am bound in gratitude to own, with much success.

Immediately on coming to Foston, as early as the year 1809, he set on foot gardens for the poor; and subsequently, Dutch gardens for spade cultivation. The former were, I believe, among the first trials of an experiment which has been since so generally adopted, as one of the most beneficial charities amongst the country population; dividing several acres of the glebe into sixteenths, and letting them, at a low rent, to the villagers, to whom they were the greatest comfort. It became quite a pretty sight afterwards to see these small gardens (which were just enough to supply a cottager with potatoes, and sometimes enable him to keep a pig) filled at dawn with the women and children cultivating them before they went out to their day's labour; and there was the greatest emulation amongst them whose garden should be most productive and obtain the prize.

Then the cheapest diet for the poor, and cooking for the poor, formed the subjects of his inquiry: and many a hungry labourer was brought in and stuffed with rice, or broth, or porridge, to test their relative effects on the appetite. In short, it would be endless to enumerate the variety of subjects and objects which the activity and energy of his mind suggested and found interest in.

In an evening, often with a child on each knee, he

would invent a tale for their amusement, composed of such ludicrous images and combinations as nobody else would have thought of, succeeding each other with the greatest rapidity; these were devoured by them with eyes and ears, in breathless interest; but at the most thrilling moment always terminated with "and so they lived very happy ever after," a kiss on each fat cheek, "and now go to bed."

The following are extracts from such few portions of his diary as have been preserved, written at various times. These slight, unfinished fragments are not, of course, given as specimens of composition; but they are, I think, of great value, as indicating the occupation and direction of his thoughts, and the wholesome training of his mind, in his leisure hours, and in solitude, of which he seems to have felt the full value for the improvement of his character. In one of his letters to Jeffrey about this period, he says:—"Living a great deal alone (as I now do) will, I believe, correct me of my faults, for a man can do without his own approbation in much society, but he must make great exertions to gain it when he is alone; without it, I am convinced, solitude is not to be endured."

"*Maxims and Rules of Life.*

"Remember that every person, however low, has *rights* and *feelings*. In all contentions, let peace be rather your object, than triumph: value triumph only as the means of peace.

"Remember that your children, your wife, and your servants, have rights and feelings; treat them as you would treat persons who could turn again. Apply these doctrines to the administration of justice as a magistrate. Rank poisons make good medicines; error and misfortune may be turned into wisdom and improvement.

"Do not attempt to frighten children and inferiors by passion; it does more harm to your own character than it does good to them; the same thing is better done by firmness and persuasion.

"If you desire the common people to treat you as a gentleman, you must conduct yourself as a gentleman should do to them.

"When you meet with neglect, let it rouse you to exertion, instead of mortifying your pride. Set about lessening those defects which expose you to neglect, and improve those excellencies which command attention and respect.

"Against general fears, remember how very precarious life is, take what care you will; how short it is, last as long as it ever does.

"Rise early in the morning, not only to avoid self-reproach, but to make the most of the little life that remains; not only to save the hours lost in sleep, but to avoid that languor which is spread over mind and body for the whole of that day in which you have lain late in bed.

"Passion gets less and less powerful after every defeat. Husband energy for the real demand which the dangers of life make upon it.

"Find fault, when you must find fault, in private, if possible; and some time after the offence, rather than at the time. The blamed are less inclined to resist, when they are blamed without witnesses; both parties are calmer, and the accused party is struck with the forbearance of the accuser, who has seen the fault, and watched for a private and proper time for mentioning it."

"My son writes me word he is unhappy at school. This makes me unhappy; but, 1st. There is much unhappiness in human life: how can school be exempt? 2ndly. Boys are apt to take a particular moment of depression for a general feeling, and they are in fact rarely unhappy; at the moment I write, perhaps he is playing about in the highest spirits. 3rdly. When he comes to state his grievance, it will probably have vanished, or be so trifling, that it will yield to argument or expostulation. 4thly. At all events, if it is a real evil which makes him unhappy, I must find out what it is, and proceed to act upon it; but I must wait till I can, either in person or by letter, find out what it is."

"Jan. 19th I passed very unhappily, from an unpleasant state of body produced by indolence.

"Feb. 15th. Lost two hours in bed, from dawdling and doubting. Maxims to make one get up:—1st. *Optimum eligite, et consuetudo faciet jucundissimum.* 2nd. I must get up at last, it will be as difficult then as now. 3rd. By getting up I gain health, knowledge, temper, and animal spirits.

"May 31st. The difficulty of getting up, and I parley with the fault; the only method is, to obey the rule instantly, and without a moment's reflection.

"Nov. 3rd. Lost a day by indolence; the only method is to spring up at once.

"I am uneasy about the sort of answer which the editor of the —— has given to my letter; but as I cannot see his answer, the best way is to wait till I can see it; and after all, it is of very little consequence. Every man magnifies too much what belongs to himself; nobody does this more than I do.

"Another reason for benevolence is, that you forget your own joy from being so accustomed to it, but the joy of others seems something new.

"—— says, 'my best patients are the poor, for God is the paymaster.'

"*Death*—it must come some time or other. It has come to all, greater, better, wiser, than I.

"I have lived sixty-six years.

"I have done but very little harm in the world, and I have brought up my family.

"I was seized with sudden giddiness, so as to fall, and for twenty-two hours was affected by violent pain. I kept my bed that day, and was weak and languid for some days after. Mr. Lyddon attributes it to indigestion. If this is the way nature punishes us for the consumption of indigestible food, I am sure it is worth while to be strictly temperate; I will therefore, in future, avoid soup and fish, and confine myself to one dish. I must not only attend to quantity, but quality. I may not be able to do this,—then I must die or be ill; but I am sure it is the best wisdom to do it.

"Not only is religion calm and tranquil, but it has an extensive atmosphere round it, whose calmness and tranquillity must be preserved, if you would avoid misrepresentation.

"Not only study that those with whom you live should habitually respect you, but cultivate such manners as will secure the respect of persons with whom you occasionally converse. Keep up the habit of being respected, and do not attempt to be more amusing and agreeable than is consistent with the preservation of respect.

"I am come to the age of seventy; have attained enough reputation to make me somebody: I should not like a vast reputation, it would plague me to death. I hope to care less for the outward world.

"Hope.

"Don't be too severe upon yourself and your own failings; keep on, don't faint, be energetic to the last.

"If you wish to keep mind clear and body healthy, abstain from all fermented liquors.

"Fight against sloth, and do all you can to make friends.

"If old-age is even a state of suffering, it is a state of superior wisdom, in which man avoids all the rash and foolish things he does in his youth, and which make life dangerous and painful.

"Death must be distinguished from dying, with which it is often confounded.

"Reverence and stand in awe of yourself.

"How Nature delights and amuses us by varying even the character of insects: the ill-nature of the wasp, the sluggishness of the drone, the volatility of the butterfly, the slyness of the bug.

"Take short views, hope for the best, and trust in God."

"A FEW UNFINISHED SKETCHES.*

"Of the Body.

"Happiness is not impossible without health, but it is of very difficult attainment. I do not mean by health merely an absence of dangerous complaints, but that the body should be in perfect tune—full of vigour and alacrity.

"The longer I live, the more I am convinced that the apothecary is of more importance than Seneca; and that half the unhappiness in the world proceeds from little stoppages, from a duct choked up, from food pressing in the wrong place, from a vext duodenum, or an agitated pylorus.

"The deception, as practised upon human creatures, is curious and entertaining. My friend sups late; he eats some strong soup, then a lobster, then some tart, and he dilutes these esculent varieties with wine. The

* From his 'Practical Essays.'

next day I call upon him. He is going to sell his house in London, and to retire into the country. He is alarmed for his eldest daughter's health. His expenses are hourly increasing, and nothing but a timely retreat can save him from ruin. All this is the lobster: and when over-excited nature has had time to manage this testaceous encumbrance, the daughter recovers, the finances are in good order, and every rural idea effectually excluded from the mind.

"In the same manner old friendships are destroyed by toasted cheese, and hard salted meat has led to suicide. Unpleasant feelings of the body produce correspondent sensations in the mind, and a great scene of wretchedness is sketched out by a morsel of indigestible and misguided food. Of such infinite consequence to happiness is it to study the body!

"I have nothing new to say upon the management which the body requires. The common rules are the best:—exercise without fatigue; generous living without excess; early rising, and moderation in sleeping. These are the apothegms of old women; but if they are not attended to, happiness becomes so extremely difficult that very few persons can attain to it. In this point of view, the care of the body becomes a subject of elevation and importance. A walk in the fields, an hour's less sleep, may remove all those bodily vexations and disquietudes which are such formidable enemies to virtue; and may enable the mind to pursue its own resolves without that constant train of temptations to resist, and obstacles to overcome, which it always experiences from the bad organization of its companion. Johnson says, every man is a rascal when he is sick; meaning, I suppose, that he has no benevolent dispositions at that period towards his fellow-creatures, but that his notions assume a character of greater affinity to his bodily feelings, and that, *feeling* pain, he becomes malevolent; and if this be true of great diseases, it is true in a less degree of the smaller ailments of the body.

"Get up in a morning, walk before breakfast, pass four or five hours of the day in some active employment; then eat and drink over-night, lie in bed till one or.two o'clock, saunter away the rest of the day in doing nothing!—can any two human beings be more perfectly dissimilar than the same individual under these two different systems of corporeal management? and is it not of as great importance towards happiness to pay a minute attention to the body, as it is to study the wisdom of Chrysippus and Crantor?"

"*Of Occupation.*

"A good stout bodily machine being provided, we must be actively occupied, or there can be little happiness.

"If a good useful occupation be *not* provided, it is so ungenial to the human mind to do nothing, that men occupy themselves *perilously*, as with gaming; or *frivolously*, as with walking up and down a street at a watering-place, and looking at the passers-by; or *malevolently*, as by teazing their wives and children. It is impossible to support, for any length of time, a state of perfect *ennui;* and if you were to shut a man up for any length of time within four walls, without occupation, he would go mad. If idleness do not produce vice or malevolence, it commonly produces melancholy.

"A stockbroker or a farmer have no leisure for imaginary wretchedness; their minds are usually hurried away by the necessity of noticing external objects, and they are guaranteed from that curse of idleness, the eternal disposition to think of themselves.

"If we have no necessary occupation, it becomes extremely difficult to make to ourselves occupations as entirely absorbing as those which necessity imposes.

"The profession which a man makes for himself is seldom more than a half profession, and often leaves the mind in a state of vacancy and inoccupation. We must lash ourselves up however, as well as we can, to a notion of its great importance; and as the dispensing power is in our own hands, we must be very jealous of remission and of idleness.

"It may seem absurd that a gentleman who does not live by the profits of farming should rise at six o'clock in the morning to look after his farm; or, if botany be his object, that he should voyage to Iceland in pursuit of it. He is the happier however for his eagerness; his mind is more fully employed, and he is much more effectually guaranteed from all the miseries of *ennui*.

"It is asked, if the object *can* be of such great importance. Perhaps not; but the pursuit *is*. The fox, when caught, is worth nothing: he is followed for the pleasure of the following.

"What is a man to do with his life who has nothing which he *must* do? It is admitted he must find some employment, but does it signify what that employment is? Is he employed as much for his own happiness in cultivating a flower-garden as in philosophy, literature, or politics? This must depend upon the individual himself, and the circumstances in which he is placed. As far as the mere occupation or exclusion of *ennui* goes, this can be settled only by the feelings of the person employed; and if the attention be equally absorbed, in this point of view one occupation is as good as another; but a man who is conscious he was capable of doing great things, and has occupied himself with trifles beneath the level of his understanding, is apt to feel envy at the lot of those who have excelled him, and remorse at the misapplication of his own powers; he has not added to the pleasures of occupation the pleasures of benevolence, and so has not made his occupation as agreeable as he might have done, and he has probably not gained as much fame and wealth as he might have done if his pursuits had been of a higher nature. For these reasons it seems right that a man should attend to the highest pursuits in which he has any fair chance of excelling; he is as much occupied, gains more of what is worth gaining, and excludes remorse more effectually, even if he fail, because he is conscious of having made the effort.

"When a very clever man, or a very great man, takes to cultivating turnips and retiring, it is generally an imposture. The moment men cease to talk of their turnips, they are wretched and full of self-reproach. Let every man be *occupied*, and occupied in the highest employment of which his nature is capable, and die with the consciousness that *he has done his best!*"

"*Of Friendship.*

"Life is to be fortified by many friendships. To love, and to be loved, is the greatest happiness of existence. If I lived under the burning sun of the equator, it would be a pleasure to me to think that there were many human beings on the other side of the world who regarded and respected me; I could and would not live if I were alone upon the earth, and cut off from the remembrance of my fellow-creatures. It is not that a man has occasion often to fall back upon the kindness of his friends; perhaps he may never experience the necessity of doing so; but we are governed by our imaginations, and they stand there as a solid and impregnable bulwark against all the evils of life.

"Friendships should be formed with persons of all ages and conditions, and with both sexes. I have a friend who is a bookseller, to whom I have been very civil, and who would do anything to serve me; and I have two or three small friendships among persons in much humbler walks of life, who, I verily believe, would do me a considerable kindness according to their means. It is a great happiness to form a sincere friendship with a woman; but a friendship among persons of different sexes rarely or ever takes place in this country. The austerity of our manners hardly admits of such a connection;—compatible with the most perfect innocence, and a source of the highest possible delight to those who are fortunate enough to form it.

"Very few friends will bear to be told of their faults; and if done at all, it must be done with infinite management and delicacy; for if you indulge often in this practice, men think you hate, and avoid you. If the evil is not very alarming, it is better indeed to let it alone, and not to turn friendship into a system of lawful and unpunishable impertinence. I am for frank explanations with friends in cases of affronts. They sometimes save a perishing friendship, and even place it on a firmer basis than at first; but secret discontent must always end badly."

"*Of Cheerfulness.*

"Cheerfulness and good spirits depend in a great degree upon bodily causes, but much may be done for the promotion of this turn of mind. Persons subject to low spirits should make the rooms in which they live as cheerful as possible; taking care that the paper with which the wall is covered should be of a brilliant, lively colour, hanging up pictures or prints, and covering the chimney-piece with beautiful china. A bay-window looking upon pleasant objects, and, above all, a large fire whenever the weather will permit, are favourable to good spirits, and the tables near should be strewed with books and pamphlets. To this must be added as much eating and drinking as is consistent with health; and some manual employment for men,—as gardening, a carpenter's shop, the turning-lathe, etc. Women have always manual employment enough, and it is a great source of cheerfulness. Fresh air, exercise, occupation, society, and travelling, are powerful remedies.

"Melancholy commonly flies to the future for its aliment, and must be encountered in this sort of artifice, by diminishing the range of our views. I have a large family coming on, my income is diminishing, and I shall fall into pecuniary difficulties. Well! but you are not *now* in pecuniary difficulties. Your eldest child is only seven years old; it must be two or three years before your family make any additional demands upon your purse.* Wait till the time comes. Much may happen in the interval to better your situation; and if nothing does happen, at least enjoy the two or three years of ease and uninterruption which are before you. You are uneasy about your eldest son in India; but it is now June, and at the earliest the fleet will not come in till September; it may bring accounts of his health and prosperity, but at all events there are eight or nine weeks before you can hear news.

Why are they to be spent as if you had heard the worst? The habit of taking very short views of human life may be acquired by degrees, and a great sum of happiness is gained by it. It becomes as customary at last to view things on the good side of the question as it was before to despond, and to extract misery from every passing event.

"A firm confidence in an overruling Providence,—a remembrance of the shortness of human life, that it will soon be over and finished,—that we scarcely know, unless we could trace the remote consequences of every event, what would be good and what an evil;—these are very important topics in that melancholy which proceeds from grief.

"It is wise to state to friends that our spirits are low, to state the cause of the depression, and to hear all that argument or ridicule can suggest for the cure. Melancholy is always the worse for concealment, and many causes of depression are so frivolous, that we are shamed out of them by the mere statement of their existence."

Scattered amongst his papers are a few fragments on metaphysical subjects, which always interested him.

"*Benevolence.*

"A child is born with the power of feeling bodily pleasure and pain. The milk he receives from his nurse delights him. The appearance of the nurse is always connected with that pleasure, and, by the laws of association, because he loves the milk he at last comes to love the nurse; that is, her presence excites in him the passion of joy. In the same manner, if his nurse, instead of suckling him, had rubbed his mouth with wormwood, the pain of the wormwood would be united with the appearance of the nurse; and because the taste of the wormwood excited in him the passion of sorrow, the appearance of the nurse would at last do the same. In this way we begin to connect our fellow-creatures with our pleasures and pains.

"But whence comes it that a child travels from joy to benevolence, and wishes to do good to the person who excites in him pleasurable sensations? Why is he not benevolent towards the pap-boat, or the nurse's gown, or any other inanimate object which his eye connects as frequently with his animal pleasures as the image of his nurse? The progress from joy to benevolence is, I believe, entirely the result of experience, and the latter is a passion of much later growth than the other. As a child grows older, he perceives that the person who ministers to his joy and sorrow has similar feelings with himself, and that it becomes his *interest* to attend to them. If he scratches, and kicks, and cries, and knocks down glasses and tea-cups, he is shaken or scolded, or sugar is refused; or he is put in the corner, or whipped. If he pleases his superior, come cakes, plums, toys, and amusing games.

"In the same manner, at school, he is every day receiving lessons of the evils of malevolence and the advantages of benevolence. Kicks, cuffs, privations, solitude, deter him on one hand; cheerful society, protection, community of joys, allure him on the other. In this way he learns the important lesson of doing good in order to promote his own good; and having loved the passion for its utility, he loves it at *last* for itself. In after-life, the poet, the orator, the moralist, and the preacher, praise and purify this fine passion, give it strength, which conceals its origin, and makes it appear primary and original.

"In order to make this more clear, let us suppose that a child was treated, to a late period, with the same uniform indulgence, however numerous his faults, and however untoward his disposition; that nurse, father, mother, schoolfellow, and schoolmaster, all studied his humours and ministered to his wants, without exacting from him in return the slightest attention to their own feelings. What motive could such a child have for benevolence? How would he learn to become benevolent? Why should he cultivate such passive human beings, more than the spoon, or the silver mug, which, tossed and tumbled about by his caprice today, are sure to appear at the dinner of tomorrow?

"In fact, such a blind submission to the will of any child would infallibly make him a tyrant, and extinguish in his mind every spark of benevolence: but if an exemption from the necessity of attending to the feelings of our fellow-creatures, destroys benevolence, the necessity of doing so may be presumed to teach it. Where one fact, admitted to be true, will explain other facts equally admitted to be true, there is no occasion to suppose other facts which are doubtful, in order to make a new series of causes and consequences. That children are born capable of feeling bodily pain and pleasure, is not disputed; that they soon learn to be benevolent towards, or to love their fellow-creatures, is an equally admitted fact. If one of these facts can be shown to be the cause of the other, there is no occasion to have recourse to a principle of benevolence as an original principle of our nature ; but this, though a curious, is not a very important question. Whether innate, or early learnt, the most pure and disinterested benevolence exists in human nature. Howard visited prisons and lazarettos, and sacrificed his life for his fellow-creatures, let the metaphysical origin of benevolence be what it may.

"'The passion of benevolence, thus excited in our nature, receives the name of gratitude, when we desire to do good to those who have done good to us. From apparent gratitude, is to be deducted the hope of future favour from the object of our gratitude, and the dread of infamy for being ungrateful. The pure passion may be explained from the united effects of association and education. Sexual love is that benevolence to persons of the opposite sex, which proceeds from the beauty of their countenance or their form.

"Paternal love is the benevolence which a father feels towards his child. This passion, like all others which are of use to mankind, is very much increased by education and general opinion, by reason and reflection, and by compassion, by habit, and association. I see no occasion for supposing the existence of any original principle of paternal love. The analogy from animals is entirely against it. Love, when applied to persons of the same sex, like affection, kindness, are all modifications of the same passions of joy, or benevolence; an agreeable, charming, or delightful person excites these passions in us, in different degrees, gives us feelings of joy, or makes us desirous of doing him some good. When benevolence excites us to give, it is called generosity. Hope is the belief, more or less strong, that joy will come; desire is the wish it may come. There is no word to designate the remembrance of joys past."

"*Of the Mind.* (*A Fragment.*)

"The mind is inhabited by ideas, by passions, and by desires. Passions are strong feelings or affections of the mind, not leading immediately to action. Desires are strong feelings of the mind, accompanied by a wish to act.

"In revenge, I can perceive that my mind is powerfully affected, and I have a wish to act, and to give pain to some person: this is a desire. When the possession of sudden wealth is announced to me, I feel transported with joy, but I have no immediate desire to act: here I only recognize the affection of my mind.

"In avarice, there is the feeling and the wish to act,—this is a desire. In grief there is only the affection or perturbation of the mind,—this is a passion. Every desire is a passion: every passion is not a desire. Emotion is another name for passion.

"The mind is of course the seat of all pain and pleasure. The pain of the gout is not in my toe, but in my mind, and I refer it to the toe as the cause. If this were otherwise, I should have ten minds instead of one, and as many on my hands.

"The pains and pleasures of the body ought to be classed among the passions. They are passions to all intents and purposes. The pains of the body have all some affinity to each other, and in consequence of that affinity have received the common name of pain. They are not degrees of the same feeling, but are different feelings, though with some general resemblance. It is an abuse of terms to call the pain excited by gout, by a cut, by a contusion, and by the stomach-ache, degrees of the same feeling. In the same manner, the pleasure arising from sweetness, smoothness, or from savoury tastes, appear to be distinct feelings, with some common relation between them, and therefore denominated pleasures.

"What is true of pain and of pleasure referred to the body, and in popular estimation *supposed* to exist *in* the body, is true also of the pains and pleasures of the mind.

"Grief, hatred, and revenge, are not degrees of the same painful feeling, but distinct feelings. So are hope, joy, and benevolence; but all the agreeable passions have some resemblance to each other,—so have all the disagreeable passions."

I find among his papers various hints for history, such as the following, which are many of them very characteristic.

"In 1758, the Chevalier Barras was burnt to death at Amiens for singing a blasphemous song. Thirty-five years afterwards the Christian religion was abolished all over France, and the church property confiscated.

"Blackstone says that for the Bull *Unigenitus* alone fifty-four thousand *lettres de cachet* were issued. Seventy thousand persons executed in the reign of Henry VIII. (*See* Brodie, vol. i.)

"In 1782, Louis XVI., exercising the right of issuing *lettres de cachet*, and in possession of full and unrestrained power; ten years after, his head was cut off.

"In 1770, the English Legislature taxed the American colonies, and made laws for them; in twelve years afterwards the colonies were declared an independent State.

"In 1797, Ireland petitioned the English Parliament for some small indulgence to their commerce; the petition was unanimously ignored: in eight years afterwards, Ireland was unanimously declared by the same Parliament to be a separate and independent kingdom.

"In America there is no waste of public money; all public matters are conducted with exemplary frugality. On days of ceremony, two constables walk before the President, and he sits down to a joint of meat and a pudding provided at the expense of twenty-two republics.

"The religious mistakes of mankind have been, that there are spirits mingling with mankind, hence *demons, witchcraft;* that God governs the world by present judgments, hence *ordeals;* that there is a connection between the fate of particular men and the heavenly bodies at the time of their birth, hence *astrology;* that God is to be worshiped by the misery and privations of the worshipers, hence *monasteries and flagellations.*

"*Account of Taxes from William the Conqueror.*

1066 . . . £200,000	1566 . . £1,500,000
1266 . . . 150,000	1666 . . 1,800,000
1366 . . . 130,000	1766 . . 17,000,000
1466 . . . 100,000	

"Four years after the Scotch Union, Lord F—— moved its repeal in the House of Lords, 54 against 54; four proxies carried it against the motion.

"Fleury became minister at seventy-three years of age.

"Galileo was made to promise, on his knees, never to teach again the motion of the Earth and the Sun; as a part of his punishment, he was directed to write every week the seven Penitential Psalms.

"The infamous Judge Jeffreys would not give up his Protestantism, and lost the favour of James II.

"At the Revolution, the debt was a million, the revenue two, *i.e.* we owed half a year's income—at present about sixteen years' income.

"Brahmins may eat beef, if killed for sacrifice,—and there are sacrifices every day.

"The Excise and Post Office began under the Commonwealth. Court of Wards abolished in the Commonwealth.

"Colbert never taxed imports as high as ten per cent. *ad valorem;* he had no prohibition.

"The Scotch members used to receive ten guineas per week, secret service money.

"Sir John Trevor, Speaker of the Lower House, was convicted of receiving a bribe of a thousand pounds from the City of London between 1700 and 1716."

Amongst his manuscripts is a sketch he wrote at a later period, giving an account of English misrule of Ireland from the earliest period of our possession up to the present day, compiled from the best existing documents, and forming so fearful a picture that he hesitated to give it to the world when done. After his death, my mother, thinking the time perhaps come when it might be published without injury, referred to what she justly felt was one of the highest historical authorities of our day, and received from Mr. Macaulay the following answer:—

"1847.

"Dear Mrs. Sydney Smith,

"I am truly grateful to you for suffering me to see the sketch of Irish history, drawn up by my admirable and excellent friend. I perfectly understand the generous feeling with which it was written, and I also think that I see why it was never published. While the Catholic disabilities lasted, he whom we regret did all that he could to awaken the conscience of the oppressors and to find excuses for the faults of the oppressed. When these disabilities had been removed, and when designing men still attempted to inflame the Irish against England, by repeating tales of grievances which had passed away, he felt that this work would no longer do any good, and that it might be used by demagogues in such a way as to do positive harm. You will see, from what I have said, that though I think this piece honourable to his memory, I do not wish to see it published, nor do I think that, though it would raise the reputation of almost any other writer of our time, it would raise his; in truth, nothing that is not of very rare and striking merit ought now to be given to the world under his name. He is universally admitted to have been a great reasoner, and the greatest master of ridicule that has appeared among us since Swift.* Many things, there-

* I find my father here, and indeed in almost every sketch of him, compared to Swift in the character of his writings. It is for others to decide upon the justness of the comparison; but there is one difference I ought, and I am proud to point out, that there is not a single line in them that might not be placed before the purity

fore, which, if they came from an inferior author, would be read with pleasure, will produce disappointment if published as works of Mr. Sydney Smith. I return the papers with most sincere thanks. Believe me ever, dear Mrs. Sydney Smith, yours very truly,
"T. B. MACAULAY."

My father had not long been established in his house at Heslington before several of his old friends found him out; amongst the first of these were Mr. Horner, Mr. Murray, and Mr. Adams. In August Mr. Abercrombie and his family spent a few days with him, which gave him much pleasure; and he had also a visit from Lord Webb Seymour, one of the friends with whom he had lived most intimately at Edinburgh, and whose early death was a source of deep regret to him.

He made the resolution, when he settled in the country, never to shoot; "first," he says, "because I found, on trying at Lord Grey's, that the birds seemed to consider the muzzle of my gun as their safest position; secondly, because I never could help shutting

of youth, or that is unfit for the eye of a woman; that he has exercised his powers of wit and sarcasm to the utmost, without ever sullying his pages with impurities, or degrading his talents and profession by irreligion; and this, I believe, can in very few instances be asserted of any other eminently humorous writer, either French or English, who have used such powers to any great extent. Lord John Russell, in writing of my father, says on this subject:—"Too much indulgence has been shown to the extravagance, dishonesty, and domestic infidelity of men of wit, as if the 'light that led astray was light from heaven.' It is not light from heaven, but flashes from a volcano which has its seat in hell."

my eyes when I fired my gun, so was not likely to improve; and thirdly, because, if you do shoot, the squire and the poacher both consider you as their natural enemy, and I thought it more clerical to be at peace with both."

In 1810 my father had the pleasure of receiving his old and valued friend, Sir Samuel Romilly, and his family; and so deep was his veneration for the unbending virtue of this great man, that it was one not easily forgotten. No two men were ever more unlike, or pursued the same ends by such different paths; yet they had many feelings in common, and a total absence of all those littlenesses which sometimes obscure and alienate even great men. I remember Sir Samuel went with my father to see Castle Howard, at which he gazed with great admiration, and after a long pause, standing on the steps of the portico and looking towards the mausoleum and at the lovely landscape around, he exclaimed, spreading out his arms, "These are indeed things that must make death terrible!"

Some years after, my father introduced the following passage, on the recent death of Sir Samuel Romilly, into a sermon on the subject of Meditation on Death, and as it has not been published, I shall insert it here, as a proof of his feelings towards that eminent man:—

"And let me ask you, my brethren, we who see the good and great daily perishing before our eyes, what comfort have we but this hope in Christ that we shall meet again? Remember the eminent men who, within the few years last past, have paid the great debt of nature. The earth stript of its moral grandeur, sunk in its spiritual pride. The melancholy wreck of talents and of wisdom gone, my brethren, when we feel how dear, how valuable they were to us, when we would have asked of God on our bended knees their preservation and . their life. Can we live with all that is excellent in human nature, can we study it, can we contemplate it, and then lose it and never hope to see it again?

"Can we say of any human being, as we may say of that great man who was torn from us in the beginning of this winter, that he acted with vast capacity upon all the great calamities of life; that he came with unblemished purity to restrain iniquity; that, condemning injustice, he was just; that, restraining corruption, he was pure; that those who were provoked to look into the life of a great statesman, found him a good man also, and acknowledged he was sincere even when they did not believe he was right? Can we say of such a man, with all the career of worldly ambition before him, that he was the friend of the wretched and the poor; that in the midst of vast occupation he remembered the debtor's cell, the prisoner's dungeon, the last hour of the law's victim; that he meditated day and night on wretchedness, weakness, and want? Can we say all this of any human being, and then have him no more in remembrance? When you 'die daily,' my brethren; when you remember my text, paint to yourselves the gathering together again of the good and the just.

"Remember that God is to be worshiped, that death is to be met, by such a life as this; remember, in the last hour, that rank, that birth, that wealth, that all earthly things will vanish away, that you will then think only of the wretchedness you have lessened and the good you have done."

I see, by letters in my possession, that on the publication of Sir Samuel's Life by his sons, my father's letter of warm admiration was the first received by the family; and the terms in which they speak of the value of my father's praise is highly gratifying to those who love his memory.

My father had by this time made a considerable acquaintance in and round York. Dining out on one occasion, he happened to meet Mr. ——, whom he always met with pleasure, as he was a man of sense, simplicity, and learning; and with such a total absence, not only of humour in himself, but in his perception of it in others, as made him an amusing subject of speculation to my father.

The conversation at dinner took a liberal turn. My father, in the full career of his spirits, happened to say, "Though he was not generally considered an illiberal man, yet he must confess he had one little weakness, one secret wish,—he should like to *roast a Quaker*."

"Good heavens, Mr. Smith!" said Mr. ——, full

of horror, "roast a Quaker?" "Yes, Sir" (with the greatest gravity), "roast a Quaker!" "But do you consider, Mr. Smith, the torture?" "Yes, Sir," said my father, "I have considered everything; it may be wrong, as you say: the Quaker would undoubtedly suffer acutely, but every one has his tastes, mine would be to roast a Quaker: one would satisfy me, only one; but it is one of those peculiarities I have striven against in vain, and I hope you will pardon my weakness."

Mr. ——'s honest simplicity could stand this no longer, and he seemed hardly able to sit at table with him. The whole company were in roars of laughter at the scene; but neither this, nor the mirth and mischief sparkling in my father's eye, enlightened him in the least, for a joke was a thing of which he had no conception. At last my father, seeing that he was giving real pain, said, "Come, come, Mr. ——, since you think this so very illiberal, I must be wrong; and will give up my roasted Quaker rather than your esteem; let us drink wine together." Peace was made, but I believe neither time nor explanation would have ever made him comprehend that it was a joke.

Though it was the general habit in Yorkshire to make visits of two or three days at the houses in the neighbourhood, yet not unfrequently invitations to dinner only came, and sometimes to a house at a considerable distance.

"Did you ever dine out in the country?" said my father; "what misery human beings inflict on each other under the name of pleasure! We went to dine last Thursday with Mr. ——, a neighbouring clergyman, a haunch of venison being the stimulus to the invitation. We set out at five o'clock, drove in a broiling sun on dusty roads three miles in our best gowns, found Squire and parsons assembled in a small hot room, the whole house redolent of frying; talked, as is our wont, of roads, weather, and turnips; that done, began to grow hungry, then serious, then impatient. At last a stripling, evidently caught up for the occasion, opened the door and beckoned our host out of the room. After some moments of awful suspense, he returned to us with a face of much distress, saying, 'the woman assisting in the kitchen had mistaken the soup for dirty water, and had thrown it away, so we must do without it;' we all agreed it was perhaps as well we should, under the circumstances. At last, to our joy, dinner was announced; but oh, ye gods! as we entered the dining-room what a gale met our nose! the venison was high, the venison was uneatable, and was obliged to follow the soup with all speed.

"Dinner proceeded, but our spirits flagged under these accumulated misfortunes: there was an ominous pause between the first and second course; we looked each other in the face—what new disaster awaited us? the pause became fearful. At last the door burst open, and the boy rushed in, calling out aloud, 'Please, Sir, has Betty any right to leather I?' What human gravity could stand this? we roared with laughter; all took part against Betty, obtained the second course with some difficulty, bored each other the usual time, ordered our carriages, expecting our post-boys to be drunk, and were grateful to Providence for not permitting them to deposit us in a wet ditch. So much for dinners in the country!"

This winter he had another visit from his friend Jeffrey, who came with an American gentleman, Mr. Simond, and his niece, Miss Wilkes. We little suspected then that this lady, great-niece to the agitator Wilkes, was so soon after to become Mrs. Jeffrey. We had also visits from Mr. Horner, Mr. Murray, and Lord Lauderdale. My father used to say of Mr. Horner that he had the Ten Commandments written on his face; in fact, that he looked so virtuous, that he might commit any crime, and no one would believe in the possibility of his guilt.

It was, I believe, in 1812 that my father's eldest brother Robert, who had gone out to India, as Advocate-General of Bengal eight years before, returned with his wife and family to this country,—a return we had all been eagerly looking forward to. Before leaving India, my uncle had with great generosity offered to remain there another year, and to bestow the proceeds of his office on my father: but my father, poor as he was, fearing the effects of the climate on his brother, and knowing his ardent desire to return to England, with equal generosity refused, without a moment's hesitation, to accept of such a sacrifice. We went to their house in town to meet them, and spent some weeks there.

My father was received with open arms by all his old friends; and the pleasure and interest of this visit to his old haunts was much enhanced by the arrival of his friend Sir James Mackintosh, likewise from India, after an absence from England of about the same time. He had arrived on the eve of a general election, and during the excitement of political changes consequent upon the murder of Mr. Percival, and the attempt to form a Ministry under Lord Wellesley.

In the summer Sir James went with Lady Mackintosh to the Highlands, and on their return spent some days with my father at Heslington. In the autumn of the following year, Madame de Staël, driven from Copet by the persecutions of Napoleon, took refuge in England, and was the object of general interest and attention. She was constantly in the society of Sir James Mackintosh, and having heard much of my father, and of his powers of conversation and argument, she was eager to make his acquaintance, and try her eloquence upon him. She used frequently to say to Sir James, with the odd jumble she made of English titles and names, " Mais, votre ami Sydney Smith, ce Prêtre-Amiral, pourquoi ne vient-il pas ?"

The Prêtre-Amiral was unable to leave his parish during her visit here, so they never met; but she took her revenge some years after at Nice, where she made the acquaintance of my father's elder brother Robert, whose wonderful powers of argument and exquisite French she revelled in through a whole winter; though often defeated by him in discussions, to the delight of all the English staying there, whom she had bullied terribly before his arrival, and who looked up to him as a sort of champion. "Ah! pourquoi ne parlez-vous pas comme ça dans la Chambre des Communes?" said Madame de Staël to him one day, after listening for some time to the eloquent flow of his language. Mr. Canning used to say, " Bobus's language is the essence of English."

Sir James Mackintosh, speaking of him in India, says, "I hear frequently of Bobus; his fame amongst the natives is greater than that of any pundit since the days of Menu."

The following year my uncle came down with his family to visit us in Yorkshire, and remained a month with us. On his return to Northampton, a typhus fever attacked his family with most fearful and fatal results, then the nurse, and lastly himself. My aunt, in communicating these dreadful tidings, entreated my father to come to their aid, and, after taking medical advice as to the best precautions against infection, he set off, in spite of my mother's earnest entreaties, without a moment's hesitation.

An intimate friend, who was staying with us at the time, and present at this scene, tells me, "Nothing in my long knowledge of him ever gave me a higher idea of your father's generosity of character and firmness of principle than this act; for, in addition to his knowledge how dependent you all were upon him, and that your mother was near her confinement, he went, not ignorant of, or despising, the danger, but with his eyes open to it, fearing it very much, and fully believing he was going to meet death. But in spite of his own fears and your poor mother's efforts, he resisted, and said, 'If any evil were to happen to Bobus, I should reproach myself all my life; but,' added he, 'Kate, mind, if I do die, you must always keep the day of my death.'"

He remained with my uncle some weeks, until he had the satisfaction of leaving him convalescent, and comfortably established in a house near Northampton, under the care of the most eminent physician there, Dr. Carr, uncle to Lady Davy; and of returning in safety to my poor mother, whose anxiety during this period may easily be imagined.

Amongst our rural delights at Heslington was the possession of a young donkey, which had been given up to our tender mercies from the time of its birth, and in whose education we employed a large portion of our spare time; and a most accomplished donkey it became under our tuition. It would walk up-stairs, pick pockets, follow us in our walks like a huge Newfoundland dog, and at the most distant sight of us in the field, with ears down and tail erect, it set off in full bray to meet us. These demonstrations on Bitty's part were met with not less affection on ours, and Bitty was almost considered a member of the family.

One day, when my elder brother and myself were training our beloved Bitty, with a pocket-handkerchief for a bridle, and his head crowned with flowers, to run round our garden, who should arrive in the midst of our sport but Mr. Jeffrey. Finding my father out, he, with his usual kindness towards young people, immediately joined in our sport, and, to our infinite delight, mounted our donkey. He was proceeding in triumph, amidst our shouts of laughter, when my father and mother, in company, I believe, with Mr. Horner and Mr. Murray, returned from their walk, and beheld this scene from the garden-door. Though years and years have passed away since, I still remember the joy-inspiring laughter that burst from my father at this unexpected sight, as, advancing towards his old friend, with a face beaming with delight and with extended hands, he broke forth in the following impromptu:—

"Witty as Horatius Flaccus,
As great a Jacobin as Gracchus;
Short, though not as fat, as Bacchus,
Riding on a little jackass."

These lines were afterwards repeated by some one to Mr. —— at Holland House, just before he was introduced for the first time to Mr. Jeffrey, and they caught his fancy to such a degree that he could not get them out of his head, but kept repeating them in a low voice all the time Mr. Jeffrey was conversing with him.

I must end Bitty's history, as he has been introduced, by saying that he followed us to Foston; and, after serving us faithfully for thirteen years, on our leaving Yorkshire was permitted by our kind friend

Lord Carlisle to spend the rest of his days in idleness and plenty, in his beautiful park, with an unbounded command of thistles.

My father meanwhile had entered into various negotiations with different clergymen to effect an exchange of livings, but the conditions imposed by Lord Eldon had hitherto prevented them from being carried into effect.

He continued, therefore, to drive over every week to do duty at his living. One Sunday (to show the very primitive state of the villagers), just as he was about to enter the church, there was a general rush of the clerk, the sexton, the churchwardens, and principal farmers after him, who, with agitated countenances, exclaimed, "Please your honour, a coach, a coach!" My father, with a calmness that filled them with wonder, said, "Well, well, my good friends, stand firm, never mind; even though there should be a coach, it will do us no harm; let us see." And certainly a carriage was seen approaching, such as rarely appeared in those parts; and as it advanced rapidly towards the little miserable hovel which had once been the parsonage-house, it was discovered to contain a very fashionable lady. The lady turned out to be Mrs. Apreece, on her way from Scotland, bringing letters of introduction to my father, whom she was anxious to hear preach; and this was the beginning of an acquaintance which afterwards ripened into intimacy, and several of the most amusing of his letters are addressed to her, under her more celebrated name of Lady Davy. She and Sir Humphry in after-times not unfrequently put up at the Rector's Head (as my father used to call his house), and no landlord could rejoice more in "a run on the road," or more cordially welcome the sight of an old friend.

CHAPTER VII.

BUILDS HOUSE.—REMOVES TO FOSTON.—DESCRIPTION OF ESTABLISHMENT.—VISIT OF SIR JAMES MACKINTOSH.—BECOMES A MAGISTRATE.—VISIT TO NEWGATE WITH MRS. FRY, AND SERMON.—VISIT TO SIR G. PHILIPS IN IMMORTAL.—FORMS THE ACQUAINTANCE OF THE EARL OF CARLISLE.—DEATH OF ONLY SISTER.—LAST VISIT FROM MR. HORNER.—BAD HARVEST AND FEVER.—EXERTIONS AMONGST THE POOR.—VISIT FROM LORD AND LADY HOLLAND.—LEAVES OFF RIDING.—DESCRIPTION OF CALAMITY.—SHOPPING AND ANECDOTES.—SENDS SON TO SCHOOL.—VISITS LORD GREY.—ACCOUNT OF TRAVELS.—VISIT FROM DR. MARCET.—CONVERSATION, AND BUNCH.—INSCRIPTION FOR DUKE OF BEDFORD'S STATUE.—ANECDOTE OF LORD ——'S SON.—ASSIZES.—HUNT'S TRIAL.—DANGER OF BAD HARVEST.—DEATH OF GRATTAN.

THUS cheered by these occasional visits of his friends, turning his back upon London and former habits, by the aid of books and of the various new duties and interests he had created for himself, he contrived to pass through three years not unpleasantly or unprofitably; but, not having succeeded in his object of exchange, he, according to his promise to the Archbishop, set vigorously to work to build his house, and accomplished it in nine months after laying the first stone. But he shall here tell his own tale, as I have heard it at various times in detached portions.

"A diner-out, a wit, and a popular preacher, I was

suddenly caught up by the Archbishop of York, and transported to my living in Yorkshire, where there had not been a resident clergyman for a hundred and fifty years. Fresh from London, not knowing a turnip from a carrot, I was compelled to farm three hundred acres, and without capital to build a parsonage-house.

"I asked and obtained three years' leave from the Archbishop, in order to effect an exchange, if possible; and fixed myself meantime at a small village two miles from York, in which was a fine old house of the time of Queen Elizabeth, where resided the last of the squires, with his lady, who looked as if she had walked straight out of the Ark, or had been the wife of Enoch. He was a perfect specimen of the Trullibers of old; he smoked, hunted, drank beer at his door with his grooms and dogs, and spelt over the county paper on Sundays.

"At first, he heard I was a Jacobin and a dangerous fellow, and turned aside as I passed: but at length, when he found the peace of the village undisturbed, harvests much as usual, Juno and Ponto uninjured, he first bowed, then called, and at last reached such a pitch of confidence that he used to bring the papers, that I might explain the difficult words to him; actually discovered that I had made a joke, laughed till I thought he would have died of convulsions, and ended by inviting me to see his dogs.

"All my efforts for an exchange having failed, I asked and obtained from my friend the Archbishop another year to build in. And I then set my shoulder to the wheel in good earnest; sent for an architect; he produced plans which would have ruined me. I made him my bow: 'You build for glory, Sir; I, for use.' I returned him his plans, with five-and-twenty pounds, and sat down in my thinking-chair, and in a few hours Mrs. Sydney and I concocted a plan which has produced what I call the model of parsonage-houses.

"I then took to horse to provide bricks and timber; was advised to make my own bricks, of my own clay; of course, when the kiln was opened, all bad; mounted my horse again, and in twenty-four hours had bought thousands of bricks and tons of timber. Was advised by neighbouring gentlemen to employ oxen: bought four,—Tug and Lug, Hawl and Crawl; but Tug and Lug took to fainting, and required buckets of sal-volatile, and Hawl and Crawl to lie down in the mud. So I did as I ought to have done at first,— took the advice of the farmer instead of the gentleman; sold my oxen, bought a team of horses, and at last, in spite of a frost which delayed me six weeks, in spite of walls running down with wet, in spite of the advice and remonstrances of friends who predicted our death, in spite of an infant of six months old, who had never been out of the house, I landed my family in my new house nine months after laying the first stone, on the 20th of March; and performed my promise to the letter to the Archbishop, by issuing forth at midnight with a lantern to meet the last cart, with the cook and the cat, which had stuck in the mud, and fairly established them before twelve o'clock at night in the new parsonage-house;—a feat, taking ignorance, inexperience, and poverty into consideration, requiring, I assure you, no small degree of energy.

"It made me a very poor man for many years, but I never repented it. I turned schoolmaster, to educate my son, as I could not afford to send him to school. Mrs. Sydney turned schoolmistress, to educate my girls, as I could not afford a governess. I turned farmer, as I could not let my land. A manservant was too expensive; so I caught up a little garden-girl, made like a milestone, christened her Bunch, put a napkin in her hand, and made her my butler. The girls taught her to read, Mrs. Sydney to wait, and I undertook her morals; Bunch became the best butler in the county.

"I had little furniture, so I bought a cart-load of deals; took a carpenter (who came to me for parish relief, called Jack Robinson) with a face like a fullmoon, into my service; established him in a barn, and said, 'Jack, furnish my house.' You see the result!

"At last it was suggested that a carriage was much wanted in the establishment; after diligent search, I discovered in the back settlements of a York coach-maker an ancient green chariot, supposed to have been the earliest invention of the kind. I brought it home in triumph to my admiring family. Being somewhat dilapidated, the village tailor lined it, the village blacksmith repaired it; nay, (but for Mrs. Sydney's earnest entreaties,) we believe the village painter would have exercised his genius upon the exterior; it escaped this danger however, and the result was wonderful. Each year added to its charms: it grew younger and younger; a new wheel, a new spring; I christened it the *Immortal;* it was known all over the neighbourhood; the village boys cheered it, and the village dogs barked at it; but 'Faber meæ fortunæ' was my motto, and we had no false shame.

"Added to all these domestic cares, I was village parson, village doctor, village comforter, village magistrate, and Edinburgh Reviewer; so you see I had not much time left on my hands to regret London.

"My house was considered the ugliest in the county, but all admitted it was one of the most comfortable; and we did not die, as our friends had predicted, of the damp walls of the parsonage."

This year (1813) was one of great exertion and anxiety to him, both in body and mind; he calculated that in the course of it he must have ridden several times round the world, in going backwards and forwards from Heslington to his living, as the offices of architect, superintendent of the works, farmer, clergyman, schoolmaster, were all centred in his person; while, to add to his anxieties and responsibilities, in September of this year another son was born to him.

Soon after engaging on the building of his house, the Archbishop, who had been made more fully aware of the difficulties of my father's situation, through the kind intervention of Mr. Harcourt and other friends, sent my father most unexpectedly his formal permission to avoid building. On hearing this, my father received many letters of remonstrance from Mr. Allen, and his kind friends at Holland House, who always hoped that some exchange might turn up, to restore him again to the south; and indeed were constantly making exertions to accomplish this object; but as the negotiations failed, I have not named them. They were most unwilling that he should embark in an undertaking which they knew would hamper him for so many years to come. But my father felt it was his duty to himself, to his parish, and to the Archbishop, whose indulgence it would be base to abuse; and being thoroughly convinced of this, he persevered, in spite of this strong temptation; though the necessity of making farm-buildings, as well as a house, absorbed not only all his available capital, but left him with a heavy debt besides.

At last, however, the deed was done, and I well remember the landing at Foston, March, 1814. Indeed how should I forget it?—a day of such difficulty, discomfort, bustle, and delight, seldom occurs twice in one life.

It was a cold, bright March day, with a biting east wind. The beds we left in the morning had to be packed up and slept on at night; waggon after waggon of furniture poured in every minute; the roads were so cut up that the carriage could not reach the door; and my mother lost her shoe in the mud, which was ankle-deep, whilst bringing her infant up to the house in her arms.

But oh, the shout of joy as we entered and took possession!—the first time in our lives that we had inhabited a house of our own. How we admired it, ugly as it was! With what pride my dear father welcomed us, and took us from room to room; old Molly Mills, the milk-woman, who had had charge of the house, grinning with delight in the background. We thought it a palace; yet the drawing-room had no door, the bare plaster walls ran down with wet, the windows were like ground-glass from the moisture which had to be wiped up several times a day by the housemaid. No carpets, no chairs, nothing unpacked; rough men bringing in rougher packages at every moment. But then was the time to behold my father!—amid the confusion, he thought for everybody, cared for everybody, encouraged everybody, kept everybody in good-humour. How he exerted himself! how his loud, rich voice might be heard in all directions, ordering, arranging, explaining, till the household storm gradually subsided! Each half-hour improved our condition; fires blazed in every room; at last we all sat down to our tea, spread by ourselves on a huge package before the drawing-room fire, sitting on boxes round it; and retired to sleep on our beds placed on the floor;—the happiest, merriest, and busiest family in Christendom. In a few days, under my father's active exertions, everything was arranged with tolerable comfort in the little household, and it began to assume its wonted appearance.

In speaking of the establishment of Foston, Annie

Kay must not be forgotten. She entered our service at nineteen years of age, but possessing a degree of sense and lady-like feeling not often found in her situation of life,—first as nurse, then as lady's-maid, then housekeeper, apothecary's boy, factotum, and friend. All who have been much at Foston or Combe Florey know Annie Kay; she was called into consultation on every family event, and proved herself a worthy oracle. Her counsels were delivered in the softest voice, with the sweetest smile, and in the broadest Yorkshire. She ended by nursing her old master through his long and painful illness, night and day; she was with him at his death; she followed him to his grave; she was remembered in his will; she survived him but two years, which she spent in my mother's house; and, after her long and faithful service of thirty years, was buried by my mother in the same cemetery as her master, respected and lamented by all his family, as the most faithful of servants and friends.

So much for the interior of the establishment. Out-of-doors reigned Molly Mills,—cow, pig, poultry, garden, and post woman; with her short red petticoat, her legs like millposts, her high cheek-bones red and shrivelled like winter apples; a perfect specimen of a "yeowoman;" a sort of kindred spirit, too; for she was the wit of the village, and delighted in a crack with her master, when she could get it. She was as important in her vocation as Annie Kay in hers; and Molly here, and Molly there, might be heard in every direction. Molly was always merry, willing, active, and true as gold; she had little book-learning, but enough to bring up two fine athletic sons, as honest as herself; though, unlike her, they were never seen to smile, but were as solemn as two owls, and would not have said a civil thing to save their lives. They ruled the farm. Add to these, the pet donkey, Bitty, already introduced to the public; a tame fawn, at last dismissed for eating the maid's clothes, which he preferred to any other diet; and a lame goose, condemned at last to be roasted for eating all the fruit in the garden; together with Bunch and Jack Robinson, already mentioned,—and you have the establishment.

As magistrates were much wanted in our neighbourhood, my father had now, in addition to his numerous avocations, taken upon himself the duties of a Justice of the Peace. He set vigorously to work to study Blackstone, and made himself master of as much law as possible, instead of blundering on, as many of his neighbours were content to do. Partly by this knowledge, partly by his good-humour, he gained a considerable influence in the quorum, which used to meet once a fortnight at the little inn, called the Lobster-house; and the people used to say they were "going to get a little of Mr. Smith's lobster-sauce." By dint of his powerful voice, and a little wooden hammer, he prevailed on Bob and Betty to speak one at a time; he always tried, and often succeeded, in turning foes into friends. Having a horror of the Game-laws, then in full force, and knowing, as he states in his speech on the Reform Bill, that for every ten pheasants which fluttered in the wood one English peasant was rotting in gaol, he was always secretly on the side of the poacher (much to the indignation of his fellow-magistrates, who in a poacher saw a monster of iniquity), and always contrived, if possible, to let him escape; rather than commit him to gaol, with the certainty of his returning to the world an accomplished villain. He endeavoured to avoid exercising his function as magistrate in his own village when possible, as he wished to be at peace with all his parishioners.

Young delinquents he never could bear to commit; but read them a severe lecture, and in extreme cases called out, "John, bring me my *private gallows!*" which infallibly brought the little urchins weeping on their knees, and, "Oh! for God's sake, your honour, pray forgive us!" and his honour used graciously to pardon them for this time, and delay the arrival of the private gallows, and seldom had occasion to repeat the threat. Indeed the subject of imprisonment occupied his mind so much, that during a visit to town, having been much interested by the account of Mrs. Fry's benevolent exertions in prisons, he requested permission to accompany her to Newgate; and I have heard him say he never felt more deeply affected or impressed than by the beautiful spectacle he there witnessed; it made him, he said, weep like a child. In a sermon he preached shortly after, he introduced the following passage:—

"There is a spectacle which this town now exhibits, that I will venture to call the most solemn, the most Christian, the most affecting which any human being ever witnessed. To see that holy woman in the midst of the wretched prisoners; to see them all calling earnestly upon God, soothed by her voice, animated by her look, clinging to the hem of her garment; and worshiping her as the only being who has ever loved them, or taught them, or noticed them, or spoken to them of God! This is the sight which breaks down the pageant of the world; which tells us that the short hour of life is passing away, and that we must prepare by some good deeds to meet God ; that it is time to give, to pray, to comfort; to go, like this blessed woman, and do the work of our heavenly Saviour, Jesus, among the guilty, among the broken-hearted and the sick, and to labour in the deepest and darkest wretchedness of life."

In February, 1815, we set out on a visit to the late Sir George Philips ; and great was the general ship, and various the contrivances to persuade the far-famed Immortal to convey us all safely over Blackstone Edge, a sort of Alps between Yorkshire and Lancashire, in the depths of winter; but under such a Hannibal, all prospered, and the Immortal covered itself with glory.

In this house we spent some weeks so agreeably,— I believe, I may say, to both parties,—that the visit was by mutual consent repeated every two or three years. There was a constant succession of agreeable guests; and our kind host so revelled in my father's humour, that he was incessantly stimulating him to attack him, which my father certainly did most vigorously; yet I believe no one present enjoyed these attacks more than Sir George himself, who laughed at them almost to exhaustion.

After our return home, the chief event in the course of the summer, which broke the even tenour of our lives, was a first visit from our great neighbours, Lord and Lady Carlisle. Though not begun under the most favourable auspices, it must be mentioned in these simple annals; as from this visit proceeded not only much agreeable society, but twenty years of such warm friendship; such delicate, unvarying, unoppressive kindness; such essential benefits, from every member of that family, both old and young, as must be always remembered with gratitude by us, contributing as they did to the pleasure and comfort of my father's life, and giving him a command of books and society, which would otherwise have been quite out of his reach.

Our infant colony was still in so rude a state, that roads, save for a cart, had hardly been thought of, when suddenly a cry was raised, that a coach and four, with outriders, was plunging about in the midst of a ploughed field near the house, and showing signals of distress. Ploughmen and ploughwomen were immediately sent off to the rescue, and at last the gold coach (as Lady Carlisle used to call it), which had mistaken the road, was guided safely up to the house, and the kind old Lord and Lady, not a little shaken, and a little cross at so rough a reception, entered the parsonage; but the shakes were soon forgotten, and good-humour restored; and after some severe sarcasms on the state of the approach to our house on the part of the old Earl, and promises of amendment on the part of my father, Lord Carlisle* drove off, and made us promise to come and stay with him at Castle Howard.

This was the first and last difficulty he ever found in coming to Foston. From this time a week seldom passed without his driving over to occupy his snug corner by the parsonage fireside, where his conversation was so epigrammatic and full of anecdotes of past times, that it was always a most agreeable half-hour to old and young. He never went away without leaving some little gift in the shape of game, fruit, flowers, or other tokens of kindness.

In 1816, my father lost his only sister, Maria, my mother's earliest friend. Charming in mind and character,† she had very delicate health, and lived unmarried with her father at Bath; my father was much attached to her, and felt her loss severely. He says, in a letter, "The loss of a person whom I would have cultivated as a friend, if nature had not given her to me as a relation, is a serious evil." We all went to see my grandfather in consequence of her death, and remained some time with him.

* Grandfather of the present Earl of Carlisle.
† Bobus used to say she had carried off all the good temper of the family.

On our return home, our poor friend Mr. Horner, whose health had been gradually failing, and had given great anxiety to all his friends, was condemned to go and end his short but noble career in a foreign land; and came to make his farewell visit to us at Foston, where he was loved and valued as a brother. His mind appeared more pure and beautiful than ever; but it was a melancholy visit, extinguishing all hope, for death was stamped on his brow. Yet, young as he was, his virtues had created, in the hearts of all who knew him, a lasting monument of love and esteem, which death only can destroy. My father says, in the sketch he wrote of Mr. Horner, "There was in his look a calm, settled love of all that was honourable and good—an air of wisdom and of sweetness; you saw at once that he was a great man, whom nature had intended for a leader of human beings. You ranged yourself willingly under his banners, and cheerfully submitted to his sway." He died at Pisa the following spring, attended by his brother, and soothed by the frequent society and regard of the Miss Allens, his early friends, who happened to be staying there: a death so mourned by his country, that I see Sir James Mackintosh says, "Never was so much honour paid in any age or nation to intrinsic claims alone : a man of thirty-eight, of obscure birth, who never filled an office, or had the power of obliging a single living creature, and whose grand title to this distinction from an English House of Commons was the belief of his virtue." My father speaks of his feelings on this loss, in the following letter to Mr. Horner's younger brother:—

"*Foston, March* 23, 1817.

"My dear Sir,

"I remember no misfortune of my life which I have felt so deeply as the loss of your brother. I never saw any man who combined together so much talent, worth, and warmth of heart; and we lived together in habits of great friendship and affection for many years. I shall always retain a most lively and affectionate remembrance of him to the day of my death. We shall be most happy to see you here if you can make us a visit; I shall always meet you with those sentiments of regard and respect which are due to yourself, but never without deep feelings of grief and emotion.

"God bless you!

"S. S.

"I beg of you to give my very kind regards to your father and mother; it is in vain to speak of their loss, to write to them: I dare not do it."

And again, in a letter to Mr. Whishaw, he says:—

"*March* 26, 1817.

"My dear Whishaw,

"I have received a melancholy fragment from poor Horner,—a letter half finished at his death. I cannot say how much I was affected by it; indeed, on looking back on my own mind, I never remember to have felt an event more deeply than his death. It is very requisite that there should be a monument to Horner: it will be some little satisfaction to us all."

And in another, he says :—

"I say nothing of the great and miserable loss we have all sustained. He will always live in our recollection; and it will be useful to us all, in the great occasions of life, to reflect how Horner would act and think in them, if God had prolonged his life."

This year, 1816, from the failure of the harvest, the distress amongst the poor was excessive. The wheat was generally sprouted throughout the country, and unfit for bread; and good flour was not only dear, but hardly to be procured. We, like our poorer neighbours, being unable to afford it, were obliged to consume our own sprouted wheat; and we lived therefore a whole year, without tasting bread, on thin, unleavened, sweet-tasting cakes, like frost-bitten potatoes, baked on tins, the only way of using this damaged flour. The luxury of returning to bread again can hardly be imagined by those who have never been deprived of it. All this bad food produced much illness amongst our poor neighbours; and a fever of a very dangerous and infectious kind broke out in our village. My father was indefatigable in his exertions amongst them, going from cottage to cottage, and providing them with food and medicine, and seeing that they were properly attended to: his medical skill stood him in good stead now. He found it impossible at first to prevent the peasants from crowding into the infected houses, till the number of deaths so alarmed them, that at last he had equal difficulty in making them go at all, or in obtaining nurses for the sick, or people even to convey the bodies to the grave, till he shamed them into it, by threatening to become one of the bearers himself.

He was much struck by the heroic conduct of some of the Quakers of the village, who, amid the general panic, were constant and active in their attention to the sick. "Are you aware of the danger?" said my father. "Oh, we have no fears; we are in the hands of God, thou knowest," was the reply.

During the summer, Lord and Lady Holland came to look at the new parsonage-house, and pass judgment upon it, in their way to the North. They left their eldest daughter under my mother's care during their absence, to our great happiness; during whose stay, Mr. Rogers spent a week at Foston, charming old and young by his kindness and inexhaustible fund of anecdote. Sir H. Davy, Mr. Warburton, and various others, also found their way to the "Rector's Head" during the summer.

My father at this period was in the habit of riding a good deal, but, either from the badness of his horses or the badness of his riding, or perhaps from both (in spite of his various ingenious contrivances to keep himself in the saddle), he had several falls, and kept us in continual anxiety. He writes, in a letter, "I used to think a fall from a horse dangerous, but much experience has convinced me to the contrary. I have had six falls in two years, and just behaved like the three per cents when they fall,—I got up again, and am not a bit the worse for it, any more than the stock in question." In speaking of this, he says, " I left off riding, for the good of my parish and the peace of my family; for, somehow or other, my horse and I had a habit of parting company. On one occasion I found myself suddenly prostrate in the streets of York, much to the delight of the Dissenters. Another time, my horse Calamity flung me over his head into a neighbouring parish, as if I had been a shuttlecock, and I felt grateful it was not into a neighbouring planet; but as no harm came of it, I might have persevered perhaps, if, on a certain day, a Quaker tailor from a neighbouring village, to which I had said I was going to ride, had not taken it into his head to call, soon after my departure, and request to see Mrs. Sydney. She instantly, conceiving I was thrown, if not killed, rushed down to the man, exclaiming, 'Where is he? where is your master? is he hurt?' The astonished and quaking snip stood silent from surprise. Still more agitated by his silence, she exclaimed, 'Is he hurt? I insist upon knowing the worst.' 'Why, please, ma'am, it is only thy little bill, a very small account, I wanted thee to settle,' replied he, in much surprise. After this, you may suppose, I sold my horse; however, it is some comfort to know that my friend Sir George is one fall ahead of me, and is certainly a worse rider. It is a great proof, too, of the liberality of this county, where everybody can ride as soon as they are born, that they tolerate me at all."

The horse Calamity, whose name has been thus introduced, was the first-born of several young horses bred on the farm, who turned out very fine creatures, and gained him great glory, even amongst the knowing farmers of Yorkshire; but this first production was certainly not encouraging. To his dismay, a huge, lank, large-boned foal appeared, of chestnut colour, and with four white legs. It grew apace, but its bones became more and more conspicuous; its appetite was unbounded,—grass, hay, corn, beans, food moist and dry, were all supplied in vain, and vanished down his throat with incredible rapidity. He stood, a large living skeleton, with famine written in his face, and my father christened him Calamity. As Calamity grew to maturity, he was found to be as sluggish in disposition as his master was impetuous; so my father was driven to invent his patent Tantalus, which consisted of a small sieve of corn, suspended on a semicircular bar of iron, from the ends of the shafts, just beyond the horse's nose. The corn, rattling as the vehicle proceeded, stimulated Calamity to unwonted exertions; and under the hope of overtaking this imaginary feed, he did more work than all the previous provender which had been poured down his throat had been able to obtain from him.

He was very fond of his young horses, and they all came running to meet him when he entered the field. He began their education from their birth: he taught them to wear a girth, a bridle, a saddle, to meet flags, music, to bear the firing of a pistol at their heads, from their earliest years, and he maintained that no horses were so well broken as his.

After our establishment at Foston, an old lady, the widow of an artist, a woman of some fortune, large dimensions, considerable talents, and much oddity, came to establish herself in a small cottage at no great distance, and was so delighted with her neighbour, that she kindly offered to drop in (as she said) frequently to tea. My father, though the most sociable of human beings, felt rather alarmed at this threatened invasion of his privacy; yet, unwilling to hurt the old lady, he at last bethought himself of writing a most comical letter, full of all sorts of imaginary facts, to her, accepting her offer, only begging to have full notice of her approach: "for," said he, "at home I sit in an old coat, which may have a hole in it; now I like to appear before you in my best. When alone we have the black kettle, we should have the urn for you; Bunch would have on her clean apron and her hair brushed, etc. etc." This answered very well to both parties. But the tale goes further. The good widow, ripe in years, at last died, leaving her property to an amiable young female friend, whom she had adopted, and who thus became our neighbour. About the same time, an Italian refugee, of very good family, had come to settle at York, and most honourably endeavoured to support himself by giving lessons in Italian. He brought letters of introduction to my father from

Lord Holland, who had known him or his family in Italy. We found him a man of talent, cultivation, and high feeling, and the more we saw of him the more we liked him. The Count and our neighbour frequently met at our house, and seeming mutually to like each other, my father thought it right to make further inquiries respecting the character of the former, and finding it most satisfactory, he promoted their intercouse, and it ended in a marriage from our house. The evening before the marriage, my father, fearing the poor Count, from the necessary preparations for his marriage, might possibly be in some little difficulty for his immediate necessities, delicately offered to assist him; but, with a burst of gratitude, in his own beautiful tongue he exclaimed joyously, "No, no; thank God, I have paid every debt I owed in the world, and have still this in my pocket," holding forth half-a-crown.

He did not live very many years to enjoy his good fortune, but we had frequent opportunities during that period of hearing of their mutual happiness.

It was somewhere about this period, I believe, that, by Lord Ossory's death, the living of Ampthill, then vacant, came into his nephew, Lord Holland's, gift; and he immediately wrote, with his usual kindness, to offer it to my father. But being untenable with Foston, and of inferior value, my father was obliged to relinquish what to him would have been a source of constant enjoyment, the vicinity to Lord Holland and to all his early friends; and to turn his mind, with renewed vigour, to the growing necessities of his little northern colony, which had suffered for the moment by this change of prospects put before him.

Nothing was more amusing than to accompany my father in a round of shopping, or providing for the ship, as he called it. On entering a shop where he was known, all were eager to serve him. Gradually, as he talked, all other business was suspended, and you often saw both customer and shop-boy forgetting their own business, and turning round to listen. In five minutes he seemed to know more of each man's trade than he knew himself, and had extracted from him, before he was aware, not only all he meant to tell, but all he meant to conceal; and was off on his road again, laden with useful knowledge, before the astonished burgher was aware of the wisdom which had gone out of him.

One day, when we were on a visit at Bishopthorpe, soon after he had preached a visitation sermon, in which, amongst other things, he had recommended the clergy not to devote too much time to shooting and hunting, the Archbishop, who rode beautifully in his youth, and knew full well my father's deficiencies in this respect, said, smiling and evidently much amused, "I hear, Mr. Smith, you do not approve of much riding for the clergy." "Why, my Lord," said my father, bowing with assumed gravity, "perhaps there is not *much objection*, provided they do not ride too well, and stick out their toes professionally." Mr. M., a Catholic gentleman present, looked out of the window of the room in which they were sitting. "Ah, I see, you think you will get out," said my father, laughing, " but you are quite mistaken; this is the wing where the Archbishop shuts up the Catholics; the other wing is full of Dissenters."

Coming down one morning at Foston, I found Bunch pacing up and down the passage before her master's door, in a state of great perturbation. "What is the matter, Bunch?" "Oh, Ma'am, I can't get no peace of mind till I've got master shaved, and he's so late this morning; he's not come down yet." This getting master shaved, consisted in making ready for him, with a large painter's brush, a thick lather in a huge wooden bowl, as big as Mambrino's helmet, which she always considered as the most important avocation of the morning.

Johnson says, "The truly strong and sound mind is the mind that can embrace equally great things and small." If this definition be just, my father's mind fully deserved these epithets, for he thought nothing unworthy of his talents that could be improved by them. "I dislike those large white blinds," I remember he said on one occasion; "I can't afford painted ones; now, girls, why not try *patchwork?* Get rich glazed cottons, combine your colours well, and select a classical pattern, and I am sure the effect will be very good." We exclaimed, laughed at him, remonstrated, declared it would be hideous, but obeyed. Each took a window; and under my mother's skilful direction, much to our own surprise, executed his idea with such success that the Combe Florey and Foston blinds excited universal admiration; and there are many now alive who, I daresay, remember them, and some who imitated them.

In the summer, hearing that an old friend, a lawyer of great eminence, with his family, had been unexpectedly detained at York by the dangerous illness of a near relation, whilst his two little girls were pining for fresh air after the hooping-cough, which they had just had, my father immediately insisted that they should be sent to Foston, and entrusted to my mother's care. This made us a little anxious, as he had never had the complaint himself: a rule therefore was made, that the dear little girls were never to approach him nearer than arm and stick length. I can see him even now, laughingly warding them off, or running away from them in the garden at Foston, to their great delight, whilst they pursued, and their bright young faces in merry conference with him at the end of his stick. Years and years have passed away since that time, and they, after having grown up into that beauty of mind and body which so fitted them for it, have long, long since, I will not say sunk into their graves, but risen to that heaven, of which their pure and blameless lives made all who knew them feel they were so worthy. No evil ensued; and this little incident only served to cement still closer a friendship of many years' standing. I only allude to it now to show my father's forgetfulness of self where his heart was concerned.

He never indulged in any pleasures in which his family did not share. Passionately fond of books, he hardly added one volume, through all his years of poverty, to the precious little store he brought down with him from London; though without a Cyclopædia, or many of those books of reference, of which he so often felt the want in his literary pursuits. These circumstances render yet more remarkable all that he has said and done during this period. When a present of books arrived (no very unfrequent event) from some of his kind old friends, who knew the pleasure it would afford, he was almost child-like in his delight, particularly if the binding was gay; and I have often been summoned (in my office of librarian, which I held, together with that of apothecary's boy) to arrange and re-arrange them on the shelves, in order to place them in the most conspicuous situation.

We had all our offices: he appointed my sister (who, from her talents, was well fitted for this office) to be his Livy; and we have often laughed over his suggestions as to how our domestic events ought to be recorded for the advantage of posterity. But his Livy was carried off too young, I fear, to have made any progress in her history. My dear mother, from her skill in domestic economy, he christened Mrs. Balwhidder, in allusion to that pretty tale by Galt, called 'Annals of the Parish,' which he delighted in. Annie Kay was prime minister; in short, my father infused something of his spirit into the most commonplace events of life, and he could not order even a dose of physic for his carter but there was fun and originality in the act.

It is said that nobody could stand with Burke under a doorway in a shower of rain without finding him out to be an extraordinary man : so, of my father, I have heard it often said that it was impossible to converse with him for five minutes, and not feel he was not like other men. I have seen him melt an exquisite of the first water, in a most amusing manner. Being very punctual (too punctual indeed,—it was the only virtue he made disagreeable), he not unfrequently arrived to dinner before the lady of the house was dressed, and received her company for her. A dandy would appear all glorious without, whose neckcloth, shirt, and white gloves were unimpeachable, and the evident result of profound study; and who, not having been introduced, of course, in true English style, appeared unconscious that another mortal was in the same room with him. My father, whose neckcloth always looked like a pudding tied round his throat, and the arrangement of whose garments seemed more the result of accident than design (yet, I ought to add, as I am now writing for those who knew him not, always looked like a gentleman, in its best sense, —that is, as one who deserved respect),—eyed him calmly for a minute, as if to take his measure, then addressed him. The dandy started, and bowed stiffly over his neckcloth. The second observation made him evidently say to himself, "Can that observation come out of that neckcloth?" The third convinced him there was something better or at least equal to neckcloths in the world; and by the time the lady of the house arrived they had sworn eternal friendship.

In the summer of this year, 1817, my uncle and his family joined us for a month at Scarborough, and afterwards returned with us to Foston; and it was during this visit that, finding my father quite unable to afford sending his eldest son Douglas to school, he most kindly offered to assist him. Not thinking himself justified in refusing Douglas so great an advantage, my father accepted a hundred a year for this purpose; and in the following year placed him at Westminster school, which he quitted some years after with great distinction, as Captain of the College.

In 1820 my father went on a visit of a few days to Lord Grey's; then to Edinburgh to see Jeffrey and his other old friends; and returned by Lord Lauderdale's house at Dunbar. Speaking of this journey, he says, " Most people sulk in stage coaches, I always talk. I have had some amusing journeys from this habit. On one occasion, a gentleman in the coach with me, with whom I had been conversing for some time, suddenly looked out of the window as we approached York and said, 'There is a very clever man, they say, but a d—s odd fellow, lives near here,—Sydney Smith, I believe.' 'He may be a very odd fellow,' said I (taking off my hat to him and laughing), 'and I daresay he is; but odd as he is, he is here, very much at your service.' Poor man! I thought he would have sunk into his boots, and vanished through the bed of the carriage, he was so distressed; but I thought I had better tell him at once, or he might proceed to say I had murdered my grandmother, which I must have resented, you know.

"On another occasion some years later, when going to Brougham Hall, two raw Scotch girls got into the coach in the dark, near Carlisle. 'It is very disagreeable getting into a coach in the dark,' exclaimed one, after arranging her bandboxes; 'one cannot see one's company.' 'Very true, Ma'am, and you have a great loss in not seeing me, for I am a remarkably handsome man.' 'No, Sir! are you really?' said both. 'Yes, and in the flower of my youth.' 'What a pity!' said they. We soon passed near a lamp-post: they both darted forward to get a look at me. 'La, Sir, you seem very stout.' 'Oh no, not at all, Ma'am, it's only my great coat.' 'Where are you going, Sir?' 'To Brougham Hall.' 'Why, you must be a very remarkable man, to be going to Brougham Hall.' 'I am a very remarkable man, Ma'am.' At Penrith they got out, after having talked incessantly, and tried every possible means to discover who I was, exclaiming as they went off laughing, 'Well, it is very provoking we can't see you, but we'll find out who you are at the ball; Lord Brougham always comes to the ball at Penrith, and we shall certainly be there, and shall soon discover your name.'"

In the summer, Dr. and Mrs. Marcet came with their two daughters to spend some days with us.

Mrs. Marcet writes:—"Mr. Smith was talking after breakfast with Dr. Marcet, in a very impressive and serious tone, on scientific subjects, and I was admiring the enlarged and philosophic manner in which he discoursed on them, when suddenly starting up, he stretched out his arms and said, 'Come, now let us talk a little nonsense.' And then came such a flow of wit, and joke, and anecdote, such a burst of spirits, such a charm and freshness of manner, such an irresistible laugh, that Solomon himself would have yielded to the infection, and called out, Nonsense for ever!"

I have been told it is the opinion of one who knew my father well, and whose opinion I value, that I have hardly done justice to the more serious part of his character. If this be so, I have indeed done him grievous wrong; for this was the foundation, or rather storehouse, from which all his wit and imagination sprang, and which gave them such value in the eyes of the world. The expression of my father's face when at rest was that of sense and dignity; and this was the picture of his mind in the calmer and graver hours of life: but when he found (as we sometimes do) a passage that bore the stamp of *immortality*, his countenance in an instant changed and lighted up, and a sublime thought, sight, or action, struck on his soul at once, and found a kindred spark within it.

Mrs. Marcet has just spoken of his rapid transition from sense to nonsense; I remember a similar instance of his rapid transition from gaiety to the deepest pathos. Some ladies walking with me, seeing my father sitting at his singular writing establishment in the bay, went in through his glorified windows, and established themselves round his table, he talking in his gayest and most animated manner;—in an instant his countenance and tone changed, and he gave expression to the thought within him, with a pathos that touched all, for there was a tear in every eye. Strange to say, vivid as this scene is to my mind, I can neither recall a word he said, nor the subject of the conversation; but it struck me as an instance of great power. His reasoning powers are sufficiently before the world in his works. He loved argument on serious and important subjects, but always after his own fashion; throwing aside all extraneous matter, and by two or three pointed questions, marching up at once to the point. He argued with perfect temper in society, or if he saw the argument becoming long or warm, in a moment he dashed over his opponent's trenches, and was laughingly attacking him on some fresh point. In sorrow or misfortune, he used to say, the great sting was self-reproach. In all the important affairs of life a man ought to make every possible exertion that he can with honour, and then, and not till then, sit down and cast his care upon God, for he careth for him. I have heard him say, "Some very excellent people tell you they dare not hope; why do they not dare to hope? To me it seems much more impious to dare to despair." I have already shown that he studied much, and had always some useful purpose in hand. The real way to improve, he said, is not so much by varied reading, as by finding out your weak points on any subject, and mastering them; this was his constant practice. But to return to Mrs. Marcet:—

"I was coming downstairs the next morning (she continues), when Mr. Smith suddenly said to Bunch, who was passing, 'Bunch, do you like roast duck or boiled chicken?' Bunch had probably never tasted either the one or the other in her life, but answered, without a moment's hesitation, 'Roast duck, please, Sir,' and disappeared. I laughed. 'You may laugh,' said he, 'but you have no idea of the labour it has cost me to give her that decision of character. The Yorkshire peasantry are the quickest and shrewdest in the world, but you can never get a direct answer from them; if you ask them even their own names, they always scratch their heads, and say, 'A 's sur ai don't knaw, Sir;' but I have brought Bunch to such perfection, that she never hesitates now on any subject, however difficult. I am very strict with her. Would you like to hear her repeat her crimes? She has them by heart, and repeats them every day.'

"'Come here, Bunch!' (calling out to her), 'come and repeat your crimes to Mrs. Marcet;' and Bunch, a clean, fair, squat, tidy little girl, about ten or twelve years of age, quite as a matter of course, as grave as a judge, without the least hesitation, and with a loud voice, began to repeat—'Plate-snatching, gravy-spilling, door-slamming, blue-bottle fly-catching, and curtsey-bobbing.' 'Explain to Mrs. Marcet what blue-bottle fly-catching is.' 'Standing with my mouth open and not attending, Sir.' 'And what is curtsey-bobbing?' 'Curtseying to the centre of the earth, please, Sir.' 'Good girl! now you may go. She makes a capital waiter, I assure you; on *state* occasions Jack Robinson, my carpenter, takes off his apron and waits too, and does pretty well, but he sometimes naturally makes a mistake and sticks a gimlet into the bread instead of a fork.'"

Once, when we were on a visit at Lord ——'s, we were sitting with a large party at luncheon, when our host's eldest son, a fine boy of between eight and nine, burst into the room, and, running up to his father, began a playful skirmish with him; the boy, half in play, half in earnest, hit his father in the face, who, to carry on the joke, put up both his hands, saying, " Oh, B——, you have put out my eye." In an instant the blood mounted to the boy's temples, he flung his little arms round his father, and sobbed in such a paroxysm of grief and despair, that it was some time before even his father's two bright eyes beaming on him with pleasure could convince him of the truth, and restore him to tranquillity.

When he left the room, my father, who had silently looked with much interest and emotion on the scene, said, " I congratulate you; I guarantee that boy; make your hearts easy; however he may be tossed about the world, with those feelings, and such a heart, he will come out unscathed."

The father, one of those who consider their fortune but as a loan, to be employed in spreading an atmosphere of virtue and happiness around them as far as their influence reaches, is now no more, and this son occupies his place; but his widowed mother the other day reminded me how true the prophecy had proved;

and the scene was so touching that I cannot resist giving it.

My father comically alludes to the solitary life we led at this time, saying in one of his letters to a friend, "Let us know when you pass, and we will write a letter to tell you whether we are at home or not. It is twenty to one against our being engaged, as we only dine out once in seven or eight years, and that septennial exertion was made last year."

As our opportunities for society were thus few, my father occasionally took lodgings for us during the assizes in York, which enabled us to see a great deal of the principal lawyers on the northern circuit. Amongst these were some of the early legal friends he had made when first settling in his little house in Doughty-street, such as Mr. Scarlett, Brougham, Parke, Tindal, and many others then beginning life, but all since become of high eminence in their profession. It was on the occasion of one of these York assizes that Lord Lyndhurst, then Sir John Copley, came there on a special retainer, and dined with us, together with a large party of lawyers; and contributed not a little, by his powers of conversation, to one of the most agreeable dinners I ever remember. Little did we then guess how much he was to contribute hereafter to the happiness and comfort of my father's life. At this time Hunt's trial was going on, and excited much interest in the public mind. My father attended through the whole trial, and has expressed in some of his letters how much he was struck by the natural and untaught ability which Hunt evinced in the conduct and defence of his cause.

This summer my father went with his family to Bishop's Lydiard, in Somersetshire, to visit my grandfather, who, though a very old man, was still in high vigour, both of body and mind; and, I think, more picturesque and agreeable than ever.

On our return in the autumn, we were in great danger of having a repetition of the disastrous harvest of 1816, from the precarious state of the weather; and it was only by my father's constant activity and energy that it was prevented. For he infused, by his presence, approbation, and good-humour, such activity and goodwill amongst his workmen, that they volunteered to continue their labours in relays all night, and persevered till the harvest was saved; while he came amongst them continually, and took care to have large tables in the barn covered with meat and drink for them.

Amongst the friends my father made at the later period of his residence in London, was Mr. Grattan. Attracted not only by what attracted all the world (Mr. Grattan's high character and great abilities), but by his ardent zeal for the two objects my father had always most at heart—Ireland, and the Catholic question,—he sought every opportunity of cultivating Mr. Grattan's society which the short visits he was now able to make to London afforded.

The death of this great man, which took place in 1820, about the period I am now arrived at, was ascribed in great measure to his coming over with a petition on the Catholic question, when in a state of health which rendered him unfit for such exertion. My father joined warmly in the general regret for the loss of such a man, and, in an article in the Edinburgh Review, on "Ireland," shortly after, expresses his admiration in a sketch of his friend, which, being as short as it is beautiful, I shall extract.

"Great men hallow a whole people, and lift up all who live in their time. What Irishman does not feel proud that he has lived in the days of Grattan? Who has not turned to him for comfort, from the false friends and open enemies of Ireland? who did not remember him in the days of its burnings, wastings, and murders? No government ever dismayed him—the world could not bribe him—he thought only of Ireland: lived for no other object, dedicated to her his beautiful fancy, his elegant wit, his manly courage, and all the splendour of his astonishing eloquence.

"He was so born, so gifted, that poetry, forensic skill, elegant literature, and all the highest attainments of human genius were within his reach; but he thought the noblest occupation of a man was to make other men happy and free; and in that straight line he kept for fifty years, without one side-look, one yielding thought, one motive in his heart which he might not have laid open to the view of God or man."

CHAPTER VIII.

LEGACY. — VISIT TO EDINBURGH. — VISITS LONDON: POPULARITY THERE.—LETTERS TO HOME, AND CARE OF PARISH.—TAKES SON TO CHARTERHOUSE.—VISITS MR. ROGERS.—APPOINTED CHAPLAIN TO HIGH SHERIFF.—PREACHES IN CATHEDRAL.—ANECDOTE AT SPENCER HOUSE.—MEETING OF CLERGY, EAST RIDING.—HIS PETITION.—SPEECH.—LIVING OF LONDESBOROUGH.—GOES TO PARIS. —LETTER ON RECEIVING IRRELIGIOUS BOOK.—DEATH OF FATHER. —DESCRIPTION OF HOUSE BY FRIEND.—LOVE OF CHESS AND SINGING.—MARRIAGE OF YOUNGEST DAUGHTER.—BECOMES CANON OF BRISTOL.—EFFECT PRODUCED AT BRISTOL.—HISTORY OF APOLOGUE, BY MR. EVERETT.

It was about this time that an old lady, Aunt Mary by name, who possessed considerable wealth, suddenly proposed to pay us a visit; and, as it seemed, so much approved all she saw in the little establishment at Foston, that on her death, the following year, she left my father a most unexpected legacy. Though not large, it then seemed to us all unbounded wealth. On receiving this accession of fortune, my father of course immediately released my uncle from the contribution he had so kindly made towards my brother's education. His next step was to call us all around him, saying, " You must all share in this windfall: so choose something you would like." We all made our selection.

In the winter of this year, we all went to Edinburgh on a visit to Lord Jeffrey, after ten years' absence on our side; and a most agreeable visit we had; for, in addition to the enjoyment of Lord Jeffrey's society at every stray moment he could steal from business, we were received with open arms by all our old Scotch friends; and when they do open their arms, there are no people so kind and so hospitable as the Scotch.

In May, next year (1822), my father went up to stay a short time in his brother's house in town, as indeed he usually did every spring. And the rush of invitations, and the struggle for his society, would have been quite enough to turn any head less strong than his. Many weeks before he set off, invitations used to come down into the country; and I have known him engaged every night during his stay, for three weeks beforehand; but in the midst of all this dissipation and popularity he never forgot his home and family. Every morning, at breakfast, appeared his letter to my mother, giving an account of his daily proceedings, together with minute directions about his farm and parish; not always, it must be admitted, in the most legible hand. A family council was often held over his directions; once, so entirely without success, that, after many endeavours on our part to decipher what they could be, as it seemed urgent, my mother cut out the passage and enclosed it to him; he returned it, saying, " he must decline ever reading his own handwriting four-and-twenty hours after he had written it." He was so aware of the badness of his handwriting, that in a letter to Mr. Travers, who wished to see one of his sermons, he says, " I would send it to you with pleasure, but my writing is as if a swarm of ants, escaping from an ink-bottle, had walked over a sheet of paper without wiping their legs." The handwriting of his friend Lord Jeffrey was, if possible, still more illegible; my father wrote to him, on receiving one of his letters, " My dear Jeffrey,—We are much obliged by your letter, but should be still more so were it legible. I have tried to read it from left to right, and Mrs. Sydney from right to left, and we neither of us can decipher a single word of it."

The interests of his villagers, too, were not neglected. On one occasion, in a broiling sun, with no other equipage than his umbrella, he paced down to one of the public offices to obtain some information about a young soldier, the only son of a poor labourer and his wife, in his village, who were in a great state of anxiety about him, not having received any tidings for months. He entered the office, hot, tired, and dusty, and I daresay very ill-dressed; and proceeded to put the necessary questions to one of the young officials, in all the splendour of whisker and waistcoat; but, after much delay and cool impertinence, obtained no satisfactory answer. He then said, giving his card, and making his bow, " I have but one other question to trouble you with, Sir, and that is your name; as I am about to proceed from this door, to call on your master. I came here, a country clergyman, to perform my duty to my parish, and I shall inform him how his servants perform theirs." These words acted like magic. In an instant the youth stood humbled before him, "entreating pardon and silence; that he had nothing to depend on but his office, and this would ruin him." My father of course yielded, but warned him to let this be a useful lesson for the future.

In the winter of the following year, about six o'clock in the evening, we were assembled round a blazing fire, waiting for dinner. The weather had been unusually severe, and the roads were so filled by drifts of snow, that they were considered quite impassable. The butcher and the baker even could hardly make their way on horseback to the house, and the front door was so blocked up by snow as to be quite unapproachable. Suddenly a tremendous peal was heard on the bell: all started at the unwonted sound in such a season and at such an hour, and were lost in conjectures what it could mean. Bunch rushed to the door, and presently entered the room breathless, exclaiming, "Please, Sir, Lord and Lady Mackincrush is com'd in a coach-and-four, and wants to stay with you, but they can't get up to the front door!" Who Lord and Lady Mackincrush could be, and why they bestowed themselves upon us, was alike a mystery. But Sydney, calling for a lantern, sallied forth, and found, to his no less joy than surprise, his old friend Sir James Mackintosh and his daughter, half buried in the snow.

They were extracted, warmed, and welcomed, as such friends ought to be; or rather, with such means as the little parsonage could furnish. The next morning, when we were sitting at breakfast, arrived, to our infinite amusement, Sir James's letter, announcing his intended visit, and asking whether we could receive him.

My father's sketch, in the Life of Sir James, shows his estimate of this great man; and the keen enjoyment his society ever afforded him was enhanced by the rarity of their meeting, now that he was so far removed from his former friends.

Sir James Mackintosh went after a few days; leaving behind not recollections only, but hat, books, gloves, papers, and various portions of his wardrobe, with characteristic carelessness. "What a man that would be," said my father, "had he a particle of gall, or the least knowledge of the value of red tape!" As Curran said of Grattan, "he would have governed the world."

In 1823, having received a presentation to the Charterhouse from the Archbishop of York, for his second son, Wyndham, he took him there in the spring. Whilst he was in town, Mr. Rogers says, "I had been ill some weeks, confined to my bed. Sydney heard of it, found me out, sat by my bed, cheered me, talked to me, made me laugh more than I ever thought to have laughed again. The next day a bulletin was brought to my bedside, giving the physician's report of my case; the following day the report was much worse; the next day declaring there was no hope, and England would have to mourn over the loss of her sweetest poet; then I died amidst weeping friends; then came my funeral; and, lastly, a sketch of my character, all written by that pen which had the power of turning everything into sunshine and joy. Sydney never forgot his friends!"

In the course of the summer a young friend came to spend a month with us, the freshness and originality of whose character both interested and amused my father; he chanced on one occasion to call her "a nice person." "Oh, don't call me '*nice*,' Mr. Sydney; people only say that where they can say nothing else." "Why? have you ever reflected what 'a *nice* person' means?" "No, Mr. Sydney," said she, laughing, "but I don't like it." "Well, give me pen and ink; I will show you," said my father, "a

"DEFINITION OF 'A NICE PERSON.'

"A nice person is neither too tall or too short, looks clean and cheerful, has no prominent feature, makes no difficulties, is never misplaced, sits bodkin, is never foolishly affronted, and is void of affectations.

"A nice person helps you well at dinner, understands you, is always gratefully received by young and old, Whig and Tory, grave and gay.

"There is something in the very air of a nice person which inspires you with confidence, makes you talk, and talk without fear of malicious misrepresentation; you feel that you are reposing upon a nature which God has made kind, and created for the benefit and happiness of society. It has the effect upon the mind which soft air and a fine climate has upon the body.

"A nice person is clear of little, trumpery passions, acknowledges superiority, delights in talent, shelters humility, pardons adversity, forgives deficiency, respects all men's rights, never stops the bottle, is never long and never wrong, always knows the day of the month, the name of everybody at table, and never gives pain to any human being.

"If anybody is wanted for a party, a nice person is the first thought of; when the child is christened, when the daughter is married,—all the joys of life are communicated to nice people; the hand of the dying man is always held out to a nice person.

"A nice person never knocks over wine or melted butter, does not tread upon the dog's foot, or molest the family cat, eats soup without noise, laughs in the right place, and has a watchful and attentive eye."

This same year, his eldest son, Douglas, having left Westminster with great distinction (and been elected Captain of the College, after struggling with unusual difficulties), went in the autumn to Christ Church, Oxford.* My father mentions, in the autumn of this

---

* "His father had always taught him the Eton grammar. The intention of sending him to Westminster was sudden. The change of grammar was a dreadful difficulty, only a few months before the competition, which was to admit him as a King's scholar. In addition to this, a most severe fever seized him shortly after he went to Westminster, and for six weeks kept him confined to his bed: but so eager was he for success, for our sakes, that even while keeping his bed from fever and weakness, he ever had his Westminster

year, in his letters, a most agreeable visit he made to Bowood, meeting there Lord Holland, Luttrell, Rogers, and some other friends.

In 1824, my father took us for a short time to town, Miss Vernon having kindly lent us her house in Hertford-street. We returned to York for the assizes, as he had been appointed by Sir John Johnstone (then High Sheriff) his chaplain; and it was upon this occasion that he preached in the Cathedral two remarkable sermons, upon the unjust judge, and the lawyer who tempted Christ. There was great curiosity to hear him, particularly amongst the lawyers on the Northern circuit, to most of whom he was personally known. The cathedral was crowded to the utmost. I well remember the startling effect on every one present when, after rising and looking round with that calm dignity so peculiar to him in the pulpit, he slowly delivered, with his powerful voice (the two judges sit-

---

grammar under his pillow; and, too ill to get up, he was incessantly working at it, in spite of all we could say. The challenges last about six weeks; there were, this year, twenty-eight candidates, of whom eight were admitted; and dear Douglas was sixth, to our inexpressible joy; for I verily believe it would have broken his heart had he failed, so very desirous was he, on this first occasion that had occurred in his young life, to repay by his success all the anxious and agitating fears his father had felt about him for the future. Having become a King's scholar, the hardships and cruelties he suffered, as a junior boy, from his master, were such as at one time very nearly to compel us to remove him from the school. He was taken home for a short period, to recover from his bruises, and restore his eye. His first act, on becoming Captain himself, was to endeavour to ameliorate the condition of the juniors, and to obtain additional comforts for them from the head-master."—*From my Mother's Journal.*

ting immediately opposite), this text: "God shall smite thee, thou whited wall; for sittest thou to judge me according to the law, and commandest me to be smitten contrary to the law?" From this opening his audience were little prepared for the following splendid eulogium which he pronounced on the office of an English judge, such as it is now exercised in this country.

"He who takes the office of a judge, as it now exists in this country, takes in his hands a splendid gem, good and glorious, perfect and pure. Shall he give it up mutilated? shall he mar it? shall he darken it? shall it emit no light? shall it be valued at no price? shall it excite no wonder? shall he find it a diamond? shall he leave it a stone?

"What should we say to the man who would wilfully destroy with fire the magnificent temple of God in which I am now preaching? Far worse is he who ruins the moral edifice of the world, which time and toil, and many prayers to God, and many sufferings of men have reared; who puts out the light of the times in which he lives, and leaves us to wander in the darkness of corruption and the desolation of sin.

"There may be, there probably is, in this church some young man who may hereafter fill the office of an English judge, when the greater part of those who hear me this day are dead and gone. Let him remember my words, and let them form and fashion his spirit. He cannot tell in what dangerous and awful times he may be placed: but, as a mariner looks to his compass in the calm, and looks to his compass in the storm, and never keeps his eye off his compass, so in every vicissitude of a judicial life,—deciding for the people, deciding against the people,—protecting the just rights of kings, or restraining their unlawful ambition,—let him ever cling to that pure, exalted, and Christian independence which towers over the little motives of life, which no hope of favour can influence, which no effort of power can control."

During one of his visits to London, at a dinner at Spencer House, the conversation turned upon dogs. "Oh," said my father, "one of the greatest difficulties I have had with my parishioners has been on the subject of dogs." "How so?" said Lord Spencer. "Why, when I first went down into Yorkshire, there had not been a resident clergyman in my parish for a hundred and fifty years. Each farmer kept a huge mastiff dog, ranging at large, and ready to make his morning meal on clergy or laity, as best suited his particular taste; I never could approach a cottage in pursuit of my calling, but I rushed into the jaws of one of these shaggy monsters. I scolded, preached, and prayed, without avail; so I determined to try what fear for their pockets might do. Forthwith appeared in the county papers a minute account of a trial of a farmer, at the Northampton Sessions, for keeping dogs unconfined; where said farmer was not only fined five pounds and reprimanded by the magistrates, but sentenced to three months' imprisonment. The effect was wonderful, and the reign of Cerberus ceased in the land." "That accounts," said Lord Spencer, "for what has puzzled me and Althorp for many years. We never failed to attend the sessions at Northampton, and we never could find out how we had missed this remarkable dog case."

In the year 1825, a meeting of the clergy of the diocese having been called in the East Riding of Yorkshire, to petition Parliament against the emancipation of the Catholics, was held at the Tiger Inn, at Beverley. My father, though much disliking such meetings, felt that, if they were called, it was his duty to attend; and, attending, to speak. Two petitions were sent up to Parliament; one to the House of Lords, to be presented by the Archbishop of York; the other to the Commons, by Sir Robert Peel; which were acceded to unanimously by all the clergy present, my father's being the *only dissentient voice.**

* "*A Petition drawn up by the Rev. Sydney Smith, to be proposed at a Meeting of the Clergy at Cleveland, in Yorkshire, in* 1825.

"We, the undersigned, being clergymen of the Church of England, resident within the Diocese of York, humbly petition your honourable House to take into your consideration the state of those laws which affect the Roman Catholics of Great Britain and Ireland.

"We beg of you to inquire whether all those statutes, however wise and necessary in their origin, may not now (when the Church of England is rooted in the public affection, and the title to the throne undisputed) be wisely and safely repealed.

"We are steadfast friends to that Church of which we are members, and we wish no law repealed which is really essential to its safety; but we submit to the superior wisdom of your honourable House, whether that Church is not sufficiently protected by its antiquity, by its learning, by its piety, and by that moderate tenour which it knows so well how to preserve amidst the opposite excesses

I see, in the very interesting Life of Dr. Bathurst, Bishop of Norwich, lately published by his daughter, that at an advanced age he stood alone in the House of Lords to advocate the cause of religious toleration against all the bench of Bishops. She speaks with honest pride of the just admiration his courage obtained from his friends, and the gratitude of the Ministry. But if this required such courage in the "*Good Bishop,*" who came to that House with all the weight of the family connection, whose influence first placed him there; and invested with the dignity of high office; will it be ungraceful in me to ask, what courage it required in my father, still young, under a Tory administration, poor, with a heavy debt still hanging over him, without family or friends to support him there, to come forward alone, in opposition to the whole clergy of his diocese, to advocate the

of mankind ;—the indifference of one age, and the fanaticism of another.

"It is our earnest hope that any indulgence you might otherwise think it expedient to extend to the Catholic subjects of this realm may not be prevented by the intemperate conduct of some few members of that persuasion; that in the great business of framing a lasting religious peace for these kingdoms, the extravagance of overheated minds, or the studied insolence of men who intend mischief, may be equally overlooked.

"If your honourable House should in your wisdom determine that all these laws which are enacted against the Roman Catholics cannot with safety and advantage be repealed, we then venture to express a hope that such disqualifying laws alone will be suffered to remain, which you consider to be clearly required for the good of the Church and State. We feel the blessing of our own religious liberty, and we think it a serious duty to extend it to others, in every degree which sound discretion will permit."

same cause?* In this speech he speaks of the advance the Catholic question had made during the session, from the astonishment of the House at the union of the Irish Catholics; and then, alluding to the effects these laws were producing in Ireland, he says, " We preach to our congregations that a tree is known by its fruits. What has your system done for Ireland ? Her children, safe under no law, live in the very shadow of death. Has it made Ireland rich? has it made Ireland loyal? has it made Ireland free? has it made Ireland happy? From the principles of this system, from the cruelty of these laws, I turn, and turn with the homage of my whole heart, to the memorable proclamation which the monarch of these realms has lately made to his dominions of Hanover, '*That no man should be subjected to civil incapacities on account of religious opinions.*' This sentiment in the mouth of a king deserves, more than all glories and victories, the notice of the historian who is destined to tell to future ages the deeds of the English people. I hope he will lavish on it every gem which glitters in the cabinet of genius; and so uphold it to the world, that it will be remembered when Waterloo is forgotten, and when the fall of Paris is blotted out from the memory of man."

About this period a very considerable and most unexpected addition was made to my father's income

---

* I hope I shall not be understood as wishing to depreciate one whom all good men must admire, but as only desirous of doing justice to my father.

by the kind intercession and exertion of our friends at Castle Howard, who obtained from the Duke of Devonshire the living of Londesborough (at no great distance from Foston, and then tenable with it), for him to hold till the Duke's nephew, Mr. Howard, should be of age to take it. This, together with Aunt Mary's legacy, put him, for the first time in his life, tolerably at his ease, as he had by this time liquidated many of the first heavy expenses entailed upon him by building. But the debt to Queen Anne's Bounty, raised on the value of the living, remained, and had up to this time obliged us to exercise the most rigid economy. These debts had weighed heavily on my father's spirits; giving him, as my mother has often told me, sleepless nights of anxiety as to the future provision for his children; and I have not unfrequently seen him in an evening, when bill after bill poured in, as he was sitting at his desk (carefully examining them, and gradually paying them off), quite overcome by the feeling of the debt hanging over him, cover his face in his hands, and exclaim, "Ah! I see, I shall end my old age in a gaol!"

This was the more striking from one the buoyancy of whose spirits usually rose above all difficulties. It made a deep impression upon us; and I remember many little family councils, to see if it were not possible to economize in something more, and lessen our daily expenses to assist him.

The following year he accomplished what he had long wished to do, but had never been able to afford,

—a visit to Paris; where he found Lord and Lady Holland, and many other English friends, and was introduced by them to some of the best French society.

He has given his impressions of Paris in his letters to my mother. These Paris letters are, I am sorry to say, almost the only ones to her which have been preserved; for though, when absent, he wrote to my mother regularly every day, yet the interesting matter they contained was so mixed up with directions and home details, that they were not considered of permanent value. The only purchase he made for himself in Paris, though he brought us all a gift, was a huge seal, containing the arms of a peer of France, which he met with in a broker's shop, and bought for four francs; and which he declared should henceforth be the arms of his branch of the Smith family. From all he witnessed in Paris, and seeing the little wisdom the Bourbons seemed to have gained from misfortune, he predicted the revolution which took place so few years afterwards. He renewed there his early acquaintance with two remarkable men, Talleyrand and Pozzo di Borgo, of whom he saw a good deal.

After his return we had a visit from Lord Jeffrey; our old and valued friend Mr. Whishaw, the Hannibal of his suppers; and Mr. John Romilly, now Master of the Rolls.

My father, who, however he might indulge in attacks on what he thought the shortcomings of the Church, never for a moment tolerated anything approaching to irreligion, even in his most private transactions, received about this time a work of irreligious tendency from the house of a considerable publisher in London, who was in the habit of occasionally presenting him with books. Many men might have passed this over as of little importance; but he felt that nothing was unimportant that had reference to such a subject. These feelings were strongly evinced on various occasions, in some of his early letters to Jeffrey, where he not only deprecates the injury to the Edinburgh Review by the admission of irreligious opinions; but declares his determination, if this were not avoided, of separating himself from a work of which he had felt hitherto so justly proud. He writes to Jeffrey, saying, "I hear with sorrow from Elmsley, that a very anti-christian article has crept into the last number of the Edinburgh Review. . . . You must be thoroughly aware that the rumour of infidelity decides not only the reputation, but the existence of the Review. I am extremely sorry, too, on my own account, because those who *wish* it to have been written by me, will say it *was* so." And again, in another letter: "I must beg the favour of you to be explicit on one point. Do you mean to take care that the Review shall not profess infidel principles? Unless this is the case, I must absolutely give up all connection with it." On the occasion just alluded to, my father immediately wrote to the publisher, saying, "that he could not be aware that he had sent him a work unfit to be sent to a clergyman of the Church of England, or, indeed, of any church;" and after counselling him against such publications, even with a view to mere worldly interests, he adds, "I hate the insolence, persecution and intolerance, which so often pass under the name of religion, and, as you know, have fought against them; but I have an unaffected horror of irreligion and impiety, and every principle of suspicion and fear would be excited in me by a man who professed himself an infidel."

In 1827 the Junction Ministry was formed, which combined a portion of the Whigs with the remains of Mr. Canning's party. My father, knowing that there were in this Ministry many upon whom he had just claims, finding his family now grown up, his son about to enter on an expensive profession,* and aware that his clerical income would shortly be diminished to nearly one-third by the resignation of the living of Londesborough to Mr. Howard, felt it due to himself and his family to make some application for preferment to his friends. He wrote, therefore, to one or two of those in the Ministry, and to his friend Lord Brougham likewise, stating to him his hopes and wishes, and requesting his influence with those in power. From Lord Brougham I have reason to believe he received the answer he had a right to expect from so very old a friend. From one of the others he received an answer politely deferring his promises to some future period, as I presume from the following reply, which is so very characteristic of my father, and so very unlike the usual mode of address from an ex-

* He was destined for the Law.

pectant clergyman to a minister of state, that I shall give it—though without a name, as I have not asked permission to insert it.

"20, *Saville-row.*

"I am much obliged by your polite letter. You appeal to my good-nature to prevent me from considering your letter as a decent method of putting me off: your appeal, I assure you, is not made in vain. I do not think you mean to put me off; because I am the most prominent, and was for a long time the only clerical advocate of that question, by the proper arrangement of which you believe the happiness and safety of the country would be materially improved. I do not believe you mean to put me off; because, in giving me some promotion, you will teach the clergy, from whose timidity you have everything to apprehend, and whose influence upon the people you cannot doubt, that they may, under your Government, obey the dictates of their consciences without sacrificing the emoluments of their profession. I do not think you mean to put me off; because, in the conscientious administration of that patronage with which you are entrusted, I think it will occur to you that something is due to a person who, instead of basely chiming in with the bad passions of the multitude, has dedicated some talent and some activity to soften religious hatreds, and to make men less violent and less foolish than he found them.

"I am, sincerely yours,
"SYDNEY SMITH."

We received a visit in the autumn from a clergyman, who, though a comparatively recent friend, was one ever highly valued by my father, and who was afterwards promoted to the bench. A letter he wrote on this occasion, descriptive of his visit, which has been most kindly sent me by his widow, is so graphic, and it is so flattering to my father that such a letter should have been written by such a man, that I cannot resist inserting it here, though it speaks of things some of which have been alluded to before.

"A man's character is probably more faithfully represented in the arrangements of his home than in any other point; and Foston is a facsimile of its master's mind, from first to last. He had no architect, but I question whether a more compact, convenient house could well be imagined. In the midst of a field, commanding no very attractive view, he has contrived to give it an air of snugness and comfort, and its internal arrangements are perfect. The drawing-room is the colour you covet, the genuine chromium, with a sort of yellow flowering pattern. It is exquisitely filled with irregular regularities—tables, books, chairs, Indian wardrobes; everything finished in thorough taste, without the slightest reference to smartness or useless finery; and his inventive genius appears in every corner; his fires are blown into brightness by *shadrachs*, tubes furnished with air from without, opening into the centre of the fire; his poker, tongs, and shovel are secured from falling with that horrid crash which is so destructive to the nerves and temper.

"His own study has no appearance of comfort; but as he reads and writes in his family circle, in spite of talking and other interruptions, this is of less consequence. In other respects it has its attractions: there, for instance, he keeps his rheumatic armour, all of which he displayed out of a large bag, giving me an illustrated lecture upon each component part. Fancy him in a fit of rheumatism, his legs in two narrow buckets, which he calls his jack-boots; round the throat a hollow tin collar; over each shoulder a large tin thing like a shoulder of mutton; on his head a hollow tin helmet, all filled with hot water; and fancy him expatiating upon each and all of them with ultra-energy.

"His bedrooms are counterparts of the lower rooms; in mine there were twenty-eight large Piranesi prints of ancient Rome, mounted just as we do ours, but without frames, and, indeed, in every vacant part of the house he has them hung up.

"His store-room is more like that of an Indiaman than anything else, containing such a complete and well-assorted portion of every possible want or wish in a country establishment.

"The same spirit prevails in his garden and farm: contrivance and singularity in every hole and corner.

"'What, in the name of wonder, is that skeleton sort of machine in the middle of your field?' 'Oh, that is my universal Scratcher; a framework so con trived, that every animal, from a lamb to a bullock, can rub and scratch itself with the greatest facility and luxury.'

"I arrived there on Saturday evening, walking from York, by which I contrived to lose my way, and take possession of another man's home and drawing-room fireside for some time before the host appeared, and the mistake was discovered.

"On Sunday we prepared for church; he was hoarse, so I was to read; against preaching I had provided by having no sermon. Good heavens! what a set-out! The family chariot, which he calls the *Immortal*, from having been altered and repaired in every possible way—the last novelty, a lining of green cloth, worked and fitted by the village tailor—appeared at the door, with a pair of shafts substituted for the pole, in which shafts stood one of his cart-horses, with the regular cart harness, and a driver by its side. In the inside the ladies were seated: on the dicky behind I mounted with him; but his servant having placed the cushions without first putting in the wooden board, on sitting down, we sank through, to his great amusement. These preliminaries being adjusted, we set out.

"The church resembles a barn more than anything else, in size and shape; though, from two old Saxon doors, it shows claim to higher antiquity than most others. About fifty people were assembled; I entered the reading-desk; he followed the prayers with a plain, sound sermon upon the duty of forgiving injuries, but in manner and voice clearly proving that he felt what he said, and meant that others should feel it too.

"His domestic establishment is on a par with the rest: his head servant is his carpenter, and never appears excepting on company days. We were waited upon by his usual *corps domestique*, one little girl, about fourteen years of age; named, I believe, Mary or Fanny, but invariably called by them Bunch. With the most immovable gravity she stands before him when he gives his orders, the answers to which he makes her repeat verbatim, to ensure accuracy.

"Not to lose time, he farms with a tremendous speaking-trumpet from his door; a proper companion for which machine is a telescope, slung in leather, for observing what they are doing.

"On Monday came Lady H. Hall, her two daughters and her two sons; the latter, Captain B. Hall, a *rara avis* I have long wished to see; and Peter Tytler, son (is he not?) to the author. What a charm there is in good society and well-informed people! what would you not have given to have heard the mass of wit, sense, anecdote, and instruction that flowed incessantly!"

The equipage alluded to in this letter requires a little explanation. Our house was above a mile from the little church, with roads to it of the stiffest and deepest clay, hardly passable to women in wet weather or winter, and my mother was in delicate health.

We could not afford horses; so my father, never ashamed of showing his poverty when he thought it right, hit upon this rude and cheap device, to enable his family to accompany him in all weathers to church. Ludicrous as this description may appear to the reader, yet the proprieties of life were attended to. The horse, the harness, the Immortal, and the carter, all wore their best and cleanest Sunday garb, and I think they excited respect rather than ridicule amidst his humble congregation.

A word, too, ought to be said in explanation of the drawing-room furniture alluded to in this letter with so much praise. It consisted of a few relics preserved from the valuable Indian furniture left by my grandmother, the greater part of which had been parted with by my mother for our benefit. All the rest was plain enough, though still in good taste. Economy, in the estimation of common minds, often means the absence of all taste and comfort; my father had the rare art to combine it with both. For instance, he found it added much to the expense of building to have high walls; he therefore threw the whole space of the roof into his bedrooms, coved the ceilings and papered them, and thus they were all airy, gay, cheap, and pretty. Cornices he found expensive; so not one in the house, but the paper border, thrown on the ceiling with a line of shade under it. This relieved the eye, and atoned for their absence. Marble chimney-pieces were too dear; so he hunted out a cheap, warm-looking Portland stone, had them cut after his own model, and the result was to produce some of the most cheerful, comfortable-looking fireplaces I remember, for as many shillings as the marble ones would have cost him pounds.

After my father became rich, at the end of life, he amusingly alludes, in one of his letters, to the joy my mother would feel on finding he had put up marble chimneypieces in his town-house.*

In his youth my father had been very fond of the game of chess, but had left it off for many years. He suddenly took it into his head to resume it this winter, and selected me, *faute de mieux*, as his antagonist. His mode of play was very characteristic—bold, rapid attack, without a moment's pause or indecision, which I suspect would have exposed him to danger from a more experienced adversary; but as it was, with a profound contempt for my skill, promising me a shilling if I beat him, he sat down with a book in his hand, looked up for an instant, made a move, and beat me regularly every night all through the winter. At last I won my shilling, but lost my playfellow; he challenged me no more.

My father was very fond of singing, but rather slow in learning a song, though when once he had accomplished it, he sang it very correctly. As he never tired of his old friends, and had always some new one on the stocks, there was a tolerable variety of songs to select from; and, with my mother's beautiful accompaniment (she was a very accomplished musician) and

* See Letter to Mrs. Holland in the Correspondence.

his own really fine voice, our trios succeeded in pleasing him so much, that he would often *encore* himself. He was so perfectly natural, that though I think (and I have heard many people remark it) the general tendency of his conversation was to underrate himself, yet whenever he was particularly pleased or satisfied with anything he had said or done, he would say so as frankly as if he had been speaking of another person. "There is one talent I think I have to a remarkable degree," I have heard him say: "there are substances in nature called amalgams, whose property is to combine incongruous materials; now I am a moral amalgam, and have a peculiar talent for mixing up human materials in society, however repellent their natures." And certainly I have seen a party, composed of materials as ill-assorted as the individuals of the 'happy family' in Trafalgar-square, drawn out and attracted together by the charm of his manner, till at last you would have believed they had been born for one another.

On the 1st of January, 1828, his youngest daughter, Emily, was married by the Archbishop of York to Mr. Hibbert, in the little barn church before mentioned. And on the 24th of the same month Lord Lyndhurst, then Chancellor, had the real friendship and courage to brave the opinions and opposition of his own party; and, though differing entirely from my father in politics, from private friendship and the respect he had for his character and talents, to bestow on him a stall which was then vacant at Bristol;—two interesting family events coming closely upon each other.

For this promotion he always felt deeply grateful to Lord Lyndhurst, as it was of the greatest importance to him; less in a pecuniary point of view (as, though rendering *permanent* what was before *temporary*, it rather diminished than increased his previous income), than from breaking that spell which had hitherto kept him down in his profession, and enabling him to show the world how well he could fulfil its duties, wherever placed. And this was strikingly exemplified at Bristol, where he arrived with a strong prejudice felt not only against himself by a large party, but against the Church generally; Bristol being full of Dissenters, and the cathedral almost deserted at the time of his arrival. There was a good deal of curiosity excited, to hear what line he would take.

He commenced his duties by preaching a sermon on the 5th of November, before the Mayor and Corporation, who came expecting to hear the usual attack on Catholics made on these occasions, and were much startled and astonished at hearing religious toleration preached from the pulpit of their cathedral, and from the lips of a dignitary of the Church. This letter, sent to me by Lord Hatherton, gives my father's account of what passed:—

"*Lower College Green, Bristol,*
"*November* 7, 1828.

" My dear Littleton,—Many thanks for your game,

and for your entertaining and interesting letter from Ireland. I direct to your country place, not knowing exactly where you will be, and presuming Mrs. Littleton will know. Putting all things together, I think something will be done. The letter from the three foolish noblemen, the failure of Penenden-heath to excite a general and tumultuous feeling, are all very favourable. I share in your admiration of Lord Anglesey's administration; I have reason to believe Ministers are a little dissatisfied with his disposition to oratory, which is thought undignified and rash in a Vice-King.

" At Bristol, on the 5th of November, I gave the Mayor and Corporation (the most Protestant Mayor and Corporation in England) such a dose of toleration, as shall last them for many a year. A deputation of *pro-Popery* papers waited on me today to print, but I declined. I told the Corporation, at the end of my sermon, that beautiful rabbinical story quoted by Jeremy Taylor, 'As Abraham was sitting at the door of his tent,' etc. etc., which, by the bye, would make a charming and useful placard against the bigoted.

" Be assured I shall make a discreet use of the intelligence you give me, and compromise you in nothing.

" Remember me, if you please, to Wilmot Horton when you write; I like him very much, and take a sincere interest in his welfare.

"Ever yours, dear Littleton, very sincerely,
"SYDNEY SMITH."

I have heard that this sermon occasioned an immense sensation at the time, "and the cathedral, from that period, whenever he was to preach (though previously almost deserted), was filled to suffocation. A crowd collected round the doors long before they were opened, and the heads of the standers in the aisle were so thick-set you could not have thrust in another; and I saw the men holding up their hats above their heads, that they might not be crushed by the pressure."

"He preached," says an eye-witness, "finely and bravely on this occasion, in direct opposition to the principles and prejudices of the persons in authority present; and ended by that beautiful apologue from Jeremy Taylor, illustrating Charity and Toleration, where Abraham, rising in wrath to put the wayfaring man forth from his tent for refusing to worship the Lord his God,* the voice of the Lord was heard in

---

* Extract from the Liberty of Prophesying, by Jeremy Taylor, D.D., ed. 1657, p. 606:—

§ 22. "I end with a story which I find in the Jew's[1] Books. When Abraham sat at his tent-door, according to his custom, waiting to entertain strangers, he espied an old man stooping and leaning on his staffe, weary with age and travelle, coming towards him, who was an hundred years of age; he received him kindly, washed his feet, provided supper, caused him to sit down; but observing that the old man eat and prayed not, nor begged for a blessing on his meat, asked him, why he did not worship the God of heaven? The old man told him that he worshiped the fire only, and acknowledged no other God: at which answer Abraham grew so zealously

---

[1] Gentius, the Latin translator of Saadi at Amsterdam, was that Jew, as appears by its being copied into Taylor's second edition, subsequent to its publication at Amsterdam in 1651.

the tent, saying, 'Abraham! Abraham! have I borne with this man for threescore years and ten, and canst not thou bear with him for one hour?'"

"And yet," says the same eye-witness of whom I have before spoken, "never did anybody to my mind look more like a High Churchman, as he walked up the aisle to the altar,—there was an air of so much proud dignity in his appearance; and when I saw him afterwards more intimately in private life, I became aware he had a lofty, brave soul, with an intense contempt for everything that was mean, base, or truckling."

The following letter from Mr. Everett gives some interesting information on this remarkable apologue, before alluded to:—

"*Cambridge*, 18*th September*, 1848.

"My dear Mrs. Smith,—I duly received, a short time since, your very interesting letter of the 7th of July, with the copy of Mr. Smith's speech, so kindly sent by you, and the memorandum relative to the Parable on Persecution. The speech, like everything from the same source, breathes a spirit of noble liberality and sound sense, which cannot be too highly praised. I am greatly indebted to you for

angry, that he thrust the old man out of his tent, and exposed him to all the evils of the night and an unguarded condition. When the old man was gone, God called to him and asked him where the stranger was; he replied, 'I thrust him away because he did not worship thee;' God answered him, 'I have suffered him these hundred years, although he dishonoured me, and couldst not thou endure him one night, when he gave thee no trouble?' Upon this, saith the story, Abraham fetcht him back again, and gave him hospitable entertainment and wise instruction. Go thou and do likewise, and thy charity will be rewarded by the God of Abraham."

giving me the opportunity of adding it to the collection of his works.

"The Parable on Persecution is one of the most curious topics in literary history. It has often been made the foundation of a charge of plagiarism against Dr. Franklin, but, as I think, without foundation. In its modern form, it was first published by Lord Kames, in 1774. He says, 'It was communicated to me by Dr. Franklin of Philadelphia;' but he does not say that Dr. F. claimed the authorship of it. It was not long after inserted in a small collection of Dr. Franklin's miscellaneous writings, published by Mr. B. Vaughan (a gentleman recollected by Lord Lansdowne) in London. Mr. Vaughan took it from Lord Kames's work. In 1788 it was traced to its source in Gentius's preface; and Dr. Franklin having been then charged with plagiarism, some friend well acquainted with his habits vindicated him in the same work, the 'Repository,' in which the charge was made. These, and some other interesting facts, are given in the new edition (Mr. Sparks's) of Franklin's works, vol. ii. p. 118, which, with the note to Bishop Heber's Life of Jeremy Taylor, in the first volume of the works, p. 365, contains, I believe, all that is known on the subject. I see one slight mistake in this learned note: it states that the famous parable did not appear in the first edition of the 'Liberty of Prophesying,' which was published in 1647, but in the second, which was printed in 1657; the work of Gentius having appeared in the interval. I have before me a volume which purports to be the second edition of the 'Liberty of Prophesying,' published in London in 1702, and not containing the parable, but this is quite immaterial.

"I lean a little to the opinion, that Bishop Taylor *may* have taken it from some Jewish book not yet discovered. There is no reason why, if he quoted Gentius, he should not have named him. It appears from Bishop Heber's learned note, that a Jewish author, whom he names, thinks he has seen the parable among the commentaries on Genesis xviii. 1; and it is quite a curious fact, that Saadi gives it as related to him, and that he, according to his own account, while in captivity at Tripoli, was compelled to work on the fortifications 'with some Jews.' Nothing seems more likely to have happened than that a learned Jew, being a fellow-prisoner with a learned Persian, should have related to him this striking parable, of which the personages were the great Jewish Patriarch, and a devotee of the old Persian superstition of fire-worship.

"Whatever be its source, there are few teachings as impressive of Jewish or Christian wisdom. It is an undoubted chapter of that great primitive Gospel, which God has written in the hearts and consciences of men, but which, like the page of revelation, is too apt to be forgotten under the influence of selfish and corrupt motives.

"I rejoice to hear that Mr. Smith's works are so frequently reprinted. In this way he will for ages to come continue to teach lessons of toleration and humanity to all who speak the English tongue. There is no one of my friends in England, with respect to whom I am more frequently questioned than Mr. Smith; and I esteem it one of the chief blessings of my residence in London to have known him, and been honoured with so much of his kindness.

"I remain, my dear Mrs. Smith, with the highest regards, ever faithfully yours,
"EDWARD EVERETT."

On his appointment to the prebendal stall at Bristol, he went for the first time to Court, and he gives an amusing account of himself on the occasion.

"I found my colleague Tate, the other day, in h[is] simplicity consulting the Archdeacon of Newfoundla[nd] what he should wear at the levee;—a man who s[pends his life] bobbing for cod, and pocketing every tenth fish. Ho[w]ever, I did worse when I went, by consulting no on[e], and, through pure ignorance, going to the levee [in] shoe-strings instead of shoe-buckles. I found, to [my] surprise, people looking down at my feet; I could n[ot] think what they were at. At first I thought they h[ad] discovered the beauty of my legs, but at last the tru[th] burst on me, by some wag laughing, and thinking [I] had done it as a good joke. I was of course exce[s]sively annoyed to have been supposed capable of su[ch] a vulgar, unmeaning piece of disrespect, and kept m[y] feet as coyly under my petticoats as the veriest pru[de] in the country, till I could make my escape; so pe[r]haps, after all, I had better have followed my frienc[['s] example."

CHAPTER IX.

HAPPINESS INCREASED BY HIS PROMOTION.—DEATH OF ELDEST SON.
—REMOVAL TO COMBE FLOREY.—REBUILDING OF HOUSE.—LORD
JEFFREY'S LAST VISIT.—INCREASED POPULARITY AT BRISTOL.—
COLLECTS CONTRIBUTIONS TO REVIEW.—FRENCH REVOLUTION.—
RIOTS AT BRISTOL.—SPEECH ON REFORM.—LETTERS ON PREFER-
MENT.—APPOINTED CANON OF ST. PAUL'S.—DEATH OF SIR JAMES
MACKINTOSH IN 1832.—MARRIAGE OF ELDEST DAUGHTER IN 1834.
—VILLAGE ANECDOTES.—CHRISTENS GRANDCHILD.—BUYS HOUSE
IN CHARLES STREET.—RECTITUDE OF STEWARDSHIP AT ST. PAUL'S.
—TOUR TO HOLLAND IN 1837.—TALLEYRAND.—CONVERSATION IN
LONDON, AND ANECDOTES.—BEGINS CONTROVERSY ABOUT CHURCH.
—PETITIONS TO HOUSE OF LORDS.—INSCRIPTION FOR STATUE OF
LORD GREY.

His promotion in the Church was a step in life which added very materially to my father's happiness. "Moralists tell you," said he, "of the evils of wealth and station, and the happiness of poverty. I have been very poor the greatest part of my life, and have borne it as well, I believe, as most people, but I can safely say that I have been happier every guinea I have gained. I well remember, when Mrs. Sydney and I were young, in London, with no other equipage than my umbrella, when we went out to dinner in a hackney coach (a vehicle, by the bye, now become almost matter of history), when the rattling step was let down, and the proud, powdered red-plushes grinned, and her

gown was fringed with straw, how the iron entere
into my soul."

"I often thank God for my animal spirits. I calle
the other day on my friend and neighbour B———, an
found him moping over the fire, wringing his hand
and in a state of the deepest melancholy. 'Wh;
B———, what is the matter? Here you are in tl
prime of life, with health, talents, education, a sens
ble wife, pleasing children, just come into possessic
of this fine old place, and a good fortune, and hav
moreover the inestimable advantage of having me f(
a neighbour; what on earth can you want more 1
make you happy?' 'Very true, Sydney, very true
but' (with a deep sigh) 'have you considered the sta
of my roads?' 'No,' I said, 'I have certainly not take
that point into consideration, but in future I will ; ε
good morning, B———.' Whilst I, who have never ha
a house, or land, or a farthing to spare, am sometim(
mad with spirits, and must talk, laugh, or burst."

He had now need of all his elasticity of spirits, fc
there came upon him what he declares was the firs
real sorrow he had known—and in truth it was
heavy one—the death of his eldest son Douglas, jus
as he had reached maturity, and gave promise of ever
excellence, both of heart and mind, that could endea
him to his parents or gratify their pride.

He died, after a long and painful illness, in town
in the year 1829. I see, in my father's note-bool
this simple entry :—" April 14th. My beloved so
Douglas died, aged twenty-four. Alas ! alas !" An

afterwards: "So ends this year of my life,—a year of sorrow, from the loss of my beloved son Douglas,—the first great misfortune of my life, and one which I shall never forget." In his last hours he often called his youngest son by the name of Douglas, showing that even then he was still in his thoughts.

It was perhaps well for all parties, that, his promotion to the Prebendal stall at Bristol having also entitled him to one of their livings, it became necessary for my father to resign Foston, and settle in Somersetshire; and here again the kindness of Lord Lyndhurst enabled him to exchange Foston for the much smaller, but more beautifully situated living, of Combe Florey, near Taunton.

We all at the time deeply regretted leaving our old haunts in Yorkshire, where we had lived so long, received so much hospitality, and made so many kind friends; but this entire change of scene, and the necessity for immediate exertion, was very useful to all under this severe affliction.

In the following letter, just sent me by one of our kind Yorkshire neighbours, he alludes touchingly to these feelings of regret for his lost son Douglas.

"*Combe Florey, August* 6, 1829.
"Dear Mrs. Thomson,*
"I never heard till I came here of the intended kindness of Mr. Thomson and yourself, with a view to

* The present Dowager Lady Wenlock.

my remaining in Yorkshire. I was sensibly touched with it, and have laid it up in the archives of my mind. As to wood and lawn, cedar and fur, and pine and branching palm, I have exchanged for the better. Good, excellent, and amiable friends, such as we met with at Escrich, I did not expect to find. Fortune may grant such favours once in a life, but they must not be counted upon. Your family are always among our sincere regrets. This is a beautiful place; the house larger than Foston, with a wood of three or four acres belonging to it close to the house, and a glebe of sixty acres surrounding it, in a country everywhere most beautiful and fertile. The people are starving,— in the last stage of poverty and depression. Mrs. Sydney, from sorrow and novelty, has forgotten her throat; I think the complaint has nearly vanished. I am busy from morning till night, in building,—not from the love of architecture, but from the fear of death,—not from a preference for any particular collocation of stones, but from an apprehension that, disdaining all collocation (as they are apt to do in ancient parsonages), they should come thundering about my head. In the meantime I have, from time to time, bitter visitations of sorrow. I never suspected how children weave themselves about the heart. My son had that quality which is longest remembered by those who remain behind,—a deep and earnest affection and respect for his parents. God save you, my dear Mrs. Thomson, from similar distress! Have you read ——'s America? If you have, I hope you dislike it as much as I do. It is amusing, but very unjust and unfair. It will make his fortune at the Admiralty. Then he temporizes about the Slave Trade; with which no man should ever hold parley, but speak of it with abhorrence, as the greatest of all human abominations. We stay here till the beginning of the year, and then go into residence at Bristol. I hope to be in town in the spring, and hereafter to pay you a visit in Yorkshire, which will be a great pleasure to me. Accept, my dear Mrs. and Mr. Thomson, our united respect and regards,

"And believe me,
"Your sincere friend,
"SYDNEY SMITH."

We had almost to begin the labours of Foston over again, as we found the parsonage-house at Combe Florey in a most ruinous state, and requiring instant attention. But my father now brought considerable experience and increased wealth to the task; and, establishing us in one corner of the house, he turned in an immense gang of workmen, and in a very short time (at the expense of about two thousand pounds more of loss to his family, having almost to rebuild it) made one of the most comfortable and charming parsonage-houses I have ever seen,—a striking contrast, I must own, in every way, to poor Foston, of which our friend Mr. Loch, when he heard we had left it, said to my father, "Are you sure you have left Foston, Mr. Smith?" "Yes." "Never to return?"

"Never." "Well, then, I may venture to say that it was, without exception, the ugliest house I ever saw."

The climate, the vegetation, and the soil were all in strong contrast to the north; and it well deserved the name of Combe Florey, for it really was a valley of flowers—a lovely little spot, where nature and art combined to realize the Happy Valley.

In the midst of our building operations, when the greater part of the roof of the house, which required renewing, was put together in rafters on the lawn, we received a visit from our friend Lord Jeffrey. I well remember our sitting out there amidst the rafters, surrounded by busy workmen, and animated by the delicious weather and the beauty of the scene around. He and my father gave full play to their fancy and imagination; and nothing could be more delightful than to sit and watch them, and listen to the playfulness and variety of their conversation. I have, I believe, omitted several of Lord Jeffrey's visits; having no other recollections of them, I am sorry to say, than that of the pleasure they always afforded to both old and young. But this, I think, was his last visit to us; and it was touching to observe these two eminent men, who had begun the struggle of life together, who had loved each other so long and so well, who had both now attained eminence and honour in their respective professions without one act of baseness, sitting together in this little earthly paradise, and, in their elder age, talking over and looking back on the past with all the pleasure and satisfaction of well-spent lives. Such scenes are pleasant and useful to dwell upon.

As a dignitary of the Church, my father now thought it more becoming to put his name to what he should hereafter write, and he therefore withdrew from the Edinburgh Review; collecting and publishing about ten years after the greater part of his contributions to it. He says, on doing so:—" I see very little in my reviews to alter or repent of. I always endeavoured to fight against evil, and what I thought evil then I think evil now. I am heartily glad that all our disqualifying laws for religious opinions are abolished, and I see nothing in such measures but unmixed good and real increase of strength to the Establishment. To set on foot such a journal in such times, to contribute towards it for many years, to bear patiently the reproach and poverty which it caused, and to look back and see that I have nothing to retract, and no intemperance and violence to reproach myself with, is a career of life which I must think to be extremely fortunate.

" Strange and ludicrous are the changes in human affairs! The Tories are now on the treadmill, and the well-paid Whigs are riding in chariots; with many faces however looking out of the windows (including that of our Prime Minister), which I never remember to have seen in the days of poverty and depression of Whiggism. Liberality is now a lucrative business. Whoever has any institution to destroy, may consider himself as a commissioner, and his fortune made; and, to my utter and never-ending astonishment, I, an old Edinburgh Reviewer, find myself fighting, in the year 1839, against the Archbishop of Canterbury and the Bishop of London for the existence of the National Church."

In the winter of the year 1830 we all accompanied my father to his residence in Bristol, where his popularity increased more and more, in spite of the firmness with which he preached many unpalatable doctrines, and the minuteness with which he felt it his duty to investigate all the affairs of the Cathedral and Chapter. These, up to this time, had been left very much to take care of themselves: and as it was nobody's business to look after them, they had fallen into great confusion and disorder.

This year the French Revolution took place (the probability of which he had foretold in his letters from Paris in 1826), producing the greatest consternation, distress, and excitement on the Continent.

In this country the riots at Bristol had broken out in the spring; and, later in the year, the resignation of the Duke of Wellington, the introduction of the Reform Bill after Lord Grey's acceptance of the Ministry, the opposition to it in the House of Lords, and the dissolution of the Parliament, were exciting the deepest interest, and producing the greatest danger of violence and disturbance in every part of England.

There was to be a large county meeting held on the

subject at Taunton; and though, as a clergyman, my father generally avoided meetings purely political, yet at the present moment he saw so much dangerous excitement at work amongst the people, and felt the crisis to be one of such vital importance to the country, that he considered it the duty of every man, who had the power so to do, to raise his voice in favour of law and order; and to urge the people with calmness and perseverance to obtain those objects they would inevitably lose by violence. In this speech, amongst other things, he says:—

"Nothing can be more different than personal and political fear: it is the artifice of our opponents to confound them together. . . . The greater part of human improvements, I am sorry to say, are made after war, tumult, bloodshed, and civil commotion. . . . Mankind seem to object to every species of gratuitous happiness, and to consider every advantage as too cheap which is not purchased by some calamity. . . . I shall esteem it a singular act of God's providence if this great nation, guided by these warnings of history, not waiting till tumult for reform, not trusting reform to the lowest of the people, shall amend their decayed institutions, at a period when they are ruled by a popular Sovereign, guided by an upright minister, and blest with profound peace. . . . If many are benefited by reform, and the lower orders are not injured, this alone is reason enough for the change. But the hewer of wood and the drawer of water are benefited by reform; and the connection between the existence of John Russell and the reduced price of bread and cheese will be as clear as it has been the object of his honest, wise, and useful life to make it. Don't be led away by nonsense. All things are dearer under a bad government, and cheaper under a good one. . . . I am old and tired,—thank me for ending; but one word more before I sit down. I am old, but I thank God I have lived to see more than my observations on human nature taught me I had any right to expect. I have lived to see an honest King, in whose word his ministers could trust. I have lived to see a King with a good heart, who, surrounded by nobles, thinks of common men; who loves the great mass of English people, and wishes to be loved by them; and who, in spite of clamour, interest, prejudice, and fear, has the manliness to carry these wise changes into immediate execution. Gentlemen, farewell! Shout for the King!"

We attended him to the meeting. I had often seen the silent effect produced by his eloquence in crowded cathedrals, but I never before saw its effect on a multitude free to express their feelings; and were I to live a thousand years, I should never forget it.

His voice seemed heard without effort in every part of the assembly; his words flowed with unbroken fluency; his language was simple and nervous; he seemed to hold the very heartstrings of the people in his hands, and to play upon them, as upon an instrument, at his pleasure; and when at last he sat down, the thunders of applause from that sea of heads beneath was perfectly thrilling. Such an exhibition of his powers filled one with regret that his voice was never likely to be raised in that assembly of his country where his talents and his character would have made him such an ornament, and where that noble voice would have been always raised for such noble purposes.

And here I must allude to what my father was too proud to speak of, except in two or three confidential letters to some of his oldest friends. Though he had at this period a firm conviction that a bishopric would be destructive of his peace and happiness, and a still firmer determination, in consequence, to reject it, should it ever be offered, yet I know he felt deeply to the hour of his death, that those by whose side he had fought for fifty years so bravely and so honestly in their adversity, and with the most unblemished reputation as a clergyman, should in their prosperity never have offered him that which they were bestowing on many, only known at that time, according to public report (whatever merits they may have since evinced), for their mediocrity or unpopularity.

He says, in one of these letters, after expressing his feeling on this subject:—" But, thank God, I never acted from the hope of preferment, but from the love of justice and truth which was bursting within me. When I began to express my opinions on Church politics, what hope could any but a madman have of gaining preferment by such a line of conduct?"

In another letter again he says :—" It is perhaps of little consequence to any party whether I adhere to it or not; but I always shall adhere to the Whigs, whoever may be put over my head; because I have an ardent love of truth and justice, and they are its best defenders. But, adhering to them under all circumstances, I cannot but feel whether I am well or ill used by them."

This silence on his part I should have observed likewise, had not Lord Melbourne, with that noble candour for which his character was so remarkable, admitted the injury my father felt, and done my father the tardy justice of stating to a gentleman, a mutual friend, and a man of great accuracy (who came direct from his house expressly to state it to me), "That Lord Melbourne said there was nothing he more deeply regretted, in looking back on his past career, than the not having made Sydney Smith a bishop."

And a juster cause of regret, I believe, was never felt. For my father's estimate of what a bishop ought to be was so high, he was so bound in honour by his own writings to become what he had required others to be, and his power of doing what he felt he ought to do was so great,[*] that, had he ever accepted the offer, which I again repeat I firmly believe he never would at this period of his life (though ardently desiring it when he was a younger man), I as firmly believe

---

[*] He says, on one occasion, " I hope I am too much a man of honour to take an office without fashioning my manners and conversation so as not to bring it into discredit."

there would have been no act in the whole of Lord Melbourne's Ministry that would have reflected more honour and distinction on him. But I bless his memory for this wish only of justice to my father.

The following short, manly statement of his case, in a letter to Lord John Russell, on the subject of his preferment, seems, as it were, to be extorted from him by that sense of justice which so powerfully influenced his feelings through life towards every person, and on every subject, less than by any wish to exalt himself, and therefore, to a certain degree, carries conviction with it. "I defy —— to quote one single passage of my writing contrary to the doctrines of the Church. I defy him to mention a single action of my life which he can call immoral. The only thing he could charge me with would be high spirits, and much innocent nonsense. I am distinguished as a preacher, and sedulous as a parochial clergyman. His real charge against me is that I am a high-spirited, honest, uncompromising man, whom he and all the bench of bishops could not turn upon vital questions: this is the reason why, as far as depends upon others, I am not a bishop. But I am thoroughly sincere in saying, I would not take any bishopric whatever."*

I find a letter, written by his friend Lord John Russell, in answer, from which I shall give an extract, as it shows that this wish to do justice to my father was shared by his old friend, Lord John, likewise:—

* I see in this letter that he urges strongly the appointment of several of his friends, and apparently not without effect.

"My dear Sydney,—I think you are quite right not to be ambitious of the prelacy, as it would lead to much disquiet for you; but if I had entirely my own way in these matters, you should have the opportunity of refusing it."

And again, my father wrote at a later period to Lord Holland, saying, "You have said and written that you wished to see me a bishop, and, I have no doubt, would try to carry your wishes into effect. If proper vacancies had occurred in the beginning of Lord Grey's administration, I believe this would have been done. Other politicians have succeeded, who entertain no such notion. But there is a still greater obstacle to my promotion, and that is, that *I have entirely lost all wish to be a bishop*. The thought is erased from my mind, and, in the very improbable event of a bishopric being offered me, I would steadily refuse it. In this I am perfectly honest and sincere, and make this communication to you to prevent your friendly exertion in my favour, and perhaps to spare you the regret of making that exertion in vain."

I lament to find that a beautiful sketch he one day drew of what he conceived the duties of a bishop to be, has been lost from among his papers. But the following short extract from his fragment on the Irish Church sufficiently shows what he felt to be the duties of so exalted a station; though even here, as usual, he draws no ideal picture of excellence, impossible to attain, but one within the reach of any man of sense and real piety.

"What a blessing to this country would a real bishop be! . . .

"But I never remember in my time a real bishop— a grave, elderly man, full of Greek, with sound views of the middle voice and preterpluperfect tense, gentle and kind to his poor clergy, of powerful and commanding eloquence, in Parliament never to be put down when the great interests of mankind were concerned; leaning to the Government when it was right, leaning to the people when they were right; feeling that if the Spirit of God had called him to that high office, he was called for no mean purpose, but rather that seeing clearly, acting boldly, and intending purely, he might confer lasting benefit upon mankind."

There were at this time so many mischievous publications circulating amongst the people, and threatening letters so frequently sent to my father and other gentlemen in the neighbourhood, that he thought it right to endeavour to counteract them, and published some cheap letters for circulation amongst the poor, called "Letters to Swing," of which the following is one which has been accidentally preserved.

From the 'Taunton Courier' of Wednesday, Dec. 8th, 1830.
"To Mr. Swing.

"The wool your coat is made of is spun by machinery, and this machinery makes your coat two or three shillings cheaper,—perhaps six or seven. Your white hat is made by machinery at half price. The coals you burn are pulled out of the pit by machinery, and are sold to you much cheaper than they could be if they were pulled out by hand. You do not complain of *these* machines, because they do you good, though they throw many artisans out of work. But what right have you to object to fanning machines, which make bread cheaper to the artisans, and to avail yourselves of *other* machines which make manufactures cheaper to you?

"If all machinery were abolished, everything would be so dear that you would be ten times worse off than you now are. Poor people's cloth would get up to a guinea a yard. Hats could not be sold for less than eighteen shillings. Coals would be three shillings per hundred. It would be quite impossible for a poor man to obtain any comfort.

"If you begin to object to machinery in farming, you may as well object to a plough, because it employs fewer men than a spade. You may object to a harrow, because it employs fewer men than a rake. You may object even to a spade, because it employs fewer men than fingers and sticks, with which savages scratch the ground in Otaheite. If you expect manufacturers to turn against machinery, look at the consequence. They may succeed, perhaps, in driving machinery out of the town they live in, but they often drive the manufacturer *out* of the town also. He sets up his trade in some distant part of the country, gets new men, and the disciples of Swing are left to starve in the scene of their violence and folly. In this way the lace manufacture travelled in the time of Ludd, Swing's grandfather, from Nottingham to Tiverton. Suppose a free importation of corn to be allowed, as it ought to be, and will be. If you will not allow farmers to grow corn here as cheap as they can, more corn will come from America; for every threshing-machine that is destroyed, more *Americans* will be employed, *not* more Englishmen.

"Swing! Swing! you are a stout fellow, but you are a bad adviser. The law is up, and the Judge is coming. Fifty persons in Kent are already transported, and will see their wives and children no more. Sixty persons will be hanged in Hampshire. There are two hundred for trial in Wiltshire—all scholars of Swing! I am no farmer: I have not a machine bigger than a pepper-mill. I am a sincere friend to the poor, and I think every man should live by his labour: but it cuts me to the very heart to see honest husbandmen perishing by that worst of all machines, the gallows,—under the guidance of that most fatal of all leaders—Swing!"

One of the earliest uses he made of his increase of wealth was to indulge himself by enlarging his library, and supplying those deficiencies before alluded to, which he had so long suffered under; and his books, which at Foston for many years had humbly occupied only the end of his little dining-room, now boldly spread themselves over three sides of a pretty odd room, dignified by the name of library,—about twenty-eight feet long and eight feet high,—ending in a bay-window supported by pillars, looking into the garden, and which he had obtained by throwing a pantry, a passage, and a shoe-hole together. In this pretty, gay room we breakfasted, he sat, and when alone we spent the evening with him. He used to say, "No furniture so charming as books, even if you never open them, or read a single word."

The cholera was now spreading rapidly over the country, and exciting the greatest alarm and anxiety. This immediately set all my father's energy to work, to have every remedy at hand for himself and the poor of his parish, and to take every precaution which the learned suggested: one of these was, never to read the accounts of its progress, which often produced such panic that the patient was half dead of fear before the cholera arrived to perfect the deed. Luckily however, neither his remedies nor his precautions proved necessary, as the cholera respected our little happy valley, and never came near us.

In October, Lord John Russell and his family came to see us; and a joyful visit it was, as the Whigs had again assumed the reins of Government under their distinguished leader Lord Grey, and, with their return, gave assurance of obtaining the Reform Bill, and thus tranquillizing the country.

Shortly after, when we were staying on a visit with Lord Morley at Saltram, my father received the news that Lord Grey* had appointed him to a Prebendal

* One of the first things Lord Grey said on entering Downing-

stall at St. Paul's, in exchange for the one of inferior value he held at Bristol, which had previously been presented to him by his friend Lord Lyndhurst.* These glad tidings, together with the charm of the place, the weather, the society of our charming hostess, and the many kind, warm old friends he found assembled there, who all seemed to rejoice really as if the benefit had been conferred on themselves, produced such an effect on his spirits, that it would be difficult to forget that week. I hardly ever remember him more brilliant. On his return he wrote the little squib of Mrs. Partington and her battle with the Atlantic, which had a success quite unlooked for, spreading in every direction; and sketches of Mrs. Partington and her mop were to be seen in the windows of all the picture-shops about the country.

1832.—This year brought with it, amongst other events, the loss of one of his early and most valued friends, Sir James Mackintosh; just at the moment when his mind seemed in the highest vigour, and he was preparing for the world some of his most important works.

Their strong friendship had been much cemented by the intimacy of my mother with the ladies of his family, and his loss was deeply lamented by both.

street, to a relation who was with him, was, "Now I shall be able to do something for Sydney Smith."

* His brother Bobus used to say that Sydney's life was the only instance of undeviating honesty that he had ever known to answer.

My father loved to think of Sir James, to speak of his virtues, and describe him; and it was a gratification to his feelings publicly to express his admiration of his old friend in the letter he addressed to his son, Mr. Mackintosh, and published in his Life of his father. In this he says:—" When I turn from living spectacles of stupidity, ignorance, and malice, and wish to think better of the world, I remember my great and benevolent friend Mackintosh." And, speaking of his love of truth, his memory, and his knowledge, he says, " Those who lived with him found they were gaining upon doubt, correcting error, enlarging the boundaries and strengthening the foundations of truth." And again he says :—" Whatever might assuage the angry passions, and arrange the conflicting interests of nations ; whatever could promote peace, increase knowledge, extend commerce, diminish crime, and encourage industry; whatever could exalt human character, and could enlarge human understanding, struck at once to the heart of your father, and roused all his faculties. I have seen him in a moment, when this spirit came upon him, like a great ship of war, cut his cable, and spread his enormous canvas, and launch into a wide sea of reasoning eloquence."

During Sir James's absence in Bombay, my father had been in the habit of writing constantly to him, to tell him all that was going on in Europe. But these letters, full of interest, though kindly returned by Mr. Mackintosh on the death of his father, have, I fear, together with all the letters of my father's boyhood, preserved carefully by his poor mother, and given to mine, fallen a sacrifice to my father's mania for burning papers. I remember these early letters of his were most original and characteristic; and it was one of our greatest pleasures as children to hear them read aloud in the evening by my mother. There was likewise a large collection of letters to his friend Horner, which he destroyed from thinking them of no value; but which would have been amongst the most interesting of his correspondence, as there were few whom he more loved, trusted, and honoured.

In 1834 my father took a house for a short time in Stratford-place, from whence his eldest daughter was married to Dr. Holland. On this occasion he writes to Lady Holland:—"We are about to be married; and Saba will be one day Lady Holland: she must then fit herself up with Luttrells, Rogers, and John Russells, &c. &c.: Sydney Smith she has." In the summer he welcomed Dr. Holland's three children, as if they had been his own, to spend the whole autumn in his house at Combe Florey.

Whilst we were there, he was writing one morning in his favourite bay-window, when a pompous little man, in rusty black, was ushered in. "May I ask what procures me the honour of this visit?" said my father. "Oh," said the little man, "I am compounding a history of the distinguished families in Somersetshire, and have called to obtain the Smith arms." "I regret, Sir," said my father, "not to be able to contribute to so valuable a work; but the Smiths never had any arms, and have invariably sealed their letters with their thumbs."

In truth, he could not have stumbled on a more perfect Goth than my father on the subject of ancestral distinctions. For though the Smiths were not literally reduced to their thumbs, yet, feeling how completely he had been the maker of his own fortunes, my father adopted the motto for his carriage of "Faber meæ fortunæ." He loved to repeat that answer of Junot to the old noblesse, when boasting of their line of ancestors: "Ah, ma foi! je n'en sais rien; moi je suis mon ancêtre."

During Lord Grey's administration, which terminated in July, 1834, there had been but two or three vacancies for bishoprics in England (Ireland, for my father, was out of the question). There were, of course, numerous claims on Lord Grey; and out of this small number, King William IV., from kindness to Lord Grey, insisted on appointing Dr. Grey, his brother, without even consulting Lord Grey. Had Lord Grey had more to bestow and remained longer in power, I have good reason to believe that his old friend Sydney Smith would not have been forgotten. This belief, it has been seen, my father stated in his letters during Lord Grey's life—and since his death I find it confirmed, from papers I possess, by one who best knew Lord Grey's feelings.

I think it was about this period that an incident happened to a poor half-mad woman, who lived at the end of our village—with a drunken husband, and a swarm of children—all sunk, in consequence, into a hopeless state of poverty, dirt, and idleness, save one son, who, strange to say, had escaped the general contagion. This boy, first at school, then as apprentice to a shoemaker in a neighbouring village, had established a high character, and was the pride of his old mother's heart. Unfortunately, on carrying home some work, he was tempted into a public-house to drink (what no Somersetshire-man can resist) a draught of cider. Some strangers were in the room, and shortly after the boy's entrance a silk handkerchief was missed, immediate search made, and the handkerchief found on young Treble, to the poor boy's utter horror. A warrant was obtained, the boy taken before the magistrates, who, upon the evidence, and the general character of the family, were about to commit him to prison. The poor old mother, frantic with grief, came before my father, imploring his assistance, and asserting the entire innocence of her son. My father, no longer a magistrate, but touched by her sorrow, and believing the possible innocence of the boy from his previous knowledge of him, undertook the affair;: went instantly to a neighbouring village, where the magistrates were sitting; obtained with some difficulty a delay, upon his undertaking to bring fresh evidence in favour of the boy; and then, with as much ardour as if his own life, and honour, and everything he held most dear, were at stake, he wrote, he investigated, he cross-examined for nearly a week, and on the day appointed attended the trial. He secured the best lawyer he could find to conduct the cause ; then, I believe, spoke for the boy himself ; and, by the evidence he produced, succeeded in showing, to the satisfaction of all, that the handkerchief had been hid where the boy could not have hid it under the circumstances; and that the real culprit was undoubtedly one of the men present, of notoriously bad character, who, to save himself, when the search was made, dexterously contrived to stuff it down the innocent boy's collar as he was pretending to assist in the search.

Treble was acquitted; and the wild joy and gratitude of the old ragged mother were deeply felt by my father, and her prayers for her protector I cannot believe were unheard in Heaven.

He never shrank from any duty, however revolting to his feelings. On one occasion he set out on a winter's night, lantern in hand, to visit a poor cottager seized with epileptic fits, of which, from some painful early associations, he had a peculiar horror; but they wished for him, and he went as usual; and I remember on his return he was much overpowered by the scene he had witnessed, which haunted him for many days. Several volumes of manuscript remain of his prescriptions for the poor, of which he always kept a record, that he might refer to them if necessary; and they now help me to bear testimony to his attentions and kindness to them.

Soon after coming to town the following year, at my request, he christened my eldest girl; and the emotion and deep feeling he evinced on the occasion added not a little, I remember, to the impressiveness of that beautiful service. On this occasion Miss Fox, Lord Holland's sister, stood as godmother to my little girl, and bestowed on her her own name. A few years ago my old friend Mr. Rogers said to me, "What a privileged person you are, to have had such a father and such an uncle!" In truth I feel it so. But he might have added, "And such a friend as Miss Fox," though I must share this last with so many; for who was ever so loved, so honoured, or so worthy to be so, as Miss Fox? Not to speak of her understanding (which was such as is rarely bestowed on women), there was such an atmosphere of purity, simplicity, and indulgent kindness about her, that all evil passions seemed to fly away at her approach, and a better and more amiable tone to be infused into society. Her heart was as a spot to repose on in the moral world, a place of refuge in distress, of sympathy in joy or sorrow, and of warm unvarying friendship in weal or woe.

In the autumn my father bought a small house in Charles-street, No. 33, near St. John's Chapel, where he had preached with so much success when a young man on first coming to London; and he gives a comical account, in one of his letters, of the short time he should require to paper, paint, furnish it, and set it in order.

In October he took my mother and Mr. and Mrs. Hibbert to Paris for a short time; and in November came to town for his residence at St. Paul's and to enter upon his new duties there, to his performance of which (even those least known to the world, and which he might have neglected almost without blame) some of his fellow-labourers have given most kind and gratifying testimony, as I find in this letter to Lady B——, sent to my mother from Mr. Cockerell, architect and superintendent of St. Paul's Cathedral, which I give, as showing a part of his character little known to the world—his powers of business.

"*Hampstead, Oct. 24th*, 1851.

"Dear Lady B——,

"I have great pleasure in committing to writing, according to your request, some of those anecdotes on the practical qualities of our lamented friend, the Rev. Sydney Smith, which you listened to with so much interest last year. Referring as they do to his *Gesta* as Canon Residentiary of St. Paul's, superintending more especially the repairs of the fabric, and my agency therein as the appointed surveyor and paymaster; they certainly exhibit the bold originality of his mind, and the integrity of his habits in the common transactions of business, in which duty and fidelity are alone concerned, with as much advantage as the better-known acts of his public life. And you justly insist upon my relation of them, however humble, and commonly considered beneath the dignity of biography; as perhaps more illustrative of conscientious motive and intrinsic merit, than the more striking talents which made him so justly valued and admired by the world, and as exhibiting his character from a point of view not hitherto perhaps taken sufficiently into account.

"The routine and technical conduct of the current business of public bodies is ordinarily committed confidentially by them to those hands which have been found worthy of the trust; but on his appointment the new Canon avowed his diffidence of them in general. His experience, acquired by the habit of careful observation, had taught him to suspect, wherever the clearest evidence of rectitude was deficient; and he investigated with the greatest minuteness all transactions which were placed under his superintendence, and that with a severity of discipline neither called for nor agreeable.

"His early communications, therefore, with myself, and I may say with all the officers of the Chapter, were extremely unpleasant; but when satisfied by his methods of investigation, and by a 'little collision,' as he termed it, that all was honest and right, nothing could be more candid or kind than his subsequent treatment; and our early dislike was at length converted into unalloyed confidence and regard. As he expressed himself to one of the most valued of our staff, 'When I heard every one speak well of you, I entertained the most vehement suspicions; and I treated you as a rogue until I had tried you so far, that you could endure such harsh treatment no longer.'

"As nothing was taken upon trust at first, great were our disputes as to contracts, materials, and prices: with all of which, from the rates in the market, to those of Portland stone, putty, and white lead, he armed himself with competent information: every item was taxed, and we owe several important improvements in the administration of the works and accounts to his acumen, punctuality, and vigour. Not only did he thus adjust and scrutinize the payment of works, but nothing new could be undertaken without his survey and personal superintendence. An unpractised head and a podagrous disposition of limbs might well have excused the survey of those pinnacles and heights of our cathedral, which are to all both awful and fatiguing; but nothing daunted him; and once, when I suggested a fear that his portly person might stick fast in a narrow opening of the western towers, which we were surveying, he reassured me by declaring, that 'if there were six inches of space, there would be room enough for him.'

"During more than a quarter of a century of my direction of these repairs, I had met with no similar sacrifice or minute attention to this department; and when it is remembered that this duty in no degree affects the funds of the Dean and Chapter, and that these repairs are from a separate fund, the administration of which only is entrusted to one of the Canons, we shall the more admire so conscientious a discharge of this duty. Such was the minor process; but the greater measures for the enduring security of this magnificent cathedral were most important and conspicuous. The disasters of York Cathedral had exhibited the unwarrantable neglect, so general in these sacred edifices, of the common security of insurance; and in 1840, I believe, Canterbury was the only cathedral church insured. St. Paul's was speedily and effectually insured in some of the most substantial offices of London: not satisfied with this security, he advised the introduction of the mains of the New River into the lower parts of the fabric, and cisterns and movable engines in the roof; and quite justifiable was his joke, that 'he would reproduce the Deluge in our cathedral.'

"The fine library of the fabric, the estimation of which was always cited by Dean Vanmildert, had long suffered by dilapidation and damp; but a stove, American indeed, and better suited to our slender finances than the dignity of our library, soon dispelled one evil, and rendered it accessible and comfortable to the studious at the same time; and the bindings were all roughly, but substantially, repaired. The restoration of the noble model, the favourite scheme of Sir Christopher Wren,—now, alas! a ruin, after one hundred and forty years of neglect,—was no less in his constant contemplation; but our funds were insufficient. The successful result of a singular dispute as to the will of Dr. Clarke, in 1675, which had been brought before the Chapter by our respected Chapter clerk, Mr. Hodgson, during Mr. Sydney Smith's administration, caused a great addition to the fabric fund, which had before been insufficient for its purposes, and effected an increase which it is hoped will secure the cathedral from dilapidation.

"A question of law was well suited to Mr. Smith's acumen and vigour, and he very materially assisted, during the progress of a suit in Chancery, instituted for the purpose of establishing the will, to its being brought to a speedy and satisfactory conclusion, to the lasting benefit of the cathedral.

"These are some of the efficient labours of our valued friend within my own professional knowledge, and they might be greatly increased by that of my colleagues in office at St. Paul's; in proof of which, I am permitted by Mr. Hodgson, who loved and honoured him, to quote a constant saying of his, 'That Mr. Sydney Smith was one of the most strictly honest men he ever met in business.' Thus established in the respect and friendship, I may truly say, of all of us, you will conceive the regret with which I received his announcement, by a note, some years before his lamented departure, that 'I should hear with pleasure, after so much trouble, that being in the expectation of his first paralytic, he was about to give up his superintendence of my department to abler hands.'

"I have great pleasure, dear Madam, in offering you these few anecdotes, in testimony of a beloved and honoured memory, however humble and insufficiently expressed. To contribute, in any truthful and impartial way, to the just appreciation of an honest and illustrious character, is one of the most delightful duties we can be called upon to perform; and surely these traits of conscience and integrity, of which I have been the witness only, in the fastidious, troublesome, and inconspicuous duties of the business transactions of fabric accounts and repairs, may, in this sense, well deserve the record to which you have so earnestly invited me. And I have the honour to be, dear Madam, your most respectful friend and servant,

"C. R. Cockerell."

The following, from his old friend, the Dean of St. Paul's, is so valuable that I cannot resist inserting it.

"No man, I should say, went on improving to so late a period of his life, both in acuteness of thought and felicity of expression. . . . Indeed the business in which I am at present engaged brings at every turn my old friend before me. I find traces of him in every particular of Chapter affairs; and on every occasion where his hand appears, I find stronger reason for respecting his sound judgment, knowledge of business, and activity of mind; above all, the perfect fidelity of his stewardship. In his care of his own interests as member of the Chapter, there was ever the most honest (rarely, if I may not say singularly honest) regard for the interests of the Chapter and the Church. His management of the affairs of St. Paul's (for at one time he seems to have been *the* manager) only commenced too late, and terminated too soon."

In the year 1837 he made a short tour into Holland, with my mother. He always lamented that the power of travelling had been denied him till his body had become almost unequal to the fatigue of doing so. He was ever most eager to see and to hear; but with the same rapidity that characterized his thoughts, he only liked first impressions, and never dwelt ten minutes together on the same scene or picture; declared he had mastered the Louvre in a quarter of an hour, and could judge of Talma's powers in ten minutes.*

On his return, by Brussels, he received much kindness and attention from his friend Mr. Van de Weyer, who was then staying there, and made acquaintance with Madame Van de Weyer, his mother, with whom he was excessively struck, both from her talent and her vigour of character. He had, whilst here, the honour of an interview with King Leopold, who afterwards sent him an invitation to dine with him at his palace at Laeken, and was kind enough to send his carriage to Brussels to take him there and bring him back. He felt this unexpected honour and attention from the sovereign of a foreign country as he ought. But am I wrong in believing that such honours do more honour even to the giver than the receiver? for are they not a pledge to the people that their sovereign prizes talents and honesty wherever they are found, and whether they have been employed, as my

* It was this love of change that made him often write and speak of Combe Florey as an earthly paradise; and again, after some weeks, describe it as *un tombeau*. Both were genuine feelings at the moment.

father says, "in protecting the just rights of kings or restraining their unlawful ambition"?

He says, in a letter from Brussels, "Holland is dear, dirty, ugly. I was much struck with the commercial grandeur of Amsterdam. You must excuse me for thinking the English to be the greatest and wisest nation that ever existed in the world; we are excelled however in many things,—in buildings, cooking, baking, and in good manners. In setting out we went by Dunkirk, over a most atrocious country. With Dunkirk I was agreeably surprised; I found an excellent inn, good shops, and noble church and tower, and altogether a handsome city. At Yprès I was delighted with the Hôtel de Ville, one of the most magnificent Gothic buildings I ever saw. At Bruges the hall and tower are quite surprising, as is the town-house here. The Flemings are hideously ugly; so is their country; the inns are all very good. All their great towns are melancholy and under-peopled.

"I dined yesterday with Sir Hamilton Seymour. Van de Weyer has been extremely kind and hospitable to us, and his old mother is an excellent person. I am to be presented to the King today."

In the autumn he came again for his residence at St. Paul's, and the eagerness to obtain his society seemed to increase with his years. He used, during his stay in town, to give an evening party once a week. These parties were always popular, though, from the numbers now assembled at them, they had not the charm of the little select suppers of his youth.

One evening, at his house, a few friends had come

in to tea; amongst others, Lord Jeffrey, Dr. Holland, and his sister. Some one spoke of Talleyrand. "Oh," said Sydney, "Lady Holland laboured incessantly to convince me that Talleyrand was agreeable, and was very angry because his arrival was usually a signal for my departure; but, in the first place, he never spoke at all till he had not only devoured but digested his dinner, and as this was a slow process with him, it did not occur till everybody else was asleep, or ought to have been so; and when he did speak he was so inarticulate I never could understand a word he said." "It was otherwise with me," said Dr. Holland; "I never found much difficulty in following him." "Did not you? why it was an abuse of terms to call it talking at all; for he had no teeth, and, I believe, no roof to his mouth—no uvula—no larynx—no trachea—no epiglottis—no anything. It was not talking, it was gargling; and that, by the bye, now I think of it, must be the very reason why Holland understood him so much better than I did," turning suddenly round on him with his merry laugh.

"Yet nobody's wit was of so high an order as Talleyrand's when it did come, or has so well stood the test of time. You remember when his friend Montrond* was taken ill, and exclaimed, 'Mon ami, je sens les tourmens de l'enfer.' 'Quoi! déjà?' was his reply. And when he sat at dinner between Madame de Staël

---

* I find that Talleyrand used to tell this story as having passed between Cardinal De la Roche-Guyon, a celebrated epicure, and his confessor.

and Madame Récamier, the celebrated beauty, Madame de Staël, whose beauties were certainly not those of the person, jealous of his attentions to her rival, insisted upon knowing which he would save if they were both drowning. After seeking in vain to evade her, he at last turned towards her and said, with his usual shrug, 'Ah, madame, *vous savez nager.*' And when —— exclaimed, 'Me voilà entre l'esprit et la beauté,' he answered, 'Oui, et sans posséder ni l'un ni l'autre.' And of Madame ——, 'Oui, elle est belle, très-belle; mais pour la toilette, cela commence trop tard, et finit trop tôt.' Of Lord —— he said, 'C'est la bienveillance même, mais la bienveillance la plus perturbative que j'ai jamais connu.' To a friend of mine he said on one occasion, 'Miladi, voulez-vous me prêter ce livre?' 'Oui, mais vous me le rendrez?' 'Oui.' 'Parole d'honneur?' 'Oui.' 'Vous en êtes *sûr?*' 'Oui, oui, miladi; mais, pour vous le rendre, il faut absolument d'abord me le prêter.'

"What a talker that Frenchman Buchon is! Macaulay is a Trappist compared to him.

"I was, many years ago, talking in Talleyrand's presence to my brother Bobus, who was just then beginning his career at the Bar, and said, 'Mind, Bobus, when you are Chancellor I shall expect one of your best livings.' 'Oui, mon ami,' said Bobus, 'mais d'abord je vous ferai commettre toutes les bassesses dont les prêtres sont capables.' On which Talleyrand, throwing up his hands and eyes, exclaimed, with a shrug, 'Mais quelle latitude énorme!'"

The conversation then turned on society in London, and its effect upon character. "I always tell Lady P—— she has preserved the two impossible concomitants of a London life—a good complexion and a good heart. Most London dinners evaporate in whispers to one's next-door neighbour. I make it a rule never to speak a word to mine, but fire across the table; though I broke it once when I heard a lady who sat next me, in a low, sweet voice, say, 'No gravy, Sir.' I had never seen her before, but I turned suddenly round and said, 'Madam, I have been looking for a person who disliked gravy all my life; let us swear eternal friendship.' She looked astonished, but took the oath, and what is better, kept it. You laugh, Miss ——; but what more usual foundation for friendship, let me ask, than similarity of tastes?"

Talking of tastes, my father quite shared in his friend Mrs. Opie's for light, heat, and fragrance. The first was almost a passion with him, which he indulged by means of little tin lamps with mutton-fat, in the days of his poverty—these, when a little richer, to our great joy, were exchanged for oil-lamps—and lastly, in the days of his wealth, for a profusion of wax-lights. The heat of his patent fireplaces has been mentioned, and his delight in flowers was extreme. He often went into the garden the moment he was dressed, and returned with his hands full of roses, to place them on the plates at breakfast. He liked to see the young people staying in his house dressed with natural flowers, and encouraged us to invent all sorts of flowery ornaments, such as earrings and necklaces, some of which were really very graceful.

The following are some fragments of my father's conversation in London.

Some one asked if the Bishop of —— was going to marry. "Perhaps he may," said my father; "yet how can a bishop marry? How can he flirt? The most he can say is, 'I will see you in the vestry after service.'"

"Oh, don't read those twelve volumes till they are made into a *consommé* of two. Lord Dudley did still better, he waited till they blew over."

Talking of tithes: "It is an atrocious way of paying the clergy. The custom of tithe in kind will seem incredible to our posterity; no one will believe in the ramiferous priest officiating in the cornfield."

"Our friend —— makes all the country smell like Piccadilly."

An argument arose, in which my father observed how many of the most eminent men of the world had been diminutive in person, and after naming several among the ancients, he added, "Why, look there, at Jeffrey; and there is my little friend ——, who has not body enough to cover his mind decently with; his intellect is improperly exposed."

"Oh, don't mind the caprices of fashionable women; they are as gross as poodles fed on milk and muffins."

"Fox wrote drop by drop."

"Simplicity is a great object in a great book; it is not wanted in a short one."

"You will generally see in human life the round man and the angular man planted in the wrong hole; but the Bishop of ——, being a round man, has fallen into a triangular hole, and is far better off than many triangular men who have fallen into round holes."

"The great charm of Sheridan's speaking was his multifariousness of style."

"When I took my Yorkshire servants into Somersetshire, I found that they thought making a drink out of apples was a tempting of Providence, who had intended barley to be the only natural material of intoxication."

"We naturally lose illùsions as we get older, like teeth, but there is no Cartwright to fit a new set into our understandings. I have, alas, only one illusion left, and that is the Archbishop of Canterbury."

Speaking of the long-debates in the House: "Why will not people remember the Flood? If they had lived before it, with the patriarchs, they might have talked any stuff they pleased; but do let them remember how little time they have under this new order of things."

"The charm of London is that you are never glad or sorry for ten minutes together: in the country you are the one and the other for weeks."

"There is a New Zealand attorney arrived in London, with 6s. 8d. tattooed all over his face."

"Yes, he has spent all his life in letting down empty

buckets into empty wells; and he is frittering away his age in trying to draw them up again."

"If you masthead a sailor for not doing his duty, why should you not weathercock a parishioner for refusing to pay tithes?"

"How is ―――?" "He is not very well." "Why, what is the matter?" "Oh, don't you know he has produced a couplet? When our friend is delivered of a couplet, with infinite labour and pain, he takes to his bed, has straw laid down, the knocker tied up, expects his friends to call and make inquiries, and the answer at the door invariably is, 'Mr. ――― and his little couplet are as well as can be expected.' When he produces an Alexandrine he keeps his bed a day longer."

"You will find a Scotchman always says what is undermost. I, on the contrary, say everything that comes uppermost, and have all sorts of bad jokes put upon me in consequence. An American published a book, and declared I had told him there were more mad Quakers in lunatic asylums than any other sect;— quite an invention on his part. Another time Prince P. M. published my conversations; so when I next met him, I inquired whether this was to be a printed or manuscript one, as I should talk accordingly. He did his best to blush."

One evening, when drinking tea with Mrs. Austin, the servant entering into a crowded room, with a boiling tea-kettle in his hand, it seemed doubtful, nay impossible, he should make his way among the numerous groups; but, on the first approach of the steaming kettle, the crowd receded on all sides, my father amongst the rest, though carefully watching the progress of the lad to the table:—"I declare," said he (addressing Mrs. Austin), "a man who wishes to make his way in life could do nothing better than go through the world with a boiling tea-kettle in his hand."

"Never neglect your fireplaces: I have paid great attention to mine, and could burn you all out in a moment. Much of the cheerfulness of life depends upon it. Who could be miserable with that fire? What makes a fire so pleasant is, I think, that it is a live thing in a dead room."

"Such is the horror the French have of our *cuisine*, that at the dinner given in honour of Guizot at the Athenæum, they say his cook was heard to exclaim, 'Ah, mon pauvre maître! je ne le reverrai plus.'"

"Lord Wenlock told me that his ground-rent cost him five pounds a foot; that is about the price of a London footman six foot high,—thirty guineas per annum."

"I believe the parallelogram between Oxford-street, Piccadilly, Regent-street, and Hyde Park, encloses more intelligence and human ability, to say nothing of wealth and beauty, than the world has ever collected in such a space before."

"When I praised the author of the New Poor Law the other day, three gentlemen at table took it to themselves, and blushed up to the eyes."

"Yes! you find people ready enough to do the Samaritan, without the oil and twopence."

"It is a great proof of shyness to crumble bread at dinner. 'Oh, I see you are afraid of me' (turning to a young lady who sat by him), 'you crumble your bread.' I do it when I sit by the Bishop of London, and with both hands when I sit by the Archbishop."

Addressing Rogers: "My dear R., if we were both in America, we should be tarred and feathered; and, lovely as we are by nature, I should be an ostrich and you an emu."

"I once saw a dressed statue of Venus in a serious house—the Venus Millinaria."

"Ah, you flavour everything; you are the vanille of society."

"I think it was Luttrell who used to say '——'s face always reminded him of boiled mutton and near relations.'"

"I fully intended going to America; but my parishioners held a meeting, and came to a resolution that they could not trust me with the canvas-back ducks; and I felt they were right, so gave up the project."

"Of course, if I ever did go to a fancy ball at all, I should go as a Dissenter."

"Some people seem to be born out of their proper century. —— should have lived in the Italian Republics, and —— under Charles II."

"My living in Yorkshire was so far out of the way, that it was actually twelve miles from a lemon.

"Don't you know, as the French say, there are three sexes—men, women, and clergymen?"

"One of my great objections to the country is, that

you get your letters but once a day; here they come every five minutes."

On some one offering him oat-cake, "No, I can't eat oat-cake, it is too rich for me."

"Harrowgate seemed to me the most heaven-forgotten country under the sun. When I saw it, there were only nine mangy fir-trees there; and even they all leant away from it."

Dining at Mr. Grenville's, he as usual arrived before the rest of the party; some ladies were shortly after announced; as Mr. Grenville, with his graceful dignity and cheerfulness, went forward to receive them, my father, looking after him, exclaimed to Mr. Panizzi, "There, that is the man from whom we all ought to learn how to grow old!" The conversation at table turned on a subject lately treated of in Sir Charles Lyell's book, the phenomena which the earth might present to the geologists of some future period; "Let us imagine," said my father, "an excavation on the site of St. Paul's. Fancy a lecture, by the Owen of some future age, on the thigh-bone of a Minor Canon, or the tooth of a Dean,—the form, qualities, the knowledge, tastes, propensities, he would discover from them." And off he went, his imagination playing on this idea in every possible way.

Some one spoke of the state of financial embarrassment of the London University at that time. "Yes, it is so great, that I understand they have already seized on the air-pump, the exhausted receiver, and galvanic batteries; and that bailiffs have been seen chasing the Professor of Modern History round the quadrangle."

Conversing in the evening, with a small circle, round Miss Berry's tea-table (who, though far advanced towards the fourscore years and ten which she afterwards attained, was still remarkable for her vigour of mind and beauty of person), my father observed the entrance of a no less remarkable person, both for talents and years, dressed in a beautiful crimson velvet gown; he started up to meet his fine old friend, exclaiming, "Exactly the colour of my preaching cushion!" and leading her forward to the light, he pretended to be lost in admiration, saying, "I really can hardly keep my hands off you; I shall be preaching on you, I fear," etc., and played with the subject to the infinite amusement of his old friend and the little circle assembled round her.

"Playfair was certainly the most delightful philomath I ever knew."

"Have you heard of Niebuhr's discoveries? All Roman history reversed; Tarquin turning out an excellent family man, and Lucretia a very doubtful character, whom Lady —— would not have visited."

The ladies having left the room, at a dinner at Sir G. Philips's, the conversation turned on the black population of America. My father, turning to an eminent American jurist, who was here some years ago, "Pray, Mr. ——, tell us why you can't live on better terms with your black population." "Why, to tell you the truth, Mr. Smith, they smell so abominably that we can't bear them near us." "Possibly not," said my father, "but men must not be led by the *nose* in that way: if you don't like asking them to dinner, it is surely no reason why you should not make *citizens* of them.

   ' Et si non alium latè jactaret odorem,
    Civis erat.' "*

"Don't talk to me of not being able to cough a speaker down: try the hooping-cough."

Mr. Monckton Milnes was talking to Alderman ——, when the latter turned away: "You were speaking," said Sydney, "to the Lord Mayor elect. I myself felt in his presence like the Roman whom Pyrrhus tried to frighten with an elephant, and remained calm."

"When so showy a woman as Mrs. —— appears at a place, though there is no garrison within twelve miles, the horizon is immediately clouded with majors."

"To take Macaulay out of literature and society, and put him in the House of Commons, is like taking the chief physician out of London during a pestilence."

"How bored children are with the wisdom of Telemachus! they can't think why Calypso is so fond of him."

Some one observing the wonderful improvement in —— since his success, "Ah!" he said, "praise is the best diet for us, after all."

One day, Mr. Rogers took Mr. Moore and my father home in his carriage, from a breakfast; and insisted on showing them, by the way, Dryden's house,

 * Virgil, Georgics ii. 132. *Laurus* in the original.

in some obscure street. It was very wet; the house looked very much like other old houses; and having thin shoes on, they both remonstrated; but in vain. Rogers got out, and stood expecting them. "Oh! you see why Rogers don't mind getting out," exclaimed my father, laughing and leaning out of the carriage, "he has got goloshes on—but, Rogers, lend us each a golosh, and we will then stand on one leg, and admire as long as you please."

"When Prescott comes to England, a Caspian Sea of soup awaits him."

"An American said to me, 'You are so funny, Mr. Smith! do you know, you remind me of our great joker, Dr. Chamberlaque.' 'I am much honoured,' I replied, 'but I was not aware you had such a functionary in the United States.'"

At Mr. Romilly's there arose a discussion on the Inferno of Dante, and the tortures he had invented. "He may be a great poet," said my father, "but as to invention, I consider him a mere bungler,—no imagination, no knowledge of the human heart. If I had taken it in hand, I would show you what torture really was; for instance (turning, merrily, to his old friend Mrs. Marcet), you should be doomed to listen, for a thousand years, to conversations between Caroline and Emily, where Caroline should always give wrong explanations in chemistry, and Emily in the end be unable to distinguish an acid from an alkali. You, Macaulay, let me consider?—oh, you should be dumb. False dates and facts of the reign of Queen

Anne should for ever be shouted in your ears; all liberal and honest opinions should be ridiculed in your presence; and you should not be able to say a single word during that period in their defence." "And what would you condemn me to, Mr. Sydney?" said a young mother. "Why, you should for ever see those three sweet little girls of yours on the point of falling downstairs, and never be able to save them. There, what tortures are there in Dante equal to these?"

"Daniel Webster struck me much like a steam-engine in trousers."

"When I began to thump the cushion of my pulpit, on first coming to Foston, as is my wont when I preach, the accumulated dust of a hundred and fifty years made such a cloud, that for some minutes I lost sight of my congregation."

"Nothing amuses me more than to observe the utter want of perception of a joke in some minds. Mrs. Jackson called the other day, and spoke of the oppressive heat of last week. 'Heat, Ma'am!' I said; 'it was so dreadful here, that I found there was nothing left for it but to take off my flesh and sit in my bones.' 'Take off your flesh and sit in your bones, Sir! Oh, Mr. Smith! how could you do that?' she exclaimed, with the utmost gravity. 'Nothing more easy, Ma'am; come and see next time.' But she ordered her carriage, and evidently thought it a very unorthodox proceeding."

"Miss ——, too, the other day, walking round the grounds at Combe Florey, exclaimed, 'Oh, why do you chain up that fine Newfoundland dog, Mr. Smith?' 'Because it has a passion for breakfasting on parish boys.' 'Parish boys!' she exclaimed, 'does he really eat boys, Mr. Smith?' 'Yes, he devours them, buttons and all.' Her face of horror made me die of laughing."

A most curious instance of this slow perception of humour occurred once in Brook-street, where a gentleman of some rank dined at our house, with a large party, of which my father and Mr. Luttrell formed a portion. My father was in high spirits, and in one of his happiest veins; and much brilliant conversation passed around from Mr. Luttrell and others. Mr. —— sat through it all with the utmost gravity. This seemed only to stimulate my father, who became more and more brilliant, till the table was in a perfect roar of laughter. The servants even, forgetting all decorum, were obliged to turn away to conceal their mirth. Mr. —— alone sat unmoved, and gazing with solemn wonder at the scene around. Luttrell was so struck by this that he said, "Mr. —— was a natural phenomenon whom he must observe;" so letting the side-dishes pass by, he took out his eye-glass to watch. At last my father accidentally struck out a subject (which, for social reasons, I must not give, though it was inimitable,) which touched the right spring, and he could resist no longer, but actually laughed out. Luttrell shouted victory in my ear; and resumed his wonted attention to the dinner, saying, he had never witnessed so curious a scene.

The conversation turned upon pictures. "I like pictures, without knowing anything about them; but I hate coxcombry in the fine arts, as well as in anything else. I got into dreadful disgrace with Sir G. B. once, who, standing before a picture at Bowood, exclaimed, turning to me, 'Immense breadth of light and shade!' I innocently said, 'Yes;—about an inch and a half.' He gave me a look that ought to have killed me."

At a large dinner party my father, or some one else, announced the death of Mr. Dugald Stewart; one whose name ever brings with it feelings of respect for his talents and high character. The news was received with so much levity by a lady of rank, who sat by him, that he turned round and said, "Madam, when we are told of the death of so great a man as Mr. Dugald Stewart, it is usual, in civilized society, to look grave for at least the space of five seconds."

"They do nothing in Ireland as they would elsewhere. When the Dublin mail was stopped and robbed, my brother declares that a sweet female voice was heard behind the hedge, exclaiming, 'Shoot the gintleman, then, Patrick dear!'"

We were all assembled to look at a turtle that had been sent to the house of a friend, when a child of the party stooped down and began eagerly stroking the shell of the turtle. "Why are you doing that, B——?" said my father. "Oh, to please the turtle." "Why, child, you might as well stroke the dome of St. Paul's, to please the Dean and Chapter."

Some one naming —— as not very orthodox, "Accuse a man of being a Socinian, and it is all over with him; for the country gentlemen all think it has something to do with poaching."

"I hate bare walls; so I cover mine, you see, with pictures. The public, it must be owned, treat them with great contempt; and even Hibbert, who has been brought up in the midst of fine pictures, and might know better, never will admire them. But look at that sea-piece, now; what would you desire more? It is true, the moon in the corner was rather dingy when I first bought it; so I had a new moon put in for half-a-crown, and now I consider it perfect."

Of my father's conversation in London, where of course such powers were most excited and most brilliant, (except in these slight specimens, principally furnished by the kindness of a friend) I have hardly attempted to give any idea; partly because the documents that would best have enabled me to do so (his daily letters, when absent, to my mother) have not been preserved;—partly because of such journals so little can and ought to be published, that they serve but to remind one of Sancho Panza's feast, where a splendid list of names promises everything, and produces nothing—and last, though not least, as his friend Lord John Russell observes, because it is hardly possible to describe his manner, or convey the slightest idea of what his powers really were, in their most brilliant moments, to those who have never witnessed them. Lord John adds,—and all who knew my father will agree with his conclusion,—that "in his peculiar style he has never been equalled, and perhaps will not be surpassed." I observe, with pleasure, that every sketch which has appeared of him has laid great stress upon the wonderful degree of truth, wisdom, and bold illustration, that was often concealed in these ludicrous pictures and apparent nonsense; and which not only made them valuable, but prevented their ever palling, or degenerating into mere buffoonery.

About this period began his contest with the Ecclesiastical Commission, which lasted nearly four years, and was carried on principally in a series of letters addressed to Archdeacon Singleton. In these letters, after touching slightly upon the injustice of forming such a Commission without any one to protect the interests of the inferior clergy—on the permanent and arbitrary powers granted to the Commission, under a Whig ministry—on the inclination the Commission evinced to appropriate the patronage, at the same time that they were claiming the honours of martyrdom (*à propos* to which he introduced the episode of the old chronicle of Dort);—touching on these, together with many other clauses very oppressive to the clergy (which were afterwards given up), he proceeds to enforce two principles. First, that if the laity desire an Establishment into which birth, wealth, station, talent, education, and character should flow; and bestow on it a revenue which, if equally divided, would hardly place the clergy on a footing with the upper servants of a nobleman's family, and would not, according to the proposed plan of spoliation, be an addition of more than £5.12s.6½d. per man—payment by hope, or inequality of division, were the only means of obtaining the desired end; and the prizes in the lottery must be left. Or, if the inequality in some instances was too great, the remedy should be applied where the greatest evil existed. Secondly, that the Commission, by attacking vested interests during the lifetime of the incumbents, were not only guilty of great present injustice, but were admitting a most dangerous precedent, and overturning a principle that all governments had hitherto respected.

These letters, which by many have been considered as evincing more talent than almost anything he has written, produced considerable effect at the time; and the many private letters I possess, as well as the testimony of the public press, show that public opinion was strongly with him—that these measures were changes, but not reforms—that they contributed nothing to the public good—and that they diminished nothing of the public hostility to the Church. How it terminated is well known. He concludes the controversy with this tribute to his old friend and opponent, Lord John Russell:—" You know very well, my dear Lord, in criticizing parts of your Church reform, I mean nothing unkind or unfriendly to you personally. I have known you for thirty years; and I do not believe that in this country, full of good men, there is one more honest, upright, and intrepid than yourself." My father, I find, states that he has the most honourable testimony from Lord John himself, that in conducting this dispute he never exceeded the bounds of free discussion ; and that he was influenced by no motive that did not affect equally the whole body to which he belonged, and whose interests he felt bound to defend.*

I am aware that these letters have afforded plausible ground for the insinuations that were made by some few, that my father, a Whig all his life, deserted his party, and attacked his friends ; and, a reformer, opposed reform the moment it affected his own interest. These are grave charges, but are best met by a few facts. He attacked the Whigs when they were in power, and had everything to bestow ; when they were poor and powerless, he was ever found fighting at their side. This does not look mean and base. He opposed not reform, but this reform ; and this reform he had opposed upon the same principle, twenty years before, in the Edinburgh Review, under a Tory administration, when in his wildest dreams he had never hoped to be a Canon of St. Paul's.† He did not, therefore, change

---

* I might add to this statement, that I have very lately received from Lord John Russell the most generous praise of these very letters (always excepting a well-known passage, which he considered unjust) ; and Lord John's last act has indeed so proved its injustice, that I feel sure my father, were he alive, would be the first to retract it, and to do honour to the sacrifice that has been made by his friend.

† There is also amongst his papers an amusing fragment on the subject of tithes, written about the period that question was being discussed, which, as it is but a fragment, is hardly worth inserting. But in this again he speaks strongly of the necessity of inequality of payment, in order to support an Establishment so ill provided for as the Church of England ; showing still further how consistent he was from first to last in his opinions on this subject as well as others.

his opinions with his position. It did not affect his personal interests, as he wanted the patronage neither for himself nor his family; and the noble use he made of valuable patronage when it did come into his hands, must sufficiently exonerate him from the suspicion of acting from interested motives in the eyes of any candid man.

The following petition from the Rev. Sydney Smith, was presented and read to the House of Lords by the Hon. the Lord Bishop of Rochester, July, 1840.

"*To the Right Honourable the Lords Spiritual and Temporal in Parliament assembled.*

"The humble petition of the Rev. Sydney Smith, Canon Residentiary of St. Paul's, humbly showeth, —That your petitioner has bestowed considerable thought and attention upon the subject of the Ecclesiastical Duties and Revenues Bill, and prays that the same may not pass into a law; for the following reasons:—

"The Bill applies to the spiritual destitution of the Church, that which was left for the ornaments and rewards of the Church; and in this way gets rid of the burden of supporting the clergy, by tampering with the sacred laws of property; making, at the same time, the multitude believe that they are reforming abuses, while they are only evading duties and weakening principles.

"By lessening the rewards of the Church, it prevents men of capital from entering into it; and makes the whole wealth of those who are engaged in the service of the Church, *less*, instead of increasing it.

"The whole mass of property which the Bill proposes to confiscate, will make the poor clergy a very little less poor, while its confiscation destroys the powerful stimulus of hope, at the beginning of an ecclesiastical life. Two-thirds of the present deans and prebendaries have been curates and small vicars: they would, at the lowest period of their fortunes, have refused to barter their hope of future competence, for the addition of a few pounds to their income; and this is *most unquestionably* the state of feeling among the lower clergy at the present moment.

"The whole of the Bill supposes that deans and chapters have made a worse use of their patronage than bishops, and this is directly contrary to truth. But what *is* true of this Bill is, that one order in the Church who have no votes in Parliament, have been completely sacrificed to those who have votes,—that deans and prebendaries, carefully excluded from the Commission, have been condemned to confiscation,—and that the Prelate Commissioners have not sacrificed one shilling of the aggregate income of the bishops to those spiritual destitutions of the Church, which they feel so strongly, but relieve with property not their own.

"The Bill destroys many ecclesiastical offices, which, with a little care and thought, might have been made eminently useful to literature; to the present plans of national education; to the care of dioceses in the decay and old-age of bishops, and to the general support of episcopal authority; or, what is of more importance (in the present unrepresented and unsupported state of the parochial clergy), to the checks upon episcopal authority.

"This Bill habituates the Legislature to the easy and inviting power of tampering with the property of the Church. It is utterly impossible to believe that this will be the last and the worst act of that nature.

"The law, as it now stands, enables dignified clergymen to bestow their patronage on their children and relations, who may be deserving of it. Under this sanction they have given to their sons very expensive educations at the Universities. The present Bill destroys these expectations; sets at nought vested rights; and, instead of applying this provision to future members of chapters, cuts off from their rights the ancient members of those bodies, who have laid out their whole plan of life upon the faith of laws unimpugned and unrepealed for centuries; and this appears to your Petitioner to be a gross act of spoliation and injustice, and contrary to the express provisions and arrangements of the Commissioners themselves.

"To give to every clergyman who has gone through the expense of an English University, and who is married and settled in the country, the income which they ought in decency and in justice to receive, would require, not only the confiscation of *all* the cathedral and episcopal property, but some millions of money in addition. A church provided for as ours now is, can obtain a well-educated and respectable clergy only by those hopes which are excited by the unequal division and lottery of preferment. This is the real cause which has brought capital and respectability into the English Church, and peopled it with the well-educated sons of gentlemen,—an object of the greatest importance in a rich country like England. Nothing would so rapidly and certainly ensure the degradation of the Church of England, as the equal division of all its revenues among all its members.

" For these reasons, your Petitioner believes the Bill in question (however well intended) to be founded on a very short-sighted policy, and that it will entail great evils upon a Church no longer unfavourable to the civil liberties of mankind—as yet untainted by fanaticism —carried forward by the labours of a highly improved clergy—and now become as useful and as active as any church establishment which the world has yet seen.

" This, as it seems to your Petitioner, is the last of all our institutions upon which an experiment so daring and so dangerous ought to be tried. For these reasons, your Petitioner humbly prays that the Ecclesiastical Duties and Revenues Bill may not pass into a law.

" SYDNEY SMITH."

In the previous year, a statue having been erected at Newcastle, in honour of Earl Grey, my father was requested to write the inscription for it. He sent the following; but as it did not entirely meet the views of all the subscribers, it was not adopted; though I have reason to believe it was much approved of by his family.

TO CHARLES, EARL GREY, K.G.,
OF HOWICK, IN NORTHUMBERLAND,
THIS MONUMENT,
IN A SPIRIT OF SOLEMN RESPECT
AND DEEP GRATITUDE,
IS ERECTED, BY MANY OF HIS FELLOW CITIZENS.
THEY HAVE SEEN HIM THROUGH A LONG LIFE
DEDICATING HIS FINE TALENTS TO PROMOTE THE BEST INTERESTS
OF MANKIND,
AND, IN EVIL DAYS, WITH HIGH MORAL COURAGE
DEFENDING THE ALMOST EXTINGUISHED LIBERTIES OF ENGLAND!
THEY OWE TO HIM THAT MEMORABLE REFORM,
WHICH, BLENDING FREEDOM WITH LOYALTY AND ORDER,
HAS INFUSED FRESH LIFE AND ENERGY INTO ALL
OUR INSTITUTIONS;
A REFORM WHICH HE PLANNED IN HIS YOUTH,
AND BROUGHT TO TRIUMPHANT PERFECTION IN HIS ADVANCED AGE.
REMEMBERING THESE THINGS,
THEY HAVE DEEMED IT AN ACT OF SACRED JUSTICE
TO RECORD, BY A PUBLIC MONUMENT,
THEIR ADMIRATION OF THIS GREAT STATESMAN:
NOT WITHOUT HOPE
THAT THE YOUNG, SEEING WHAT THOSE QUALITIES ARE
WHICH COMMAND THE GRATITUDE OF MANKIND,
MAY STRIVE TO BE AS GOOD AND PURE AS HE
WHOSE IMAGE IS HERE PLACED BEFORE THEIR EYES.

279

CHAPTER X.

VISIT TO COMBE FLOREY.—KINDNESS TO GRANDCHILDREN.—SUDDEN WEALTH.—RECOLLECTIONS OF HIS PARISHIONERS AT FOSTON.—DEATH OF LORD HOLLAND: HIS PORTRAIT.—LETTER TO MR. WEBSTER.—SKETCH OF REVUE DES DEUX MONDES.—LETTER OF MR. GRENVILLE.—VISIT FROM MR. MOORE, AND VERSES.—BESTOWS THE LIVING OF EDMONTON ON MR. TATE'S SON.—LETTER TO MRS. SYDNEY SMITH.—ADDRESS OF PARISHIONERS, AND ANSWER.—LETTER OF MRS. MARCET.—RECEIPT FOR MAKING EVERY DAY HAPPY.—DEFINITION OF HAPPINESS.—PETITION TO THE AMERICAN CONGRESS IN 1843.—EFFECTS.—SPEECH FROM MR. TICKNOR.—LETTER FROM MR. WAINWRIGHT.—ABUSE AND GIFTS FROM AMERICA.—EFFECT OF PREACHING IN OLD-AGE.—LETTER OF MISS EDGEWORTH.—CORRESPONDENCE WITH SIR R. PEEL.—EXTRACT FROM JOURNAL, WITH ANECDOTES.

IN the summer we went again to spend some months with my father at Combe Florey, which every year became more beautiful under his fostering care. His love of children I have before alluded to ; and particularly of his little grandchildren, whose happiness he delighted to promote. He hardly ever dressed in a morning without having them round him to assist him ; or to play at shaving his table with his shaving-brush and huge wooden bowl, which still remained, though the reign of Bunch had ceased. Amongst these grandchildren was an odd, clever little girl, about five years old, who amused him much by her peculiarities; one of which was, that she insisted upon understanding everything she heard, and that when baffled, as she often necessarily was, she took to roaring and kicking. On one of these occasions, he was walking round his garden with his two arms swung behind over his black crutch-stick (his usual manner of walking), and hearing these sounds from his merry little favourite, he stopped under the open window, and called out, "What is the matter with my little girl?" "Oh," said her mother, "she cannot understand something about the Hebrews. I have tried to explain it to her; but as she has lost her temper, I have told her she must wait till she is a little older." He looked excessively amused at the mental ambition of the five-years-old, but walked off in silence. Two hours after, the mother found him closeted with the little culprit in his favourite library, in his large arm-chair, with the child on his knee, with maps, dictionary, and books piled around him; he explaining and she listening with apparently equal pleasure, till the difficulty was overcome, and the child satisfied. I must add, in justice to the little girl, that though she has retained her love of investigation, she has fortunately left off the habit of roaring and kicking under mental difficulties.

The sudden death of his youngest brother Courtenay about this time (whose debt of thirty pounds he had paid with so much difficulty at College fifty years before) without a will, put him in possession of the third part of the very large, but to himself useless, fortune, which he had accumulated in India; and thus, as my father has said, "in my grand climacteric I became unexpectedly a rich man." Having the means of spending now, he spent as liberally as if he had been used to wealth all his life; for his rigid economy in poverty had never the effect of making him penurious.

This summer, when travelling through Yorkshire, I went with my children to see our old haunts at Foston; and it was very gratifying to find, though nearly ten years had elapsed since he left them, how fresh my father's memory still was in the hearts of his villagers. From almost every cottage some one came out to greet me, and to remind me of some saying, or some act of kindness, or to show me his parting gift, or to remember how he "doctored" them, and to lament his loss. And as to old Molly Mills, who was still alive, it was quite affecting to see the mixture of joy and sorrow in her face, as she recalled old stories, or thought of her present loss,—"the smile on her lip, and the tear in her eye." I felt these were humble, but not the less precious tributes to his character.

Each year now thinned the ranks of the great men with whom he had begun life;—men not only endeared to him by social intercourse, but by that deep interest which a struggle for the same cause during so many years usually inspires. But amongst these losses, none ever fell more deeply and heavily on his heart than that of Lord Holland. He loved him (as indeed all did who had the privilege of knowing him intimately), and he felt deeply his debt of gratitude to him in early life. Lord Holland's last illness was, I believe, short; and on his dressing-table were found these few lines, which were sent to me by his sister, Miss Fox, after his death:—

> "Nephew of Fox, and friend of Grey,—
> Enough my meed of fame
> If those who deign'd to observe me say
> I injured neither name."

In a letter to Mrs. M., one of our oldest friends, he says, speaking of Lord Holland's death,—"It is indeed a great loss to me; but I have learned to live, as a soldier does in war, expecting that on any one moment the best and the dearest may be killed before his eyes. . . . I have gout, asthma, and seven other maladies, but am otherwise very well.—SYDNEY SMITH."

I see amongst my father's papers a sketch of Lord Holland, from which I shall make some extracts, as, I trust, they can only give pleasure.

"A Portrait.

"Great powers of reasoning, great quickness and ingenuity of proof, and a memory in the highest degree retentive; a knowledge varied and extensive, and in English history and constitutional law profound. . . . An invincible hatred of tyranny and oppression, the most ardent love of public happiness, and attachment to public rights. His conversation was lively and incessant. . . .

"As a speaker, he wanted words, which he was often forced to stop for; and he was too slow; but he atoned for these defects by sense, knowledge, simplicity, logic, vehemence, and unblemished character. There never existed in any human being a better heart, or one more purified from all the bad passions, more abounding in charity and compassion, or which seemed to be so created as a refuge to the helpless and the oppressed.

* * * * *

" He was very acute in the discernment of character; more so, I cannot help thinking, than any public man of his time whom it has fallen to my lot to observe. He was one of the most consistent and steady politicians living in any day; in whose life, exceeding sixty-five years, there was no doubt, varying, nor shadow of change. It was one great, incessant, and unrewarded effort to resist oppression, promote justice, and restrain the abuse of power."

When Mr. Webster was Secretary of Foreign Affairs for the United States, my father heard it reported from America that an accidental mistake he had made, in introducing Mr. Webster, on his coming to this country some time before (I believe, to Lord Brougham) under the name of Mr. Clay, was intentional, and by way of joke. Annoyed that so much impertinence and bad taste should be imputed to him, he wrote a few lines of explanation to Mr. Webster, to which he received the following answer:—

"*Washington*, 1841.

" My dear Sir,

" 'Though exceedingly delighted to hear from you,

I am yet much pained by the contents of your note; not so much however as I should be, were I not able to give a peremptory denial to the whole report. I never mentioned the incident to which you refer, as a joke of yours,—far from it; nor did I mention it as anything extraordinary.

"My dear, good friend, do not think me such a —— as to quote or refer to any incident falling out between you and me to your disadvantage. The pleasure of your acquaintance is one of the jewels I brought home with me. I had read of you, and read you, for thirty years. I was delighted to meet you, and to have all I knew of you refreshed and brightened by the charms of your conversation. If any son of —— asserts that either through ill-will, or love of vulgar gossip, I tell such things of you as you suppose, I pray you let him be knocked down *instanter*. And be assured, my dear Sir, I never spoke of you in my life but with gratitude, respect, and attachment.

"D. WEBSTER."

My father wrote in answer :—

"Many thanks, my dear Sir, for your obliging letter. I think better of myself because you think well of me. If, in the imbecility of old-age, I forgot your name for a moment, the history of America will hereafter be more tenacious in its recollections—tenacious, because you are using your eloquent wisdom to restrain the high spirit of your countrymen within the limits of justice, and are securing to two kindred nations, who ought to admire and benefit each other, the blessings of peace. How can great talents be applied to nobler ends, or what existence can be more truly splendid?

"Ever sincerely yours,
"SYDNEY SMITH."

I have mentioned that my father, for reasons already given, had made a collection of his writings in the Edinburgh Review and elsewhere; and retracted what little he felt he had been led by party prejudice to say unjustly; and I cannot resist inserting here a short passage from a French Review (I believe, the 'Revue des Deux Mondes'), because I think it is a trait in his character that has been unnoticed by his countrymen.

"Quoi de plus fréquent que de se dire, au fond du cœur, j'ai été trop loin—ceci n'était pas vrai, ceci était injuste? mais quoi de plus rare que de l'imprimer? Voilà ce que Sydney a noblement fait : trente ans après ses regards rencontrent une plaisanterie qu'un juge moins sévère de ses propres fautes aurait pu croire innocente, il ne peut s'empêcher de dire, 'Il n'y a rien qui dépare plus les lettres de Plymley que cette attaque dirigée contre M. Bourne, qui est une personne d'honneur et de talent ; mais voilà où mènent les mauvaises passions de l'esprit de parti.' Castlereagh n'était pas un homme vénal, cependant il l'avait représenté comme capable de recevoir de toutes mains ; 'Je l'ai injustement accusé,' avoue-t-il franchement. Il est beau d'entendre de la sorte un mot fameux, et de reconnaître, en se condamnant soi-même, qu'on doit surtout la vérité à son ennemi mort."

He sent a copy of his works to each of my children in 1842, as the best memorial of himself that he could give them: alas! in how few years was it the only memorial left.

I find among the papers left me a pretty letter from his old friend Mr. Grenville, to whom my father had sent what he believed to be a rare and valuable edition of Lucan, which we had found amongst his books. The following is an extract from it.

"My dear Sir,

"Lucan was first printed in 1469; but although, under these circumstances, Aldus of 1515 may not be highly estimated in bibliographical reputation, still it comes to me with all the value of a unique copy; for I know nobody else who would have so disposed of a book with a perfect indifference to its being worth one hundred pounds or one hundred pence, but with an evident wish that it might turn out to be ranked under the first of these two classes. Most gladly and gratefully therefore shall Lucan, 1515, repose upon my shelves; with the unique distinction which I am proud to attribute to it from its highly-valued donor.

"Ever most truly yours,
"THOMAS GRENVILLE."

"*Hamilton Place*, 1842."

In the summer of 1843, we had a visit from Mr. Moore, a visit often before promised, but never accomplished. The weather and the place were lovely, and seemed to inspire the charming little poet, who talked and sang in his peculiar fashion, like any nightingale of the Flower Valley, to the delight of us all. In true poet style, when he departed, he left various articles of his wardrobe scattered about. On my father writing to inform him of this, he sent the following answer :—

"*Sloperton*, 1843.

"My dear Sydney,

"Your lively letter (what else could it be?) was found by me here on my return from Bowood; and with it a shoal of other letters, which it has taken me almost ever since to answer. I began my answer to yours in rhyme, contrasting the recollections I had brought away from you, with the sort of treasures you had supposed me to have left behind. This is part of it :—

"Rev. Sir, having duly received by the post
Your list of the articles missing and lost
By a certain small poet, well known on the road,
Who visited lately your flowery abode;
We have balanced what Hume calls '*the tottle o' the whole*,'
Making all due allowance for what the bard stole;
And hoping th' enclosed will be found quite correct,
Have the honour, Rev. Sir, to be yours with respect.

"Left behind a kid glove, once the half of a pair,
An odd stocking, whose fellow is—Heaven knows where;

And (to match these odd fellows) a couplet sublime,
Wanting nought to complete it but reason and rhyme.

"Such, it seems, are the only small goods you can find,
That this runaway bard in his flight left behind;
But in settling the account, just remember, I pray,
What rich recollections the rogue took away;
What visions for ever of sunny Combe Florey,
Its cradle of hills, where it slumbers in glory,
Its Sydney himself, and the countless bright things
Which his tongue or his pen, from the deep shining springs
Of his wisdom and wit, ever flowingly brings.

"I have not time to recollect any more; besides I was getting rather out of my depth in those deep shining springs, though not out of yours. Kindest regards to the ladies, not forgetting the pretty Hebe* of the breakfast-table the day I came away.
"Yours ever most truly,
"THOMAS MOORE."

"*Bowood, August, Tuesday* 22nd, 1843.

"My dear Sydney,

"You said, in your acknowledgment of my late versicles, that you had never been be-rhymed before. This startled me into the recollection that I had myself once before made free with you in that way; but where the evidence was of my presumption, I could not remember. The verses however, written some three or four years ago, have just turned up, and here they are for you. I forgot, by the bye, to tell you that, a day or two after my return from Combe Florey

* Sir Henry Holland's youngest daughter.

(*I like to write that name*), I was persuaded to get into a gig with Lady Kerry, and let her drive me some miles. Next day I found out that, but a day or two before, it had run away with her!—no bad taste, certainly, in the horse;—but it shows what one gets by consorting with young countesses and frisky ecclesiastics.*

"Yours ever,
"THOMAS MOORE.

* * * * * * *

"And still let us laugh, preach the world as it may,
   Where the cream of the joke is, the swarm will soon follow;
Heroics are very fine things in their way,
   But the laugh, at the long-run, will carry it hollow.

"Yes, Jocus! gay god, whom the Gentiles supplied,
   And whose worship not even among Christians declines;
In our senates thou 'st languish'd, since Sheridan died,
   But Sydney still keeps thee alive in our shrines.

"Rare Sydney! thrice honour'd the stall where he sits,
   And be his every honour he deigneth to climb at!
Had England a hierarchy form'd all of wits,
   Whom, but Sydney, would England proclaim as its primate?

"And long may he flourish, frank, merry, and brave,
   A Horace to feast with, a Pascal† to read!
While he *laughs*, all is safe; but, when Sydney grows grave,
   We shall then think the Church is in danger indeed."

About this time the very valuable living of Edmonton fell vacant, by the death of my father's fellow-

* Mr. Smith had driven Mr. Moore with a somewhat frisky horse. Mr. Moore got out of the gig, and walked home.

† "Some parts of the 'Provinciales' may be said to be of the highest order of *jeux d'esprit*."—*Note by Mr. Moore.*

canon, Mr. Tate; and by the rules of the Chapter of St. Paul's, it lay with my father either to take it himself or present it to a relation or friend. Remembering the honest intrepidity of his old colleague, who, in spite of poverty and many children, had many years before joined him in a minority of two against the clergy of Yorkshire, under a Tory administration, in favour of Catholic Emancipation; and grieving at the poverty his family would be reduced to by his death; he determined to bestow the living on his eldest son, who had acted as his father's curate, if he found on inquiry that he was fitted for it by his character. He has given a most touching account of his interview with the unhappy widow and her family on this occasion, in a letter to my mother, from which I shall give some extracts.

"Green-street, October 23.

"Dearest Kate,

"I meant to have gone to Munden today, but am not quite stout, so have postponed my journey there till next Saturday, the 28th. I went over yesterday to the Tates at Edmonton. The family consists of three delicate daughters, an aunt, the old lady, and her son, then curate of Edmonton; the old lady was in bed. I found there a physician, an old friend of Tate's, attending them from friendship, who had come from London for that purpose. They were in daily expectation of being turned out from house and curacy. . . I began by inquiring the character of their servant;

then turned the conversation upon their affairs, and expressed a hope the Chapter might ultimately do something for them. I then said, 'It is my duty to state to you (they were all assembled) that I have given away the living of Edmonton; and have written to our Chapter clerk this morning, to mention the person to whom I have given it; and I must also tell you, that I am sure he will appoint his curate. (A general silence and dejection.) It is a very odd coincidence,' I added, 'that the gentleman I have selected is a namesake of this family; his name is Tate. Have you any relations of that name?' 'No, we have not.' 'And, by a more singular coincidence, his name is Thomas Tate; in short,' I added, 'there is no use in mincing the matter, you are vicar of Edmonton.' They all burst into tears. It flung me also into a great agitation of tears, and I wept and groaned for a long time. Then I rose, and said I thought it was very likely to end in their keeping a buggy, at which we all laughed as violently.

"The poor old lady, who was sleeping in a garret because she could not bear to enter into the room lately inhabited by her husband, sent for me and kissed me, sobbing with a thousand emotions. The charitable physician wept too. . . . I never passed so remarkable a morning, nor was more deeply impressed with the sufferings of human life, and never felt more thoroughly the happiness of doing good.

"God bless you!

"SYDNEY SMITH."

On this act becoming known, my father received an address from the principal parishioners of Edmonton, stating that they had intended to address the Dean and Chapter, respectfully soliciting their patronage in favour of the son of their late vicar, and adding: "But what shall we say, Reverend Sir, of that munificent act of liberality on your part, by which the necessity of such a memorial is superseded? Though however that necessity is superseded, we feel, Reverend Sir, bound in gratitude to present to you personally our united thanks, for the great benefit you have bestowed on our parish, and the high gratification you have afforded us." To which my father replied:—

"Gentlemen,

"I am very much pleased by the address you have done me the honour to send me. . . . In the choice of a clergyman for the parish of Edmonton, I was actuated by many considerations. I had to consult the character and dignity of the Chapter, which would have been compromised by the nomination of a person merely because he was my friend and relation. I was to find a serious and diligent man, in the prime of life, able and eager to fulfil the burdensome duties of so large a parish; and I was to seek in him those characters of gentleness and peace which are of such infinite importance to the character of the Church, and the happiness of those who live under the beautiful influence of these qualities. Lastly, I had to show my strong respect for the memory of one of the kindest and best men that ever lived; and to lift up, if I could, from poverty and despair, his widow and his children.

"The address I have the honour to receive from you today convinces me that I have succeeded in combining these objects; and makes me really happy in thinking that my conduct has obtained the approbation of so many honourable men, so well acquainted with the circumstances of the case.

"I am, Gentlemen, with great respect,
"Your obedient humble servant,
"SYDNEY SMITH."

I must add a touching little note from his old friend Mrs. Marcet, to my mother, on this occasion.

"What a happy woman you must be, my dear Mrs. Smith, to have such a husband! All the world know his talents, but it is not many who know that heart, so overflowing with generous and magnanimous feelings, with tender mercies, and Christian charities. God bless him! . . . I will write it, though it makes my hand ache;* it fills my heart with joy, and my eyes with tears.
"Ever affectionately yours,
"J. MARCET."

The following letter was very kindly sent to me

* Mrs. M. had sprained her wrist.

by the Bishop of London, from which I give extracts:—

"My dear Lord,
"I am very glad you approve of my choice. Every one of the persons who have pews in his church have concurred in the same sentiment, as I learn from a memorial sent to me to that effect. I never saw a greater scene of distress than when I went down to them;—the poor mother ill in bed of a fever, three delicate sisters, a poor and aged aunt, and the curate—all expecting to be turned out of house and curacy, with £100 per annum between them all. The transition from despair to joy was awful; I shall never forget it. . . . Have mercy, my dear Lord, and take £100;* it leaves only £700 per annum to the Vicar of Edmonton and his brothers; this will make W—— Hill equal to Southgate, where the curacy is made up £200 per annum.

"Yours, my dear Lord, very sincerely,
"SYDNEY SMITH."

It is beautifully said somewhere:—"Happiness is what all men seek; all men have the jewel in their casket, but how few find the key to open it!" The following paragraph, which, I find my mother says, "was cut out of our papers and preserved by Sydney," shows at least that he had not sought for the key quite in vain.

* The Bishop of London had wished to divide the Living.

"*Receipt for making every Day Happy.*

"When you rise in the morning, form a resolution to make the day a happy one to a fellow-creature. It is easily done;—a left-off garment to the man who needs it, a kind word to the sorrowful, an encouraging expression to the striving; trifles in themselves light as air will do it, at least for the twenty-four hours; and, if you are young, depend upon it it will tell when you are old; and, if you are old, rest assured it will send you gently and happily down the stream of human time to eternity. By the most simple arithmetical sum, look at the result: you send one person, only one, happily through the day; that is three hundred and sixty-five in the course of the year; and supposing you live forty years only after you commence that course of medicine, you have made 14,600 human beings happy, at all events for a time. Now, worthy reader, is this not simple? It is too short for a sermon, too homely for ethics, and too easily accomplished for you to say, 'I would if I could.'"

I know that my mother thought her husband's life the best comment on these precepts. I see amongst his scattered notes on this subject, "The haunts of Happiness are varied, and rather unaccountable; but I have more often seen her among little children, home fire-sides, and country houses, than anywhere else; at least I think so."

On his return to Combe Florey, in July, he spent

a few days at Nuneham, on a visit to his former diocesan, the Archbishop of York. He met there a large and agreeable party; and a discussion arising, amongst other subjects, on hardness of character, my father, at the request of Miss G. Harcourt, wrote the following definition of it.

"*Definition of Hardness of Character.*

"*Hardness* is a want of minute attention to the feelings of others. It does not proceed from malignity or a carelessness of inflicting pain, but from a want of delicate perception of those little things by which pleasure is conferred or pain excited.

"A hard person thinks he has done enough if he does not speak ill of your relations, your children, or your country; and then, with the greatest good-humour and volubility, and with a total inattention to your individual state and position, gallops over a thousand fine feelings, and leaves in every step the mark of his hoofs upon your heart. Analyse the conversation of a well-bred man who is clear of the besetting sin of hardness; it is a perpetual homage of polite good-nature. He remembers that you are connected with the Church, and he avoids (whatever his opinions may be) the most distant reflections on the Establishment. He knows that you are admired, and he admires you as far as is compatible with good-breeding. He sees that, though young, you are at the head of a great establishment, and he infuses into his manner and conversation that respect which is so pleasing to all who exercise authority. He leaves you in perfect good-humour with yourself, because you perceive how much and how successfully you have been studied.

"In the meantime the gentleman on the other side of you (a highly moral and respectable man) has been crushing little sensibilities, and violating little proprieties, and overlooking little discriminations; and, without violating anything which can be called a *rule*, or committing what can be denominated a *fault*, has displeased and dispirited you, from wanting that fine vision which sees little things, and that delicate touch which handles them, and that fine sympathy which this superior moral organization always bestows.

"So great an evil in society is *hardness*, and that want of perception of the minute circumstances which occasion pleasure or pain!"

Towards the end of this year (1843) my father sent a petition to the American Congress, for payment of the debt due to England by the repudiating States.

It was said of Régnault St. Jean d'Angely, President of the French Institute, "qu'il avait passé la vie en venant toujours au secours *du plus fort*." The reverse might justly be said of my father: he passed his life in minorities, and in the cause of the oppressed. He says, in speaking of his motives for undertaking the one in question: "I am no enemy to America; I loved and admired honest America when she respected the laws of pounds, shillings, and pence, and I thought the United States the most magnificent picture of human happiness. I meddle now in these matters because I hate fraud; because I pity the misery it has occasioned; because I mourn over the hatred it has excited against free institutions."

This petition and the letters which followed it produced a most extraordinary sensation, and brought upon him much abuse from the American press; though we had reason to believe, from many sources, that they spoke the feelings of every honourable man in America.

"And all this storm," says the editor of the 'Morning Chronicle' of the time, "has been raised by a few words from a *private* English gentleman! Why is it that his words have had such a talismanic effect? It is true, they were words of choice and singular excellence; but no mastery of language or weight of literary reputation could so have moved America, if they did not happen to be employed in the utterance of home truths, which are, or ought to be, sharper than a two-edged sword. We repeat, that the power of these letters lies mainly in the deep moral feeling that pervades them; and one proof of this is, the warm response they have called forth from those in America, in whom the moral sense is strong enough to make them speak out."

As one specimen of this, I shall insert a speech or letter of Mr. Ticknor's, extracted from the 'Boston Semi-weekly Advertiser,' and sent to my father by Mr. Everett.

"The short and pungent petition to Congress of the Rev. Sydney Smith, in relation to his claim on the state of Pennsylvania, for interest-money due to him, has already excited no little remark among us, and is likely to excite yet more. This is probably one of the effects its author intended it should produce; perhaps it is one of the effects that we ourselves, as honest men and patriots, ought to desire; for the subject of his petition is a grave one, that cannot excite too much discussion in any part of the United States. But we should be careful, for our own sakes, to assume the right tone when speaking of a man like Mr. Smith, who only asks to be paid that to which he is as justly entitled as any one of us is entitled to anything he possesses.

"It has therefore appeared to many persons unseemly that the 'Boston Courier' should speak of Mr. Smith's petition, to have payment made to him of the interest, which has been solemnly promised on the faith and honour of the State of Pennsylvania, merely as 'impudence, bombast, and impertinence.' The claims of a creditor are not always welcome to his debtor, and, when other means have failed, they are not always set forth by the injured party in the most civil and gracious words; writs and executions, for instance, are not drawn up in terms chosen for the sake of pleasing 'ears polite.' Mr. Smith would, no doubt, have much preferred to use the good set terms of these instruments of established authority; and nobody would then have fancied he was doing anything unreasonable, since he would be doing just what everybody else does who cannot in other ways get his rights. But the great and rich State of Pennsylvania, like the other States of our Union, has taken some pains to place herself above the reach of such vulgar processes for coercing her to be honest. She *cannot* be sued: her creditor therefore is compelled to use his own words, instead of the more stringent words of the law. No doubt Mr. Sydney Smith, when doing this, does not present himself with a very cringing air: he uses strong phrases, stronger than we like to hear, stronger than is respectful; but the real difficulty in the case is, that the strongest words he uses are true words; for just so long as the Pennsylvanians refuse to lay a tax of one cent on every hundred dollars of their wealth to pay their honest debts, just so long they may be called 'men who prefer any load of infamy, however great, to any pressure of taxation, however light;' and this is the hardest and sharpest phrase in Mr. Smith's petition. To be sure, it would not be easy, on the same subject, to say anything more cutting or more terse; but, after all, the bitterness of the words lies in their truth.

"The 'New York Evening Post' is more severe on Mr. Smith than the 'Boston Courier.' His petition is there treated as the 'ravings of one who had been disappointed in reaping that profit from his speculations which he expected and desired;' and, because he has told us that we are 'unstable in the very foundations of social life,' the writer in the 'Post' inquires, whether 'the Bible used by the reverend gentleman teaches him that dollars and cents are the very foundation of social life?' Now, it is disagreeable to witness such injustice coupled with such violence of language; the thing is wrong in itself, and it does us much harm. The Rev. Sydney Smith is no more a speculator than every man is who lends money to his neighbour at the regular rate of interest; nor does he rave any more than every man raves, who insists, in round terms, that he will be paid what is plainly and lawfully due to him. Then, too, as to the 'foundations of social life,' the New York assailant of Mr. Smith really does not seem to suspect that honesty and good faith are among them, and that all the English clergyman asks of Pennsylvania is to be honest, in the lowest and commonest sense of that reproachful word which we can no longer, as one would think from the tone of this writer in the 'Post,' bear to have uttered in our presence.

"But let us now look at the matter just as it really stands. The Rev. Sydney Smith, as anybody may learn who will inquire, is a man known throughout Europe for his wit, logic, and the general vigour of his mind. He was, above forty years ago, one of the founders and main supporters of the Edinburgh Review; and he is now one of the most popular and powerful writers of his time, read alike on both sides of the Atlantic. He is an old Whig; and for the sin of maintaining manfully, against all his worldly interests, the cause of free institutions, the cause of Irish emancipation, and the cause of Parliamentary reform, he was kept low in the Church, as long as the Tories had power; and supported himself and his family, in no small degree, by his pen. He was, in fact, for many years a very poor parson, in a very poor parish in Yorkshire, where he was much loved by his parishioners for his active goodness; taking pains, among other things, to study medicine, in order to be able to practise it gratuitously among them, as there was no physician in their neighbourhood, and they could not afford to send abroad for one. When he was about sixty years old, the Whigs came into office, and gave him a good living. From this, it seems, he made in his old-age some savings: and, having confidence in free institutions and American honesty, he invested a part, or the whole, of these savings in Pennsylvania stocks. But his interest there is not paid, and his capital is shrunk to a merely nominal value. He of course complains. He tells us even that we are not honest. We answer, you 'rave,' you are 'impertinent,' you are 'impudent,' you are 'a reverend slanderer.' But what, in the meantime, do honourable men everywhere say better about us? and how comfortably does an American, always before so proud to call himself such, feel, who is now travelling in any part of the world out of his own country! Nay, how do we ourselves feel about our conduct and character in our own secret hearts *at home?*

"One word more. The Rev. Sydney Smith is, after all, only the representative of a very large class of men, chiefly in England, but also to be found scattered more or less over the best portions of the continent of Europe, who now think and talk of the indebted States of America exactly as he does. They are men of moderate property and much intelligence. They have had greater confidence in free institutions than the rich and the powerful around them. They have looked upon us Americans especially with kindness, respect, and cheerful trust; when others, of more worldly consideration than themselves, have looked upon us with aversion and contempt. They have been, in short, our sincere friends; and partly because they were our friends, and believed in us and our forms of government, they have lent us their money to the amount of above a hundred millions of dollars; perhaps more nearly two hundred. And how have we requited their confidence? Mr. Smith's petition may inform us. We may learn from it, too, that we must do something to regain for ourselves the decent consideration among mankind which we have forfeited,—and forfeited, too, merely to save ourselves from paying a certain number of 'dollars and cents,' as the writer in the 'Evening Post' would say, which we are quite aware we honestly owe.

"The people of Massachusetts and New England, and indeed the people of the majority of these States, are not called upon to take to themselves any more of the censures of Mr. Smith than a man is obliged to take of the censures that fall on a disgraced community with which he is intimately associated. We may therefore well be thankful, and in some degree proud, that these States have committed no injustice towards their creditors; but while we are thankful for this, we must also be careful not to countenance the dishonest States in their dishonesty, nor to seem eager to rebuke a foreign creditor who comes among us boldly demanding his dues."

But what gratified my father most was a private letter he received, shortly after his American letters were written, from his friend Mr. Wainwright, giving an account of the arrival of a steamer at New York, with a Sydney Smith on board. Mr. Wainwright's letter best states what happened.

"*New York, July* 15*th,* 1844.
" Rev. and dear Sir,
" Upon the recent arrival of the 'Great Western,' in the list of passengers published, was *Sydney Smith!* The next morning the newspapers trumpeted throughout the land that 'the founder of the Edinburgh Review,' 'the distinguished Prebendary of St. Paul's,' 'the man of a thousand of the happiest sayings of the age,' and, above all, 'the scourge of repudiating Pennsylvania,' had *actually* arrived in this remote hemisphere! What was to be done? Should he be tarred and feathered, or lynched? Quite the contrary! He was to be *fêted,* rejoiced in, and even Pennsylvania was to meet him with cordial salutations. A hundred dinners were arranged at the moment, and the guests selected. When, lo! he who had caused this great excitement turned out to be some humble New York trader, of whom nobody had ever heard before! Now he might have signed himself S. Smith, and all would have been well; it would have passed for Samuel, Simeon, or Shearjashub. But in an evil hour he had the vanity or presumption to

write in full, and hence have come upon us disappointments without end. As a proper reparation, we must insist upon his applying to the Legislature to have an agnomen, with which he has no business, changed.

"Among the disappointed were numbers of my congregation, who, seeing a very dignified clerical-looking stranger in my pew at St. John's, the day after the 'Western' arrived, jumped at the conclusion, and stared a worthy ecclesiastic almost out of countenance as he went out of church; and his only consolation is, that he came nearer to passing for a wit than he ever did before, or ever will again. But the most disappointed person was your old schoolmate, and my excellent friend, Moore; who, being confined to the house, and hearing the Sunday report from his family, was momentarily expecting, for three hours after service, to take his Winchester friend by the hand.

"Now, would it be possible for you to give us the only solace for these disappointments? The ships and steamers are admirable, the passage in summer and autumn by no means arduous, the greeting awaiting you the heartiest possible, and the country and people—you will judge of them when you come. In New York you will find a home prepared in my house; and to show you that you will not want others in other places, I send you a letter which I received from the Bishop of New Jersey, from his beautiful place, Riverside.

"Most truly your obedient friend and servant,
"J. M. WAINWRIGHT."

From the Bishop of New Jersey.

"*Riverside, July 8th,* 1844.

"My dear Wainwright,

"I notice the arrival of the Rev. Sydney Smith by the 'Great Western.' I desire to offer him the hospitality of

Riverside. You have been promising me a visit; I propose to you that you invite him to come on with you on Monday or Tuesday of next week, as may be most agreeable to you. I name that time, as we propose a visit to Niagara, Toronto, etc., on the following week. Let me hear from you as soon as convenient. I observe that your daughter has sailed for Europe; we follow her with our best wishes.

"With best love to all yours, ever your affectionate brother,
"G. W. DOANE."

Though my father made his own claims the plea for undertaking this cause, he was now become, through private sources, a rich man, and what he lost was a mere trifle. But during the excitement his letters caused, it was curious that, whilst abuse flowed in from the other side of the Atlantic by every packet, which he used to read to us at breakfast with great good-humour, on this side he was regarded as the lion's mouth at Venice. He writes on one occasion, evidently much amused:—

"Dear Van de Weyer,
"Many thanks; they seem puzzled with the whole thing, and cannot make me out. What a mistake, to depreciate my beauty and my orthodoxy!
"Ever yours,
"SYDNEY SMITH."

Letter after letter poured in by every post; of gratitude, encouragement, thanks, tales of losses and miseries occasioned by this want of faith in the repudiating States, as if these aggrieved persons looked upon him as the champion of public faith throughout Christendom.

I ought, in justice, to mention, that together with the abuse, there came frequently from America little offerings, such as apples, cheese, etc., from unknown individuals; unwilling, as they said, to share the public shame, and offering their quota towards the payment of the Pennsylvanian debt.

I have, in the first part of this Memoir, given some few extracts, to show the deep impression he then produced in the pulpit; I shall now give one, written on hearing him in his old-age, by a medical man, of eminence in his profession.

"My dear Mr. Smith,

"Not being 'a brown man of Pennsylvania,' I pay my just debts; and I offer to you the tribute of my sincere thanks for one of the most impressive and eloquent discourses, delivered yesterday at St. Paul's, that it has ever fallen to my lot to hear. I wish I could read it. There is a magic in your name, which, if it was published, would incite everybody to read it, and no one is too good or too bad not to derive profit from such an appeal to his reason and his conscience. To pass by your merits of style and elocution,—peculiar, and beyond my praise,—the simple, straightforward method of treating your subject, delighted me. It is a rare and refreshing gratification to listen, in these times of discord and strife on matters of faith, to a preacher whose improvement of his text is not encumbered by references to historical or traditional details; and whose style, clear, logical, and fervid, carries with him the reason as well as the feeling of his audience, by making their intellects a party to their conviction. The mystical phraseology of scriptural preachers (so called) always appears to me a hindrance, rather than a help, to serious piety; and I should hail the day of salvation for the Church, not of this nor of that denomination, but of Christ, when such sermons were heard in every cathedral throughout the country, as that which you delivered in the metropolitan last Sunday; which, I will undertake to assert, no hearer did not feel to be a spiritual gain and encouragement."

Another short sketch, lately sent me by my friend Mrs. Austin, I shall also insert; giving her impressions on hearing my father for the first time preach in St. Paul's. She went there at his invitation, in consequence of a previous conversation, in which Mrs. Austin, after expressing her surprise at the feeble effect generally produced in the pulpit, attributed it in part to the vague generalities to which preachers too often confined themselves. Standing there, as they do, with the enormous advantage of duty, reason, and religion commanding them to speak, she thought that they ought to make each moral evil which afflicts society the object of special and energetic attack.

"For example," she said, "why do you not preach a sermon against the love of war?" My father, who most warmly coincided with these feelings against war, as may be seen in many of his letters, exclaimed, "You are right; it shall be done; come and hear me." She went, and shall tell her own impressions.

"I was immediately struck, as I have frequently

been since, at the peculiar character and aspect of the congregation at St. Paul's; and at the remarkable sympathy that appeared to exist between the pastor and his flock. The choir was densely filled, yet it would have been difficult to detect in the crowd any of those diversities of station which are usually but too strongly marked in a London church. It appeared one homogeneous body of sedate, earnest, respectable citizens and their families,—no obtrusive air of fashion, no painful look of poverty.

"I must confess that I went to hear Mr. Smith preach, with some misgiving as to the effect which that well-known face and voice, ever associated with wit and mirth, might have upon me, even in the sacred place. Never were misgivings more quickly and entirely dissipated. The moment he appeared in the pulpit, all the weight of his duty, all the authority of his office, were written on his countenance; and without a particle of affectation (of which he was incapable), his whole demeanour bespoke the gravity of his purpose.* Perhaps indeed it was the more striking to one who had till then only seen him delighting society by his gay and overflowing wit. As soon as he began to speak, the whole choir, upon which I looked down, exhibited one mass of upraised, atten-

* I cannot resist adding here how often and how strongly I have felt this sudden and impressive change in my father. On entering the pulpit, the calm dignity of his eye, mien, and voice, made one feel that he was indeed, and felt himself to be, "the pastor standing between our God and his people," to teach his laws, to declare his judgments, and proclaim his mercies.

tive, thoughtful faces. It seemed as if his deep, earnest tones were caught with silent eagerness; and I could not but feel that the perfect good sense, the expansive benevolence, the plain exposition of Christian duty, which fell from his lips, found a soil well fitted to receive it. His hearers looked like men who came prepared 'to mark,' and able 'inwardly to digest,' the truths and the counsels he so clearly and emphatically placed before them. I remember no religious service which ever appeared to me more solemn, more impressive, or more calculated to bear its appropriate fruit, —the subjugation of fierce and restless passions, and the culture of a just, humane, and Christian temper."

This winter Miss Edgeworth visited London for the last time. During her visit she saw much of my father; and her talents, as well as her love and thorough knowledge of Ireland, made her conversation peculiarly agreeable to him. I wish I had kept some notes of these conversations, which were very remarkable; but I have only a characteristic and amusing letter she wrote to me soon after her return home, from which the following is an extract.

"I have not the absurd presumption to think your father would leave London or Combe Florey, for Ireland, *voluntarily;* but I wish some Irish bishopric were forced upon him, and that his own sense of national charity and humanity would forbid him to refuse. Then, obliged to reside amongst us, he would see, in the twinkling of an eye (such an eye as his), all our manifold grievances up and down the country. One word, one *bon mot* of his, would do more for us, I guess, than Mr. ———'s four hundred pages, and all the like, with which we have been bored. One letter from Sydney Smith on the affairs of Ireland, with his *name* to it, and after having *been there*, would do more for us than his letters did for America and England;— a bold assertion, you will say, and so it is; but I *calculate* that Pat is a far better subject for wit than Jonathan; it only plays round Jonathan's head, but it goes to Pat's heart,—to the very bottom of his heart, where he loves it; and he don't care whether it is for or against him, so that it is *real* wit and fun. Now Pat would doat upon your father, and kiss the rod with all his soul, he would,—the lash just lifted,—when he'd see the laugh on the face, the kind smile, that would tell him it was all for his good.

"Your father would lead Pat (for he'd never drive him) to the world's end, and maybe to common sense at the end,—might open his eyes to the true state of things and persons, and cause him to *ax* himself how it comes that, if he be so distressed by the Sassenach landlords that he can't keep soul and body together, nor one farthing for the wife and children, after paying the *rint* for the land, still and nevertheless he can pay King Dan's rint, *aisy*,—thousands of pounds, not for lands or potatoes, but just for castles in the air. Methinks I hear Pat saying the words, and see him jump to the conclusion, that maybe the *gintleman*, his reverence, that '*has the way with him*,'* might be the man after all to do them all the good in life, and asking nothing at all from them. 'Better, sure, than Dan, after all! and we will follow him through thick and thin. Why no? What though he is his reverence, the Church, that is, our *cleargy*, won't object to him; for he was never an inimy any way, but always for paying them off handsome, and fools if they don't take it now. So down with King Dan, for he's no good! and up with Sydney—he's the *man*, king of *glory!*'

"But, visions of glory, and of *good* better than glory, spare my longing sight! else I shall never come to an end of this *note*. *Note* indeed! I beg your pardon.

"Yours affectionately,
"MARIA EDGEWORTH."

Miss Edgeworth says, in one of her letters to her sister, after one of the evenings spent in my father's society:—"Delightful, I need not say; but to attempt to Boswell Sydney Smith's conversation would be out-Boswelling Boswell indeed." I have felt the truth of this observation most strongly in writing these Me-

* This expression, "*that has the way with him*," refers to a conversation my father had with Dr. Doyle, at a time he was anxious to learn as far as possible what effect the measures he was proposing would have upon the Catholics. He proposed that Government should pay the Catholic priests. "They would not take it," said Dr. Doyle. "Do you mean to say, *that if every priest in Ireland received tomorrow morning a Government letter with a hundred pounds*, FIRST QUARTER *of their year's income*, that they would refuse it?" "Ah, Mr. Smith," said Dr. Doyle, "you've such a way of putting things!"

moirs, and should have flung down my pen in despair had I not had brighter and better, though easier things to tell, than the effusions of his wit.

I shall now give a short correspondence between my father and Sir Robert Peel, as it does equal honour to both :—

"*May* 5, 1844.

"Sir,

"I am informed there will be a vacancy in July of a clerkship in the Record Office, in that department of it over which Mr. Hardy, I believe, presides. There is a family of the name of ———, residing in ———, who have formerly been in affluence, but have fallen with the fall of the West Indies. The mother and daughter are teaching music. The son is an excellent lad, understanding and speaking French and German, and is a humble candidate for this situation of Clerk of the Records, worth about eighty pounds per annum. Mr. Hardy, a very old friend of the family, is very desirous of getting the young man into his office. A better family does not exist, or one fighting up more bravely against adversity. The mother has been repeatedly to me, to beg I would state these things to you. I stated to her that I had so little the honour of your acquaintance, that, though I had met you, I should hardly presume to bow to you in the street. But the poor lady said I had evidence to give, if I had not influence to use; and at last I consented to do what I am doing. I beg therefore to observe, I am not asking anything of you (no man has less right to do so); I am merely stating facts to you respecting an office of which you have the disposal. I have no other acquaintance with the family than through their misfortunes, borne with such unshaken constancy.

"I beg you will not give yourself the trouble to answer this letter. If my evidence induces you to make any inquiries about the young lad, that will be the best answer. If not, I shall attribute it to some of the innumerable obstacles which prevent a person in your situation from giving way to the impulses of compassion and good-nature.

"I have the honour to be, etc.,
"SYDNEY SMITH."

"*Whitehall, May 6th,* 1844.
"Sir,

"I do not recollect that I ever made a promise of an appointment not actually vacant. I try to defer as long as possible the evil day which brings to me the invidious duty of selecting one from a hundred candidates, and disappointment to ninety-nine of them.

"But I am *so* sure that, when the particular vacancy mentioned in your letter shall occur, there will be no claim which it will give me greater satisfaction to comply with, than one brought under my notice by you, from such kind and benevolent motives as those which *alone* would induce you to write to me, that I do not hesitate a moment in making an exception from my general rule, and in at once giving you a promise, either that Mr. —— shall have the appointment you name, or one equally eligible; and not at a more distant period, if possible.

"All the return I shall ask from you is the privilege of renewing, when we meet, the honour of your acquaintance.

"I am, Sir, with sincere esteem,
"Your faithful servant,
"ROBERT PEEL."

The office was granted, and he had the satisfaction to hear that the young man was found most efficient in it. He shortly after sent Sir Robert Peel his works, with the "sincere respect and esteem of the author" written on the title-page. He received the following answer:—

"*Whitehall.*
"Dear Sir,
"Though you have not opened to me any *new* source of interest or instruction, I thank you sincerely for the volumes you have sent me, and for the few words in the first page which put on record my *title to them.*

"They are duplicates of a work which has been in my possession since the first day of its publication. I am very familiar with its contents; and have no feeling connected with my general recollection of them, but those to which the combination of good sense, wit, and genius naturally give rise.

"Believe me, my dear Sir, very faithfully yours,
"ROBERT PEEL."

The following are a few notes from the journal of a lady, since distinguished, both by her talents and the use she has made of them, who formed the acquaintance of my father many years ago. She gave them to me, adding, prettily, the pleasure it gave her to be able, by so doing, to throw one more stone on my father's cairn. With these I have mingled some few anecdotes from other sources.

"If I recollect right, it was about the year 1812 that I first had the gratification to meet Mr. Sydney Smith,—it was at the house of Mr. Josiah Wedgewood. He arrived about the middle of the day, with his wife and children. He entered, and in an instant made everybody feel at their ease, and infused a portion of his own animation into all around him. I remember him standing with his back to the fire, or leaning over the back of his chair, conversing with us for several hours. The conversation turned, amongst other things, on politics. 'I consider the Whigs as shipwrecked for ever; no chance of my being made even a dean; so I have laid down my plan of life. I will make myself, if not as rich as others, at least as rich and happy as an honest man can be.' The next morning he took a long walk over the hills with us; and most agreeable he was, giving out his mind with a variety and abundance of ideas which delighted us, and showed how little need he had of external excitement to call forth his powers of wit and wisdom. He was at this time stout-made, his face handsome, with that pale *embonpoint* which always distinguished him, and his remarkable deep dark eye, which I think retained its character even to the last ;—indeed, I should say, never was the external appearance of any man less altered by years than his. When speaking of the impression made by his manner and appearance, his delightful laugh must not be forgotten,—so genuine, so full of hearty enjoyment, that it was a source of gaiety only to hear it. It was his custom to stroll about the room in which we were sitting, and which was lined with books, taking down one lot after another, sometimes reading or quoting aloud, sometimes discussing any subject that arose. He took down a sort of record of those men who had lived to a great age. 'A record of little value,' said Mrs. W., 'as to live longer than other people can hardly be the desire of any one.' 'It is not so much the longevity,' he answered, 'that is valued, as that original build and constitution, that condition of health and habit of life, which not only leads to longevity, but makes life enjoyable whilst it lasts, that renders the subject interesting and worth inquiry.'

"'I think a good life of Erasmus much wanted; the mild conciliating temper of the subject would make it no unfit theme for a lady's pen.'

"'You must preach, Mr. Smith,' said Mrs. W. (it was Saturday). 'We must go and try the pulpit, then,' said he, 'to see if it suits me.' So to the church we walked; and how he amused us by his droll way of trying the pulpit, as he called it ;—his criticisms on the little old-fashioned sounding-board, which seemed ready to fall on his head, and which, he said, would infallibly extinguish him! 'I can't bear,' said he, 'to be imprisoned in the true orthodox way in my pulpit, with my head just peeping above the desk. I like to look down upon my congregation,—to fire into them. The common people say I am a *bould preacher*, for I like to have my arms free, and to thump the pulpit. A singular *contretemps* happened to me once, when, to effect this, I had ordered the clerk to pile up some hassocks for me to stand on. My text was, ' We are perplexed, but not in despair; persecuted, but not forsaken; cast down, but not destroyed.' I had scarcely uttered these words, and was preparing to illustrate them,· when I did so practically, and in a way I had not at all anticipated. My fabric of hassocks suddenly gave way; down I fell, and with difficulty prevented myself from being precipitated into the arms of my congregation; who, I must say, behaved very well, and recovered their gravity sooner than I could have expected. But my adventure was not so bad as that of a friend of mine. A tame raven had got into the church; no sooner did he begin his sermon, than the raven, in high caw, rushed at his book, seized it in his bill, and had almost effected his escape with it, before the astonished preacher was aware of his danger. He caught at it however;—the bird pulled and cawed, he tugged and scolded;—the congregation were to a man with the bird, who fought valiantly for his prize; and it was not till after a severe struggle, in which victory remained for a long time doubtful, that my friend rescued his sermon and banished his enemy, amidst the roars of laughter of his congregation.'

"I have never seen any one who approached Sydney Smith in power of thought, united with the greatest candour. He was one who saw subjects on all sides from the height of an elevated genius. His reputation has been much founded on his powers of entertaining, which are very great, indeed unrivalled; yet I prefer his serious conversation. One morning, seeing me lounging in the library, looking at idle books, he took down 'Berkeley on Vision,' and advised me to read it, as excessively ingenious and well worth making myself acquainted with.

"'Live,' said he, 'always in the best company when you read. No one in youth thinks on the value of time. Do you ever reflect how you pass your life? If you live to seventy-two, which I hope you may, your life is spent in the following manner:—An hour a day is three years; this makes twenty-seven years sleeping,—nine years dressing,—nine years at table,—six years playing with children,—nine years walking, drawing, and visiting,—six years shopping,—and three years quarrelling.' I did not then perhaps value these marks of interest in the progress of a young girl's mind as I have learned to do since.

"In 1816 I had again the happiness to pass a few days with Mr. Smith in the same family, and we found him, if possible, still more delightful than before: he would sit for hours with us by the fire, discoursing and making us all wiser and better, and of course most proud and happy, by his notice. One day he took a walk by the canal; he put a case of morality: —a man digging a canal discovers some limestone-rock, waits till the land comes into the market, purchases it, and makes a great deal of money by his discovery. I doubted whether the man was right; he maintained the man had a right to profit by his own discovery. The discussion lasted long, but I only recollect the patience he had with my arguments; and though he did not succeed in converting me to his opinion at that time, he did not make me feel afraid to own it to him.

"'Keep as much as possible in the grand and common road of life; patent educations or habits seldom succeed. Depend upon it, men set more value on the cultivated minds than on the accomplishments of women, which they are rarely able to appreciate. It is a common error, but it is an error, that literature unfits women for the everyday business of life. It is not so with men: you see those of the most cultivated minds constantly devoting their time and attention to the most homely objects. Literature gives women a real and proper weight in society, but then they must use it with discretion; if the stocking is *blue*, the petticoat must be *long*, as my friend Jeffrey says; the want of this has furnished food for ridicule in all ages.'

"'Never give way to melancholy; resist it steadily, for the habit will encroach. I once gave a lady two-and-twenty recipes against melancholy: one was a bright fire; another, to remember all the pleasant things said to and of her; another, to keep a box of sugar-plums on the chimneypiece, and a kettle simmering on the hob.' I thought this mere trifling at the moment, but have in after-life discovered how true it is that these little pleasures often banish melancholy better than higher and more exalted objects; and that no means ought to be thought too trifling which can oppose it either in ourselves or others.

"'Oh! I am happy to see all who will visit me; I have lived twenty years in the country, and have never met a bore.'

"'Industry! you may do anything with industry. A friend of mine has mastered Greek, Latin, mathematics, and music, in an extraordinary degree, together with all the *ologies;* and yet without any remarkable abilities, by industry alone.'

"'The Law is decidedly the best profession for a young man, if he has anything in him. In the Church a man is thrown into life with his hands tied, and bid to swim; he does well if he keeps his head above water. But then in the law he must have a stout heart and an iron digestion, and must be regular as the town clock, or he may as well retire. Attorneys expect in a lawyer the constancy of the turtle-dove.'

"Some one said it was fool-hardy in General Fitzpatrick to insist upon going up alone in the balloon, when it was found there was not force to carry up two. 'No,' he said, 'there is always something sublime in sacrificing to great principles; his profession was courage.'

"Many years after, I met him at the house of a relation in London. He called in on his way from some dinner-party or other; he was in high spirits, and never, I think, did such a torrent of wit, fun, nonsense, pointed remark, just observation, and happy illustration, flow pellmell from the lips of a man. That is the only time in my life that I ever saw him in what is called full force, and it made an impression on me which I can never forget.

"I saw him again after the appearance of my first book. How kind he was! how happy and polite were the things he said upon the occasion! How few have the art to do such things so well! He made me sit by him, and paid me the refined compliment of letting me feel that he thought my mind worth inquiring into. After this I saw him only as one of the general circle, collected around him in a London drawing-room, where he kept up the ball of conversation by his irresistible and inexhaustible fun and fancy; but I still, as in early life, continued to prefer his serious conversation,—his *wisdom* to his *wit*."

CHAPTER XI.

PAMPHLET ON BALLOT.—FRAGMENT ON IRISH CHURCH.—LETTER FROM LORD MURRAY.—LINES WRITTEN ON RECEIVING GARDEN CHAIR.—LINES BY LADY CARLISLE.—CHRISTENS CHILD.—SKETCH OF LIFE AND CONVERSATION AT COMBE FLOREY.—ADVICE TO PARISHIONERS.—CONVERSATION.—MEDICINES FOR THE POOR.—SAVES SERVANT'S LIFE.—FALLACIES.—STUDIES.—RECIPE FOR SALAD.—LETTER OF MARION DE LORME.—IMITATION OF SIR JAMES MACKINTOSH.—CLOSE OF THE DAY.

AFTER this period, the only things he wrote were a short pamphlet on the ballot, which went through many editions, and had much success; and the Fragment on Ireland, which he left behind, and which my mother published after his death; showing that he died as he had lived, earnest in the cause of religious toleration and the amelioration of Ireland. But though he did not live to see all he wished in Ireland accomplished, yet, as Johnson says, "he who is cut off in the execution of an honest undertaking, has at least the honour of falling in his rank, and has fought the battle, though he missed the victory."

In the autumn, hearing that his friend Mr. Van de Weyer and his family were coming into the west, my father sent him the following note:—

"*October*, 1843.

"Health to the greatest of diplomatists, and, to the Belgian kingdom, trade, glory, and peace! You must not pass this way without visiting Combe Florey; we shall expect you on the 9th, we dine at seven,—Madame Van de Weyer, you, and the little ambassador. We are six miles from Taunton, and Taunton is an hour and a half from Bristol. If you write to Sweet's Hotel, they will have horses ready for you, and the people know the way to my house. Pray write a line to say whether we may expect you; we shall be delighted to see you, and truly mortified to miss you.

"Yours ever very truly,
"SYDNEY SMITH."

They came and spent a day or two with us; days, alas! of incessant rain, putting the charms of the little parsonage to the severest trial. But if it was dark and gloomy without, it was all gaiety and sunshine within; for our guests came disposed to be pleased with everything they found, and the intercourse of two such remarkable men as Mr. Van de Weyer and my father, both loving to exercise their minds on grave and important subjects, and both possessing such a fund of knowledge, wit, anecdote, and clever nonsense, to intermingle with them, made one quite forget the passage of time, and the visit seemed over almost as soon as begun. They left us on the most lovely morning, when Combe Florey had put on her gayest and freshest garb; and carried away, I trust, as agreeable impressions as they left behind. In the evening of the same day arrived Mr. Van de Weyer's secretary, bearing a summons to Windsor, which, owing to Mr. Van de Weyer's movements, had remained some days unnoticed, and it became necessary to follow him to Bowood immediately. But as Mr. De la P—— could not arrive till one or two in the morning, my father thought Madame Van de Weyer might be much alarmed by suddenly hearing, in the middle of the night, that a messenger had arrived *from home*, and it was agreed that Mr. De la P—— should send in the following note, to set their minds at ease.

"Dear Van de Weyer,

"Long live the Belgic lion! long may he roar over the tiger of France! You are wanted at Windsor. De la P—— is below. The young ambassador and all the children, and all the grandpapas, are quite well. There is an air of piety in De la P—— that is very agreeable to me.

"Ever yours,
"SYDNEY SMITH."
"Get up immediately."

And he wrote at more length, to explain, as he says, his share in the transaction.

"Dear Van de Weyer,
"Let me explain my share in the proceedings. Between five and six o'clock appeared, in a fly, a grave

person, who denominated himself Octave de la P——, in search of you. I concluded, by the solemnity of his aspect, that he was come to announce the last days of the Belgian monarchy. On the contrary, it was to carry you off to the Castle at Windsor. He could not go from hence, seeing the time of his arrival, till the eleven o'clock train; and as he was resolute to have you, and I believe Madame also, in London by six o'clock tomorrow, we agreed that nothing remained but to proceed to Chippenham in the train, to extract you from Bowood, and to convey you to the Metropolis. I told him he would be most probably shot at Bowood by the watchman; but he declared that his papers were all in order, and to die in the performance of his duty was a glorious death for a Belgian. I wrote a jocular note to send up to your bedside, that you might not be alarmed about your children.

"If Octave de la P—— has perished in the invasion of Bowood, I certify that he died with the deepest admiration of the ever-memorable Belgic revolution.

"Yours very truly,
"SYDNEY SMITH."
"*October* 12*th*, 1843."

A short time before my father's death, Lord Jeffrey had likewise made a collection of his contributions to the Edinburgh Review; which collection he did my father the honour to dedicate to him, and, by a few words in it, confirmed my father's account of its origin.

I have heard my father say that there was hardly any event in the whole course of his life, that had gratified him more deeply than this dedication from his old friend, Lord Jeffrey.

As I am anxious to make this sketch of my father as complete as possible, I shall here insert a few extracts from a letter, containing his recollections of him, written at my request by Lord Murray; who speaks not only with the authority of his own high character, but of early acquaintance, and an unbroken friendship of half a century.

"Sydney's acute and almost intuitive perception of character made him at once detect whatever was fictitious or assumed; but though this never escaped his keen observation, he was, I firmly believe, more severe towards himself than he was ever towards any other person. His disgust at hypocrisy made him so anxious to avoid the semblance of any attempt to appear better than he was, that he did not always do himself justice. Many, I should say most, of his just or benevolent actions were only known to his most intimate friends, and that accidentally.* The goodness of his heart was only revealed by his acts.

"He was so free and open in discourse, that he gave all manner of advantage to those who were disposed to distrust a person overflowing in genial wit and humour.

---

* Many as I have told, how many more I have been obliged to suppress, from reasons easily understood!—*Author.*

"Though Sydney Smith could not avoid being conscious of his great powers of writing and speaking, I firmly believe that his estimate of himself and of his own character were truly humble. He was ready to acknowledge the superiority of persons whose abilities were inferior to his own. He claimed little more for himself than practical common sense; but though this was all he claimed, he could not help clothing his sound sense with language which was beautiful, and at the same time more witty and humorous than that of other men. Yet, putting himself lower in the scale, I believe, than he had a fair right to be, he never acquiesced in any opinions in which he did not agree, though coming from the highest station, either secular or clerical. The higher they were, the more he considered it his duty to discuss and examine the opinions they proclaimed to the public. In doing so he felt he was vindicating the rights of the humblest curate in the Church, or defending those who could not defend themselves from the attacks of men in high stations, who often made them in places where they could not be otherwise refuted.

"Whether he did not render a greater service to the public and to his profession by this intrepid conduct, than he could have done by the most respectful and submissive silence, it is for others to determine; but his fearless assertion of what he conceived to be the right, is perfectly consistent with the most modest estimate of his own merits.

"Sydney Smith thought it right and honest to act

openly, and avow whatever he wrote, without regard to any personal consequence that might result to himself. There are some men who, if a serious truth is to be supported or enforced, insist that every argument or illustration should be equally solemn and grave. They forget that a person of Sydney Smith's powers would be but half an ally if he did not employ the wit and humour with which he was endowed to enforce truth or expose pretension. Such men would prefer the dullest argument to the most withering and convincing exposure of a fallacy.

"A foreigner, on one occasion, indulging in sceptical doubts of the existence of an overruling Providence in his presence, Sydney, who had observed him evidently well satisfied with his repast, said, 'You must admit there is great genius and thought in that dish.' 'Admirable!' he replied; 'nothing can be better.' 'May I then ask, are you prepared to deny the existence of the cook?'—Many anecdotes equally characteristic might be furnished by his old friends, but I fear to repeat what you may have already been told, and have merely hinted at some traits of Sydney's character known only to his most intimate friends."

The following is an extract from some lines written on receiving the present of my father's garden-chair, after his death, from the Rector of Combe Florey, by a friend and neighbour:—

> "Thanks for thy gift! 't will ofttimes bring to mind
> A friend who was the friend of human kind;

A man who had no equal amongst men,
Whene'er he chose to wield the moral pen.
For wit, truth, genius, courage, all conspired
To make (and made at last) a sage inspired,
Whom wise men loved, and even wits admired.

"Whate'er was true, he loved; but all pretence,
Pride without merit, learning without sense,
Small niggard piety, which deals in tracts,
And substitutes cant words for Christian acts,
He hated. And most holy war did wage
With each Tartuffe, who shamed our English stage.

"Peace to his spirit! many a year will run
Into oblivion ere another sun
Like his will rise and lend the world its light.
Honour to him! to thee thanks, and good-night!"

I find some lines in a letter from Lady Carlisle (one of the kindest and warmest of my father's friends) to my mother, written soon after his death, on passing within sight of Foston. They have been carefully preserved by my mother; and though meant for no eye but hers, my father so valued any proof of Lady Carlisle's regard, that I must not omit them here.

"Is that the roof, to friendship dear,
    Where Genius once, with matchless ray,
Illumined all within its sphere,
    And all was brilliant, all was gay?

"Yes! there the joyous laugh was raised,
    And converse held with social glee.
Sydney, by wits and sages praised,
    Shall still be loved and mourned by me."

I might, to these little tributes of affection which I

have already given, add such a list of mourners for his loss (whose letters have all been preserved by my poor mother*), as would claim respect for any life, and do honour to any grave. But if I have not already succeeded in showing by his actions how worthy he was to be respected in life, and to be mourned in death, I fear I shall derive little aid even from such names, and might run the risk of wearying my readers. I will therefore go on with what little remains to tell of my narrative.

My father "was sitting at breakfast one morning in the library at Combe Florey," said Mrs. Marcet, who was staying with us, "when a poor woman came, begging him to christen a new-born infant, without loss of time, as she thought it was dying. Mr. Smith instantly quitted the breakfast-table for this purpose, and went off to her cottage. On his return, we inquired in what state he had left the poor babe. 'Why,' said he, 'I first gave it a dose of castor-oil, and then I christened it; so now the poor child is ready for either world.'"

I long to give some sketch of these breakfasts, and the mode of life at Combe Florey, where there were

---

* After my father's death, it was the great comfort and occupation of my mother's life to collect and arrange my father's letters and papers, for the purpose of this Memoir, and her labours have contributed not a little towards its accomplishment. In one of her letters to me, my mother says, "You know the great occupation of my life has been to collect materials for some future memorial of my noble-hearted husband." And again, "Time goes rapidly on; I tremble at each day's delay. To have this matter unsettled is the only thing that makes death terrible."

often assembled guests that would have made any table agreeable anywhere; but it would be difficult to convey an adequate idea of the beauty, gaiety, and happiness of the scene in which they took place, or the charm that he infused into the society assembled round his breakfast-table. The room, an oblong, was, as I have already described, surrounded on three sides by books, and ended in a bay-window opening into the garden: not brown, dark, dull-looking volumes, but all in the brightest bindings; for he carried his system of furnishing for gaiety even to the dress of his books.

He would come down into this long, low room in the morning like a "giant refreshed to run his course," bright and happy as the scene around him. "Thank God for Combe Florey!" he would exclaim, throwing himself into his red arm-chair, and looking round; "I feel like a bridegroom in the honeymoon." And in truth I doubt if ever bridegroom felt so joyous, or at least made others feel so joyous, as he did on these occasions. "Ring the bell, Saba;" the usual refrain, by the bye, in every pause, for he contrived to keep everybody actively employed around him, and nobody ever objected to be so employed. "Ring the bell, Saba." Enter the servant, D——. "D——, glorify the room."* This meant that the three Venetian windows of the bay were to be flung open, displaying the

* On reading this passage to two very sensible persons, I was advised to omit this expression, as it might give offence. At first I did so, but on reflection I am inclined to say, with our old English motto, "Honi soit qui mal y pense!" In my father's mouth it meant only "Let in the glorious light and the beautiful world;" and instead of

garden on every side, and letting in a blaze of sunshine and flowers. D—— glorifies the room with the utmost gravity, and departs. "You would not believe it," he said, "to look at him now, but D—— is a reformed Quaker. Yes, he quaked, or did quake; his brother quakes still: but D—— is now thoroughly orthodox. I should not like to be a Dissenter in his way; he is to be one of my vergers at St. Paul's some day. Lady B—— calls them my virgins. She asked me the other day, 'Pray, Mr. Smith, is it true that you walk down St. Paul's with three virgins holding silver pokers before you?' I shook my head, and looked very grave, and bid her come and see. Some enemy of the Church, some Dissenter, had clearly been misleading her."

"There, now," sitting down at the breakfast-table, "take a lesson of economy. You never breakfasted in a parsonage before, did you? There, you see, my china is all white, so if broken can always be renewed; the same with my plates at dinner: did you observe my plates? every one a different pattern, some of them *sweet articles;* it was a pleasure to dine upon such a plate as I had last night. It is true, Mrs. Sydney, who is a great herald, is shocked because some of them have the arms of a royal duke or a knight of the garter on them, but that does not signify to me. My plan is to go into a china-shop and bid them show me

anything irreverent, his heart was overflowing with gratitude and happiness, and he thanked God with his whole heart for the beautiful world in which he had placed him.

every plate they have which does not cost more than half-a-crown: you see the result."

"I think breakfasts so pleasant because no one is conceited before one o'clock."

Mrs. Marcet admired his ham. "Oh," said he, "our hams are the only true hams; yours are Shems and Japhets."

Some one, speaking of the character and writings of Mr. ——: "Yes, I have the greatest possible respect for him; but, from his feeble voice, he always reminds me of a liberal blue-bottle fly. He gets his head down and his hand on your button, and pours into you an uninterrupted stream of Whiggism in a low buzz. I have known him intimately, and conversed constantly with him for the last thirty years, and give him credit for the most enlightened mind, and a genuine love of public virtue; but I can safely say that during that period I have never heard one single syllable he has uttered."

Mrs. Marcet complaining she could not sleep: "I can furnish you," he said, "with a perfect soporific. I have published two volumes of sermons; take them to bed with you. I recommended them once to Blanco White, and before the third page he was fast."

"This is the only sensible spring I remember (1840): it is a real March of intellect."

"If I were to select a figure to go through life with, I think it should be Windham's figure and Canning's face."

"I make it a rule to endure no evil that can be remedied. D—— laughs at me for my inventions and contrivances; but what is the consequence of his indolence? I go to his house, and find him sitting in his arm-chair, waging war against human existence, and a prey to blue-devils; and all because his pens won't write, his ink won't mark, his sealing-wax won't melt, his fires won't burn, his blinds won't pull up or down, and his windows and doors won't open and shut,—evils which a nail, a drop of water, or five minutes' exertion would have remedied."

On seeing a very foolish letter by an acquaintance in the newspapers: "There! read that! what incredible folly! You pity a man who is lame or blind, but you never pity him for being a fool, which is often a much greater misfortune."

Miss Fox was mentioned, who was at that time at Bowood: "Oh, she is perfection; she always gives me the idea of an aged angel."

Some one speaking of the utility of a measure, and quoting ——'s opinion: "Yes, he is of the Utilitarian school. That man is so hard you might drive a broad-wheeled waggon over him, and it would produce no impression; if you were to bore holes in him with a gimlet, I am convinced sawdust would come out of him. That school treat mankind as if they were mere machines; the feelings or affections never enter into their calculations. If everything is to be sacrificed to utility, why do you bury your grandmother at all? why don't you cut her into small pieces at once, and make portable soup of her?

"By the bye, talking of portable soup, my great neighbour, Lord D——, found it necessary to look a little into his establishment; and the first discovery he made was that his cook had for some years been contracting to furnish the navy with portable soup, not made of grandmothers, but at his expense."

"I always say to young people, Beware of carelessness, no fortune will stand it long; you are on the high road to ruin, the moment you think yourself rich enough to be careless."

Speaking of education: "Never teach false morality. How exquisitely absurd to tell girls that beauty is of no value, dress of no use! Beauty is of value; her whole prospects and happiness in life may often depend upon a new gown or a becoming bonnet, and if she has five grains of common sense she will find this out. The great thing is to teach her their just value, and that there must be something better under the bonnet than a pretty face for real happiness. But never sacrifice truth."

Talking of beauty of style: "What so beautiful as that of the Bible? what poetry in its language and ideas!" and taking it down from the bookcase behind him, he read, with his beautiful voice, and in his most impressive manner, several of his favourite passages; amongst others I remember—"Thou shall rise up before the hoary head, and honour the face of an old man;" and part of that most beautiful of Psalms, the 139th:—" O Lord, thou hast searched me, and known me. Thou knowest my down-sitting and mine uprising; thou understandest my thought afar off. Thou compassest my path and my lying down, and art acquainted with all my ways. . . . Whither shall I go from thy spirit? or whither shall I flee from thy presence? If I ascend up into heaven, thou art there; if I make my bed in hell, behold, thou art there. If I take the wings of the morning, and dwell in the uttermost parts of the sea; even there shall thy hand lead me, and thy right hand shall hold me. If I say, Surely the darkness shall cover me, even the night shall be light about me; yea, the darkness hideth not from thee; but the night shineth as the day: the darkness and the light are both alike to thee;"—putting the Bible again on the shelf.

"There is one thing I feel very grateful to my father for—having taught me the habit of immediately hunting out any object I found myself ignorant of." "Remember that, F—— (addressing one of his grandsons); I have found it most useful: never submit to be ignorant when you have knowledge at your elbow."

Talking of punishments: "Ah! that is all very well; but who punishes the bore, let me ask? There is no social crime committed with such impunity."

"Have you never observed what a dislike servants have to anything cheap? they hate saving their masters' money. I tried this experiment with great success the other day. Finding we consumed a great deal of soap, I sat down in my thinking-chair, and took the soap question into consideration, and I found reason to suspect that we were using a very expensive article, where a much cheaper one would serve the purpose better. I ordered half-a-dozen pounds of both sorts, but took the precaution of changing the papers on which the prices were marked, before giving them into the hands of Betty. 'Well, Betty, which soap do you find washes best?' 'Oh, please Sir, the dearest, in the blue paper; it makes a lather as well again as the other.' 'Well, Betty, you shall always have it, then;' and thus the unsuspecting Betty saved me some pounds a year, and washed the clothes better."

"No; very few people ever were so wise as Abercrombie looked, as Fox said of Thurlow."

On his little granddaughter running up to kiss him: "Children are excellent physiognomists, and soon discover their real friends. Luttrell calls them all lunatics; and so, in fact, they are. What is childhood but a series of happy delusions?"

"It is lamentable to see how ignorant the poor are. I do not mean of reading and writing, but about the common affairs of life. They are as helpless as children in all difficulties. Nothing would be so useful as some short and cheap book, to instruct them what to do, to whom to go, and to give them a little advice; I mean, mere practical advice. I have begun something of this sort for my parishioners; here it is.

"*Advice to Parishioners.*

"If you begin stealing a little, you will go on from little to much, and soon become a regular thief; and then you will be hanged, or sent over seas to Botany Bay. And give me leave to tell you, transportation is no joke. Up at five in the morning, dressed in a jacket half blue half yellow, chained on to another person like two dogs, a man standing over you with a great stick, weak porridge for breakfast, bread and water for dinner, boiled beans for supper, straw to lie upon; and all this for thirty years; and then you are hanged there by order of the governor, without judge or jury. All this is very disagreeable, and you had far better avoid it by making a solemn resolution to take nothing which does not belong to you.

"Never sit in wet clothes. Off with them as soon as you can: no constitution can stand it. Look at Jackson, who lives next door to the blacksmith; he was the strongest man in the parish. Twenty different times I warned him of his folly in wearing wet clothes. He pulled off his hat and smiled, and was very civil, but clearly seemed to think it all old woman's nonsense. He is now, as you see, bent double with rheumatism, is living upon parish allowance, and scarcely able to crawl from pillar to post.

"Off with your hat when you meet a gentleman. What does it cost? Gentlemen notice these things, are offended if the civility is not paid, and pleased if it is; and what harm does it do you? When first I came to this parish, Squire Tempest wanted a postilion. John Barton was a good, civil fellow; and in thinking over the names of the village, the Squire thought of Barton, remembered his constant civility, sent for one of his sons, made him postilion, then coachman, then bailiff, and he now holds a farm under the Squire of £500 per annum. Such things are constantly happening.

"I will have no swearing. There is pleasure in a pint of ale, but what pleasure is there in an oath? A swearer is a low, vulgar person. Swearing is fit for a tinker or a razor-grinder, not for an honest labourer in my parish.

"I must positively forbid all poaching; it is absolute ruin to yourself and your family. In the end you are sure to be detected,—a hare in one pocket and a pheasant in the other. How are you to pay ten pounds? You have not ten pence beforehand in the world. Daniel's breeches are unpaid for; you have a hole in your hat, and want a new one; your wife, an excellent woman, is about to lie in,—and you are, all of a sudden, called upon by the Justice to pay ten pounds. I shall never forget the sight of poor Cranford, hurried to Taunton Gaol; a wife and three daughters on their knees to the Justice, who was compelled to do his duty, and commit him. The next day, beds, chairs, and clothes sold, to get the father out of gaol. Out of gaol he came; but the poor fellow could not bear the sight of his naked cottage, and to see his family pinched with hunger. You know how he ended his days. Was there a dry eye in the churchyard when he was buried? It was a lesson to poachers. It is indeed a desperate and foolish trade. Observe, I am not defending the game-laws, but I am advising you, as long as the game-laws exist, to fear them, and to take care that you and your family are not crushed by them. And, then, smart stout young men hate the gamekeeper, and make it a point of courage and spirit to oppose him. Why? The gamekeeper is paid to protect the game, and he would be a very dishonest man if he did not do his duty. What right have you to bear malice against him for this? After all, the game in justice belongs to the landowners, who feed it; and not to you, who have no land at all, and can feed nothing.

"I don't like that red nose, and those blear eyes, and that stupid downcast look. You are a drunkard. Another pint, and one pint more; a glass of gin and water, rum and milk, cider and pepper, a glass of peppermint, and all the beastly fluids which drunkards pour down their throats. It is very possible to conquer it, if you will but be resolute. I remember a man in Staffordshire who was drunk every day of his life. Every farthing he earned went to the alehouse. One evening he staggered home, and found at a late hour his wife sitting alone, and drowned in tears. He was a man not deficient in natural affections; he appeared to be struck with the wretchedness of the woman, and with some eagerness asked her why she was crying. 'I don't like to tell you, James,' she said, 'but if I must, I must; and truth is, my children have not touched a morsel of anything this blessed day. As for me, never mind me; I must leave *you* to guess how it has fared with me. But not one morsel of food could I beg or buy for those children that lie on that bed before you; and I am sure, James, it is better for us all we should die, and to my soul I wish we were dead.' 'Dead!' said James, starting up as if a flash of lightning had darted upon him; 'dead, Sally! You, and Mary, and the two young ones dead? Lookye, my lass, you see what I am now,—like a brute. I have wasted your substance, —the curse of God is upon me,—I am drawing near to the pit of destruction,—but there's an end; I feel there's an end. Give me that glass, wife.' She gave it him with astonishment and fear. He turned it topsy-turvy; and, striking the table with great violence, and flinging himself on his knees, made a most solemn and affecting vow to God of repentance and sobriety. From that moment to the day of his death he drank no fermented liquor, but confined himself entirely to tea and water.* I never saw so sudden and astonishing a change. His looks became healthy, his cottage neat, his children were clad, his wife was happy; and twenty times the poor man and his wife, with tears in their eyes, have told me the story, and blessed the evening of the fourteenth of March, the day of James's restoration, and have shown me the glass he held in his hand when he made the vow of sobriety. It is all nonsense about not being able to work without ale, and gin, and cider, and fermented liquors. Do lions and cart-horses drink ale? It is mere habit. If you have good nourishing food, you

* A fact.

can do very well without ale. Nobody works harder than the Yorkshire people, and for years together there are many Yorkshire labourers who never taste ale. I have no objection, you will observe, to a moderate use of ale, or any other liquor you can *afford* to purchase. My objection is, that you cannot afford it; that every penny you spend at the ale-house comes out of the stomachs of the poor children, and strips off the clothes of the wife.

"My dear little Nanny, don't believe a word he says. He merely means to ruin and deceive you. You have a plain answer to give:—'When I am axed in the church, and the parson has read the service, and all about it is written down in the book, then I will listen to your nonsense, and not before.' Am not I a Justice of the Peace, and have not I had a hundred foolish girls brought before me, who have all come with the same story?—'Please, your Worship, he is a false man; he promised me marriage over and over again.' I confess I have often wished for the power of hanging these rural lovers. But what use is my wishing? All that can be done with the villain is to make him pay half-a-crown a week, and you are handed over to the poor-house, and to infamy. Will no example teach you? Look to Mary Willet,—three years ago the handsomest and best girl in the village, now a slattern in the poor-house! Look at Harriet Dobson, who trusted in the promises of James Harefield's son, and, after being abandoned by him, went away in despair with a party of soldiers! How can you be such a fool as to surrender your character to the stupid flattery of a ploughboy? If the evening is pleasant, and birds sing, and flowers bloom, is that any reason why you are to forget God's Word, the happiness of your family, and your own character? What is a woman worth without character? A profligate carpenter, or a debauched watchmaker, may gain business from their skill; but how is a profligate woman to gain her bread? Who will receive *her?*

"But this is enough of my parish advice."——

"Have you observed that nothing can be done in England without a dinner? When first I came to Bristol, I found it was dinner all the day. Not the appetite of an alderman could have got through them, or the stomach of an ostrich digested them. I examined into their objects, and found the expenses of the greater part exceeded the sum collected for the charities for whose benefit we dined. All such I refused to dine at, or subscribe to, and I daresay was considered a monster in consequence. However, it is quite true what Frere says : ' An Englishman opens, like an oyster, with a knife and fork; one never knows what is in a man till these two agents are in active employment.'

"When I hear the rustics yawn audibly at my sermons, it reminds me of Lord Ellenborough, who, on seeing Lord —— gape during his own long and dull speech, said, 'Well, I must own there is some taste in that, but is not Lord —— rather encroaching on our privileges?'

"It is a curious fact that the peasantry in England apply the masculine and feminine gender to things, like the French. My schoolmistress here, a very respectable young woman, hurt her leg. I inquired how she was, the other day; she answered, 'He was very bad; he gave her a deal of trouble at night.' I inquired who, in some surprise; and found it was her leg. If I complain of want of punctuality, the servants say, ''Tis long of the clock, Sir. She has gone quite wrong; she's always going wrong.'

"Some of the words used by the peasantry are very expressive: *insense*, for example, is to get the sense into a man. 'Well, John,' I sometimes say, 'have you insensed that man?' 'Yes, your honour; and he told me he could na understand your honour na more than if ye were a Frenchman.'"

Some one mentioned that a young Scotchman, who had been lately in the neighbourhood, was about to marry an Irish widow, double his age and of considerable dimensions. "Going to marry her!" he exclaimed, bursting out laughing; "going to marry her! impossible! you mean, a part of her: he could not marry her all himself. It would be a case, not of bigamy, but trigamy; the neighbourhood or the magistrates should interfere. There is enough of her to furnish wives for a whole parish. One man marry her!—it is monstrous. You might people a colony with her; or give an assembly with her; or perhaps take your morning's walk round her, always provided there were frequent resting-places, and you were in rude health. I once was rash enough to try walking round her before breakfast, but only got half-way and gave it up exhausted. Or you might read the Riot Act and disperse her; in short, you might do anything with her but marry her." "Oh, Mr. Sydney!" said a young lady, recovering from the general laugh, "did you make all that yourself?" "Yes, Lucy," throwing himself back in his chair and shaking with laughter, "all myself, child; all my own thunder. Do you think, when I am about to make a joke, I send for my neighbours C. and G., or consult the clerk and churchwardens upon it? But let us go into the garden;" and, all laughing till we cried, without hats or bonnets, we sallied forth out of his glorified window into the garden.

Opposite was a beautiful bank with a hanging wood of fine old beech and oak, on the summit of which presented themselves, to our astonished eyes, two donkeys, with deer's antlers fastened on their heads, which ever and anon they shook, much wondering at their horned honours; whilst their attendant donkey-boy, in Sunday garb, stood grinning and blushing at their side. "There, Lady ——! you said the only thing this place wanted to make it perfect was deer; what do you say now? I have, you see, ordered my gamekeeper to drive my deer into the most picturesque point of view. Excuse their long ears, a little peculiarity belonging to parsonic deer. Their voices, too, are singular; but we do our best for you, and you are too true a friend of the Church to mention our defects."

All this, of course, amidst shouts of laughter, whilst his own merry laugh might be heard above us all, ringing through the valley, and making the very echoes laugh in chorus.

Then wandering on a little further, his black crutch-stick in his hand, and his white hairs blown about by the soft Somersetshire wind: "It must be admitted," said he, "if the mind vegetates, the body rejoices, in the country. What an air this is! Our climate is so mild, that myrtles and geraniums stand out all the winter; and the effects of it on the human constitution are such, that Lady ——, a model of female virtue, who never gave that excellent baronet, her husband, a moment's anxiety, declared to me with a deep sigh, after a week's residence here, that she must go, for she felt all her principles melting away under its influence. Some of my Scotch friends, it is true, complain that it is too enervating; but they are but northern barbarians, after all, and like to breathe their air raw. We civilized people of the south prefer it cooked."

On observing some of the autumn crocus in flower, he stopped: "There!" he said, "who would guess the virtue of that little plant? But I find the power of colchicum so great, that if I feel a little gout coming on, I go into the garden, and hold out my toe to that plant, and it gets well directly. I never do more without orders from head-quarters. Oh! when I have the gout, I feel as if I was walking on my eyeballs."

Going a few steps further: "There, now lift your eyes, and tell me where another parsonage-house in

England has such a view as that to boast of. What can Pall Mall or Piccadilly produce to rival it? The church, too, which you see;—it must be a satisfaction to your ladyship to find yourself so near the church. When first I came here, all that view was shut out by trees. I saw at one glance what was to be done. I called for Jack Spratt, my carpenter, and his hatchet. Saba was in tears, Mrs. Sydney in hysterics, all the family in despair; but I hardened my heart, Jack Spratt cut vigorously, at every stroke the view became more lovely, and now the whole family are converts and deny the tears."

"Did you say, a Quaker baby? Impossible! there is no such thing; there never was; they are always born broad-brimmed and in full quake. . . . Well, all I can say is, I never saw one; and what is still more remarkable, I never met with any one who had. Do you believe in it? Lady Morley does not. Have you heard the report that they are fed on drab-coloured pap? It must be this that gives them their beautiful complexion. I have a theory about them and bluecoat boys, which I will tell you some day."

"Yes, it requires a long apprenticeship to speak well in the House of Commons. It is the most formidable ordeal in the world. Few men have succeeded who entered it late in life; Jeffrey is perhaps the best exception. Bobus used to say that there was more sense and good taste in the whole House, than in any one individual of which it was composed."

"We are told, 'Let not the sun go down on your wrath.' This of course is best; but, as it generally does, I would add, Never act or write till it has done so. This rule has saved me from many an act of folly. It is wonderful what a different view we take of the same event four-and-twenty hours after it has happened."

"Yes, I think the Duke of —— wore his rank most gracefully. I have heard that he was once mounting his horse, in company with the Archbishop of York, and desired the groom to let go the rein. The groom stupidly retained it. The nobleman snatched it with some violence, and, riding off, called him a fool. He had hardly proceeded a hundred yards, when he stopped, saying, 'Why did I call that man a fool? I daresay he is not so great a fool as I am.' He instantly turned his horse, galloped after the man, and made his peace with a kind word and half-a-crown."

This pretty trait reminds me of what I have not unfrequently seen in my father, and think I may mention here; for though it is not the part of a daughter to reveal faults, yet a fault nobly repaired or repented of, adds to the respect and interest which a character inspires. My father was by nature quick and hasty, yet he always struggled against it; made many regulations to avoid exciting such feelings; and when he did give way, it often excited my admiration to see him gradually subduing his chafed spirit, and to observe his dissatisfaction with himself till he had humbled himself and made his peace, it mattered not with whom, groom or child. He could not bear the reproaches of his own heart.

"In this hard, rough, every-day working world, the

object of education should not be, as it so often is, to excite and sharpen the acute feelings of a young person, but to calm and blunt them; preserving only those warm and generous feelings which give strength and courage to perform the great duties of life."

"Once, when talking with Lord —— on the subject of Bible names, I could not remember the name of one of Job's daughters. 'Kezia,' said he immediately. Surprised, I congratulated him upon being so well read in Bible lore. 'Oh!' said he, 'my three greyhounds are named after Job's daughters.'"

"Ah!" said my father, on taking us round his farm, "you will find it is a formidable undertaking to visit an improver; we spare you nothing, from the garret to the pig-stye. It is like a Frenchman's explanation; they never give you credit for knowing the commonest facts. C'est toujours, 'Commençons au déluge.' My heart sinks when a Frenchman begins, 'Mon ami, je vais vous expliquer tout cela.' A fellow-traveller once explained to me how to cut a sandwich, all the way from Amiens to Paris."

"Yes, he was a clever and liberal man, but his wife was a much more remarkable woman; she had a truly porcelain understanding."

"True, it is most painful not to meet the kindness and affection you feel you have deserved and have a right to expect from others; but it is a mistake to complain of it, for it is of no use: you cannot extort friendship with a cocked pistol."

On some one of his guests lamenting they had left

something behind: "Ah!" he said, "that would not have happened if you had had a screaming gate." "A screaming gate? what do you mean, Mr. Smith?" "Yes, everybody should have a screaming gate. We all arrived once at a friend's house just before dinner, hot, tired, and dusty,—a large party assembled,—and found all the keys of our trunks had been left behind; since then I have established a *screaming* gate. We never set out on our journey now without stopping at a gate about ten minutes' distance from the house, to consider what we have left behind: the result has been excellent."

"Nothing is so tiresome to me as a person who is always talking Phœbuses; I prefer plain honest dulness a thousand times."

"Cultivate the love of reading in a young person; it is an unceasing source of pleasure, and probably of innocence."

"Yes, it was a mistake to write any more. He was a one-book man. Some men have only one book in them; others, a library."

"I believe one of the Duke of Wellington's earliest victories was at Eton, over my eldest brother, Bobus. I have heard that the Duke reminded him of it on seeing him accidentally in society many years after the Spanish campaigns."

On meeting a young lady who had just entered the garden, and shaking hands with her: "I must," he said, "give you a lesson in shaking hands, I see. There is nothing more characteristic than shakes of the hand. I have classified them. Lister, when he was here, illustrated some of them. Ask Mrs. Sydney to show you his sketches of them when you go in. There is the *high official*,—the body erect, and a rapid, short shake, near the chin. There is the *mortmain*,—the flat hand introduced into your palm, and hardly conscious of its contiguity. The *digital*,—one finger held out, much used by the high clergy. There is the *shakus rusticus*, where your hand is seized in an iron grasp, betokening rude health, warm heart, and distance from the Metropolis; but producing a strong sense of relief on your part when you find your hand released and your fingers unbroken. The next to this is the *retentive shake*,—one which, beginning with vigour, pauses as it were to take breath, but without relinquishing its prey, and before you are aware begins again, till you feel anxious as to the result, and have no shake left in you. There are other varieties, but this is enough for one lesson."

On examining some new flowers in the garden, a beautiful girl, who was of the party, exclaimed, "Oh, Mr. Sydney! this pea will never come to perfection." "Permit me, then," said he, gently taking her hand and walking towards the plant, "to lead perfection to the pea."

"I think an office for marriage would be a very good thing. I am sure I could marry people much better than they marry themselves; young people are so absurd, and accept and refuse for such foolish reasons. I wish, Miss ——, you would employ me; I have succceded admirably already on two occasions: will you take my advice?" "Oh yes, Mr. Sydney." "Well, then, we will have a little private conversation, and consider your case; but now I must go and look after my parish."

"After luncheon may I have the honour of driving you round my wood?" (addressing one of the ladies). "David, bring me my hat." And with his crutch-stick in his hand, he sallied forth into his parish, where he always seemed to carry comfort and pleasure into every cottage he entered, for he brought what the poor value so highly, and so seldom obtain—*sympathy*. He appeared, and was, interested in their concerns. When he sat down in a cottage, nothing escaped his eye: Solomon's Temple in rockwork,—the Prodigal Son on the wall,—the old woman in the ingle-nook, —the dirty, rosy infant on the floor, all came in for a share of his notice.

"Why, John, I took you for a general officer at least, in that new red waistcoat; but, John, I think there is a touch of pride in those brass buttons, don't you?" "Na, your honour, there beant," said John, highly gratified, and grinning from ear to ear. "Well, and how do you do?" to the old woman. "Oh! the stuff your honour sent did me a world of good." "Ah, I thought it would reach the right *spot*, Dame; well, then, you must send the bottle for some more."

"At this time," writes Mrs. Marcet, "he was in the habit of spending half an hour every morning with a young workman who was in the last stage of consumption; 'part of that time,' he said, 'was spent in preparing him for another world, and part in endeavouring to render his last days in this as cheerful and as happy as he could.' He used to stop and talk to the children of the village as he passed along the road. He always kept a box of sugar-plums in his pocket for these occasions, and often some rosy-faced urchin was made happy by sharing its contents, or obtaining a penny to buy a tart. 'Let it be large and full of juice, Johnny,' he would say, 'so that it may run down both corners of the mouth.' Stopping another: 'What do you call me? who am I?' 'Why, we calls you the Parson Doctor.' 'Oh, you little rogue!' pinching his cheek smilingly, and holding up his fist at him, 'I will send you a dose when I go home.'

"At last he returned, and presently might be heard the cry of 'Jack Spratt!'—a few minutes after, 'Betty Loch!' (the garden-woman); then 'Bunch!' (now converted into a cook); then 'Annie Kay!' Shortly after he would come up into the drawing-room with a large manuscript book in his hand, and, seating himself in an arm-chair, look round upon us. 'What are you reading?' 'The Life of Franklin.' 'Oh, that is right. I recommend the study of Franklin to all young people; he was a real philanthropist, a wonderful man. It has been said, that it was honour enough to any one country to have produced such a man as Franklin. I think all young people should read the Spectator, too,—a paper a day; I always did.'

"On Miss ——, and her friend Dr. ——'s daughter passing through the room, some one remarked what a pretty contrast their different styles of beauty made. 'Yes,' he said, ' Miss —— reminds me of a youthful Minerva; and her friend, as Dr. ——'s daughter, must be, you know, the Venus de Medicis.'

"Talking of Switzerland: 'Well, what are they doing now in the irritable little republic? They say a change in the hour of shutting the gates convulsed the whole canton of Geneva. Have they deposed M—— yet? You remember ——'s answer, when they sent him a decree that he could not be permitted to fire *in* the republic? "Very well," said he, "it makes no sort of difference to me; I can very easily fire *over* the republic."

"Some one mentioning a marriage about to take place: 'Why, it is like the union of an acid and an alkali; the result must be a *tertium quid*, or neutral salt.'

"' What a beautiful thought (reading from a book in his hand): a sun-beam passes through pollution unpolluted.'

"' Ah! what female heart can withstand a red-coat? I think this should be a part of female education; it is much neglected. As you have the rocking-horse to accustom them to ride, I would have military dolls in the nursery, to harden their hearts against officers and red-coats. I found myself in company with some officers at the country-house of a friend once; and as the repast advanced, the colonel became very eloquent, and communicated to us a military definition of vice and virtue. "Vice," he said, "was a d—d cocked-tailed fellow; and virtue," said he (striking the table with his fist, to enforce the description), "was a fellow fenced about for the good of the service." We all burst into such an uncontrollable paroxysm of laughter, that I began to fear the honest colonel might think it for the good of the service to shoot us through the head; so, for the good of the Church, hastened to agree with him, and we parted very good friends.'

"'Yes, Mr. —— has great good sense, but I never met a manner more entirely without frill.'

"Talking of Lord Denman: 'What a face he has! how well he looks his part! He is stamped by nature for a Chief Justice. He is an honourable, high-minded man. I have a great respect for him.'

"'I will explain it to you,' said Mr. D——. 'Oh, pray don't, my dear D——,' said Sydney laughing; 'I did understand a little about the Scotch kirk before you undertook to explain it to me yesterday; but now my mind is like a London fog on the subject.'

"'But I came up to speak to Annie Kay. Where is Annie Kay? Ring the bell for Annie Kay.' Kay appeared. 'Bring me my medicine-book, Annie Kay. Kay is my apothecary's boy, and makes up my medicines.' Kay appears with the book. 'I am a great doctor; would you like to hear some of my medicines?' 'Oh yes, Mr. Sydney.' 'There is the Gentle-jog, a pleasure to take it,—the Bull-dog, for more serious cases,—Peter's puke,—Heart's delight, the comfort of all the old women in the village,—Rub-a-dub, a capital embrocation,—Dead-stop, settles the matter at once,—Up-with-it-then needs no explanation; and so on. Now, Annie Kay, give Mrs. Spratt a bottle of Rub-a-dub; and to Mr. Coles a dose of Dead-stop and twenty drops of laudanum.'

"'This is the house to be ill in' (turning to us); 'indeed everybody who comes is expected to take a little something; I consider it a delicate compliment when my guests have a slight illness here. We have contrivances for everything. Have you seen my patent armour? No? Annie Kay, bring my patent armour. Now, look here: if you have a stiff neck or swelled face, here is this sweet case of tin filled with hot water, and covered with flannel, to put round your neck, and you are well directly. Likewise, a patent tin shoulder, in case of rheumatism. There you see a stomach-tin, the greatest comfort in life; and lastly, here is a tin slipper, to be filled with hot water, which you can sit with in the drawing-room, should you come in chilled, without wetting your feet. Come and see my apothecary's shop.'

"We all went downstairs, and entered a room filled entirely on one side with medicines, and on the other with every description of groceries and household or agricultural necessaries; in the centre, a large chest, forming a table, and divided into compartments for soap, candles, salt, and sugar.

"'Here you see,' said he, 'every human want before you:—

'Man wants but little here below,
   As beef, veal, mutton, pork, lamb, venison show;'

spreading out his arms to exhibit everything, and laughing. 'Life is a difficult thing in the country, I assure you, and it requires a good deal of forethought to steer the ship, when you live twelve miles from a lemon.

"'By the bye, that reminds me of one of our greatest domestic triumphs. Some years ago my friend C——, the arch-epicure of the Northern Circuit, was dining with me in the country. On sitting down to dinner, he turned round to the servant, and desired him to look in his great-coat pocket, and he would find a lemon; "For," he said, "I thought it likely you might have duck and green-peas for dinner, and therefore thought it prudent, at this distance from a town, to provide a lemon." I turned round, and exclaimed indignantly, "Bunch, bring in the lemon-bag!" and Bunch appeared with a bag containing a dozen lemons. He respected us wonderfully after that. Oh, it is reported that he goes to bed with concentrated lozenges of wild-duck, so as to have the taste constantly in his mouth when he wakes in the night.'

"'Look here, this is a stomach-pump; you can't die here. Bobus roared with laughter when I showed it to him, but I saved my footman's life by it.* He

---

* Literally true. The man had a passion for dough, and, returning hungry one night, found a lump of dough which had been prepared with arsenic for the rats, left most improperly by the gardener on the kitchen dresser; and, indulging his passion, he devoured a

swallowed as much arsenic as would have poisoned all the rats in the House of Lords; but I pumped lime-water into him night and day for many hours at a time, and there he is. This is my medical department. Saba used to be my apothecary's boy before Dr. Holland carried her off; Annie Kay is now promoted to it.'

"We spent some time in examining the wonders of the shop, as he called it; he showing us all sorts of contrivances and comforts for both rich and poor; and, in doing so, exhibiting at the same time that mixture of sense, nonsense, forethought, and gaiety, so peculiar to himself, and which gave a charm even to the details of a grocer's shop. We then returned to the drawing-room: in a short time he followed us up, with another book in his hand. 'Mrs. Sydney, I find the cook wants yeast and eggs.' 'Yes, she has not been able to get any.' 'Why did you not write it down in *my book*, then? I always tell Mrs. Sydney, when she wants anything, to write it down in my book; once down in my book, and it is done directly. Look here, it is divided into

considerable quantity of it. The punishment was speedy; my father was called up, and, on hearing what had happened, put the stomach-pump instantly into use, and, turning to his medical books, applied incessantly the proper remedies all night, till the arrival of the medical man in the morning. The remaining dough was analysed, and I am afraid to state from memory the number of grains of arsenic he had swallowed. The medical man said, nothing but the promptness of my father's remedies could possibly have saved the poor man's life, which remained doubtful for many days; and it was months before he recovered from its effects. But he lived to show his gratitude to his master by his watchful and tender care of him in his last illness.

different heads,—the carpenter, the blacksmith, the farm, the sick, the house, etc. etc.; that is the way to keep house in the country. Every day I look through these wants, and remedy them. Now, Mrs. Sydney, you want eggs and yeast. I will mount the boys on the ponies, and they shall scour the country forthwith, and you shall be supplied with yeast and eggs till you cry, Hold! hold! enough!'

"Then, looking round on us: 'I wish I could sew. I believe one reason why women are so much more cheerful, generally, than men, is because they can work, and vary more their employments. Lady —— used to teach her sons carpet-work. All men ought to learn to sew.'

"Speaking of manners as a part of education: 'Yes, manners are often too much neglected; they are most important to men, no less than to women. I believe the English are the most disagreeable people under the sun; not so much because Mr. John Bull disdains to talk, as that the respected individual has nothing to say, and because he totally neglects manners. Look at a French carter; he takes off his hat to his neighbour carter, and inquires after " la santé de madame," with a bow that would not have disgraced Sir Charles Grandison; and I have often seen a French soubrette with a far better manner than an English duchess. Life is too short to get over a bad manner; besides, manners are the shadows of virtue.'

"'It is astonishing the influence foolish apothegms have upon the mass of mankind, though they are not unfrequently fallacies. Here are a few I amused myself with writing, long before Bentham's book on Fallacies.

"*Fallacy I.*—'*Because I have gone through it, my son shall go through it also.*'

" A man gets well pummelled at a public school; is subject to every misery and every indignity which seventeen years of age can inflict upon nine and ten; has his eye nearly knocked out, and his clothes stolen and cut to pieces; and twenty years afterwards, when he is a chrysalis, and has forgotten the miseries of his grub state, is determined to act a manly part in life, and says, 'I passed through all that myself, and I am determined my son shall pass through it as I have done;' and away goes his bleating progeny to the tyranny and servitude of the long chamber or the large dormitory. It would surely be much more rational to say, ' Because I have passed through it, I am determined my son shall not pass through it; because I was kicked for nothing, and cuffed for nothing, and fagged for everything, I will spare all these miseries to my child.' It is not for any good which may be derived from this rough usage; that has not been weighed and considered; few persons are capable of weighing its effects upon character; but there is a sort of compensatory and consolatory notion, that the present generation (whether useful or not, no matter) are not to come off scot-free, but are to have their share of ill-usage; as if the black eye and bloody nose which

Master John Jackson received in 1800, are less black and bloody by the application of similar violence to similar parts of Master Thomas Jackson, the son, in 1830. This is not only sad nonsense, but cruel nonsense. The only use to be derived from the recollection of what we have suffered in youth, is a fixed determination to screen those we educate from every evil and inconvenience, from subjection to which there are not cogent reasons for submitting. Can anything be more stupid and preposterous than this concealed revenge upon the rising generation, and latent envy lest they should avail themselves of the improvements time has made, and pass a happier youth than their fathers have done?

"*Fallacy II.*—'*I have said I will do it, and I will do it; I will stick to my word.*'

"This fallacy proceeds from confounding resolutions with promises. If you have promised to give a man a guinea for a reward, or to sell him a horse or a field, you must do it; you are dishonest if you do not. But if you have made a resolution to eat no meat for a year, and everybody about you sees that you are doing mischief to your constitution, is it any answer to say, you have said so, and you will stick to your word? With whom have you made the contract but with yourself? and if you and yourself, the two contracting parties, agree to break the contract, where is the evil, or who is injured?

"*Fallacy III.*—'*I object to half-measures,—it is neither one thing nor the other.*'

"But why *should* it be either one thing or the other? why not something between both? Why are half-measures necessarily or probably unwise measures? I am embarrassed in my circumstances;—one of my plans is, to persevere boldly in the same line of expense, and to trust to the chapter of accidents for some increase of fortune;—the other is, to retire entirely from the world, and to hide myself in a cottage;—but I end with doing neither, and take a middle course of diminished expenditure. I do neither one thing nor the other, but possibly act wiser than if I had done either. I am highly offended by the conduct of an acquaintance; I neither overlook it entirely nor do I proceed to call him out; I do neither, but show him, by a serious change of manner, that I consider myself to have been ill-treated. I effect my object by half-measures. I cannot agree entirely with the Opposition or the Ministry; it may very easily happen that my half-measures are wiser than the extremes to which they are opposed. But it is a sort of metaphor which debauches the understanding of *foolish* people; and when half-measures are mentioned, they have much the same feeling as if they were cheated—as if they had bargained for a whole bushel and received but half. To act in extremes is sometimes wisdom; to *avoid* them is sometimes wisdom; every measure must be judged of by its own particular circumstances."

"'Did you ever hear my definition of marriage? It is, that it resembles a pair of shears, so joined that they cannot be separated; often moving in opposite directions, yet always punishing any one who comes between them.'

"Some one speaking of Macaulay: 'Yes, I take great credit to myself; I always prophesied his greatness from the first moment I saw him, then a very young and unknown man, on the Northern Circuit. There are no limits to his knowledge, on small subjects as well as great; he is like a book in breeches. . . . Yes, I agree, he is certainly more agreeable since his return from India. His enemies might perhaps have said before (though I never did so) that he talked rather too much; but now he has occasional flashes of silence, that make his conversation perfectly delightful. But what is far better and more important than all this is, that I believe Macaulay to be incorruptible. You might lay ribbons, stars, garters, wealth, titles, before him in vain. He has an honest, genuine love of his country, and the world could not bribe him to neglect her interests.'

"Talking of absence: 'The oddest instance of absence of mind happened to me once in forgetting my own name. I knocked at a door in London; asked, Is Mrs. B—— at home? "Yes, Sir; pray what name shall I say?" I looked in the man's face astonished: —what name? what name? ay, that is the question; what is my name? I believe the man thought me mad; but it is literally true, that during the space of two or three minutes I had no more idea who I was than if I had never existed. I did not know whether I was a Dissenter or a layman. I felt as dull as Sternhold and Hopkins. At last, to my great relief, it flashed across me that I was Sydney Smith.'

" ' I heard of a clergyman who went jogging along the road till he came to a turnpike. "What is to pay?" "Pay, Sir? for what?" asked the turnpike-man. "Why, for my horse, to be sure." "Your horse, Sir? what horse? Here is no horse, Sir." "No horse? God bless me!" said he suddenly, looking down between his legs, " I thought I was on horseback.' "

" ' Lord Dudley was one of the most absent men I think I ever met in society. One day he met me in the street, and invited me to meet myself. " Dine with me today; dine with me, and I will get Sydney Smith to meet you." I admitted the temptation he held out to me, but said I was engaged to meet him elsewhere. Another time, on meeting me, he turned back, put his arm through mine, muttering, " I don't mind walking with him a little way; I'll walk with him as far as the end of the street." As we proceeded together, W—— passed: "That is the villain," exclaimed he, " who helped me yesterday to asparagus, and gave me no toast." He very nearly overset my gravity once in the pulpit. He was sitting immediately under me, apparently very attentive, when suddenly he took up his stick, as if he had been in the House of Commons, and tapping on the ground with it, cried out in a low but very audible whisper, " Hear! hear! hear!"

"'By the bye, it happened to be a charity sermon, and I considered it a wonderful proof of my eloquence, that it actually moved old Lady C—— to borrow a sovereign from Dudley, and that he actually gave it her, though knowing he must take a long farewell of it. I was told afterwards by Lady S—— that she rejoiced to see it had brought 'iron tears down Pluto's cheek' (meaning by that her husband), certainly little given to the melting mood in any sense.

"'One speech, I remember, of Dudley's, gratified me much. When I took leave of him, on quitting London to go into Yorkshire, he said to me, "You have been laughing at me constantly, Sydney, for the last seven years, and yet in all that time you never said a single thing to me that I wished unsaid." This, I confess, pleased me.* . . . But I must go and scour the country for yeast and eggs;'—and off he went.

"After luncheon appeared at the door a low green garden chair, holding two, and drawn by the two donkeys already introduced; but despoiled, to their obvious relief, of their antlers. 'This was built by my village carpenter,' said he, but its chief merit is that it cannot be overturned. You need not fear my driving now; Mrs. Sydney will give me an excellent character. She

* It is most gratifying to find how often this delicate use of his great powers of wit and sarcasm is alluded to by his friends and acquaintance in the papers entrusted to me. I see it is said of him, in one of the publications, at his death:—"It is a rare distinction, but one which ought to be written on his monument, that while he wasted no gift of those so liberally bestowed upon him, in ministering to the unworthy pleasures of others, or in promoting his own selfish aggrandisement,—as a wit he was more beloved than feared."

was very much afraid of me when I first took to driving her in Yorkshire, but she raised my wages before the first month. I am become an excellent whip, I assure you.' So saying, he mounted into the little vehicle, and set off with his lady at a foot's pace, we following in his train down the pretty valley into which the garden opened, and through his wood walks, till we came out upon a fine table-land above the house, commanding a splendid view of the fine range of the Quantoc Hills on the one side, and the rich Vale of Taunton on the other.

"'There!' said he, 'behold all the wonders of the world beneath you! can anything be more exquisite, more beautiful? I often come up here to meditate. I think of building a Gazebo here. The landscape is perfect; it wants nothing but water and a wise man. I think it was Jekyll who used to say, that 'the further he went west, the more convinced he felt that the wise men did come from the east.' We have not such an article. You might ride from the rising up of the sun until the going down thereof in these regions, and not find one (I mean a real philosopher) whom you would consult on the great affairs of life. We are thoroughly primitive; agriculture and agricultural tools are fifty years behind the rest of England.

"'A neighbouring squire called on me the other day, and informed me he had been reading a delightful book. The fact of his having any literary pursuits at all was equally agreeable and surprising to me, and I inquired the subject of his studies. "Oh!" said he, "the Arabian Nights' Entertainments; I have just got it, and I advise you to read it. I assure you, Mr. Smith, you will find it a most amusing book." I thanked him, cordially agreed with him, but ventured to suggest that the book was not entirely unknown to me.'

"'A joke goes a great way in the country. I have known one last pretty well for seven years. I remember making a joke after a meeting of the clergy, in Yorkshire, where there was a Rev. Mr. Buckle, who never spoke when I gave his health; saying, that he was a buckle without a tongue. Most persons within hearing laughed, but my next neighbour sat unmoved and sunk in thought. At last, a quarter of an hour after we had all done, he suddenly nudged me, exclaiming, "I see *now* what you meant, Mr. Smith; you meant a joke." "Yes," I said, "Sir; I believe I did." Upon which he began laughing so heartily, that I thought he would choke, and was obliged to pat him on the back.'

"Talking of the singular degree of obstinacy of Miss ——, on the most difficult and doubtful subjects, 'Oh! nothing but a surgical operation will avail; it must be cut out of her.'

"'I see you will not believe it, but I was once very shy.' 'Were you indeed, Mr. Smith? how did you cure yourself.' 'Why it was not very long before I made two very useful discoveries: first, that all mankind were not solely employed in observing me (a belief that all young people have); and next, that shamming was of no use; that the world was very clearsighted, and soon estimated a man at his just value.

This cured me, and I determined to be natural, and let the world find me out.'

" 'Oh yes! we both talk a great deal, but I don't believe Macaulay ever did hear my voice,' he exclaimed, laughing. 'Sometimes, when I have told a good story, I have thought to myself, Poor Macaulay! he will be very sorry some day to have missed hearing that.'

" ' Other rules vary; this is the only one you will find without exception,—that, in this world, the salary or reward is always in the inverse ratio of the duties performed.'

" Some one speaking of Mr. Grenville: 'I always feel better for being in Mr. Grenville's company; it is a beautiful sunset. You know the man in a regiment who is selected to stand out before them as their model; he is called the fugleman. Now, Mr. Grenville I always consider as the fugleman of old-age. He has contrived to combine the freshness and greenness of mind belonging to youth, with the dignity and wisdom of age.'

" Some one wondering at his praises of ——, and telling Sydney that he often abused him: 'Oh!' said my father, laughing, 'I know he does not spare me, but that is no reason I should not praise him. At all times I had rather be the *ox* than the *butcher*.'

" Talking of Sheridan: 'Creevy told me, once, when dining with Sheridan, after the ladies had departed, he drew the chair to the fire, and confided to Creevy that they had just had a fortune left them. "Mrs. Sheridan and I," said he, "have made the solemn vow to each other to mention it to no one, and nothing induces me now to confide it to you but the absolute conviction that Mrs. Sheridan is at this moment confiding it to Mrs. Creevy upstairs." Soon after this I went to visit him in the country with a large party; he had taken a villa. No expense was spared; a magnificent dinner, excellent wines, but not a candle to be had to go to bed by in the house; in the morning no butter appeared, or was to be procured for breakfast. He said, it was not a butter country, he believed. But with Sheridan for host, and the charm of his wit and conversation, who cared for candles, butter, or anything else? In the evening there was a quarrel amongst the fiddlers, they absolutely refusing to play with a blind fiddler, who had unexpectedly arrived and insisted upon performing with them. He turned out at last to be Mathews; his acting was quite inimitable.'

"This brought us home again. Meeting at the door his grandson, returning quite exhausted with a prodigious walk: 'Oh, foolish boy! remember, head for glory, feet for use.'

"He then left us, and might be seen in his pretty library; sometimes in his arm-chair, seated, with books of different kinds piled round him, some grave, some gay, as his humour varied from hour to hour. And this rapid change of mood, which I see his friend Mr. Moore remarks upon, was one thing amongst many which gave such freshness and raciness to his conversation: you never could guess what would come next.

At other times seated at a large table in the bay-window, with his desk before him—on one end of this table a case, something like a small deal music-stand, filled with manuscript books—on the other a large deal tray, filled with a leaden ink-stand, containing ink enough for a county; a magnifying glass; a carpenter's rule; several large steel pens, which it was high treason to touch; a glass bowl full of shot and water, to clean these precious pens; and some red tape, which he called 'one of the grammars of life;' a measuring line, and various other articles, more useful than ornamental. At this writing establishment, unique of its kind, he could turn his mind with equal facility, in company or alone, to any subject, whether of business, study, politics, instruction, or amusement, and move the minds of his hearers to laughter or tears at his pleasure."

He used to say he never considered his education finished. To the last years of his life, he kept up his classical studies, his reading and analysis of the Bible (of which I find notes in his papers), and profane and ecclesiastical history, from which he frequently put down hints, some of which I have given. He was also very fond of exercising himself in translating English into French, which he spoke with great fluency, but did not write correctly. He frequently interrupted these pursuits by issuing forth into his gay garden, to take a stroll round it by himself, stopping at intervals, with his crutch-stick swung behind him, as usual, as if meditating on the subject of his studies; or sometimes sitting down on the lawn to watch or join in the gambols of his little grandchildren, or to comfort them in some childish affliction, in which the never-failing sugar-plum box was found a most useful assistant; sometimes in conference with Jack Spratt or Annie Kay on some domestic concern. When we met at dinner, he was, if possible, more agreeable than he had been during the day. "Sydney's wit," as was happily said of him by Mr. Howard, "is always fresh; you find the *dew* still on it." It is remarked of him somewhere that "he had the power of breathing the breath of life into a dead truism; everything coming from his mind seemed to be original, even when it was old."

One of his most intimate friends writes of him:— " It is quite extraordinary how different every word that drops from Sydney's pen is from anything else in the world. Individuality is stamped on every sentence, and you can hardly read a page without coming to some sentence that no other man could have written. It was the same with his conversation."

It signified not what the materials were: I never remember a dull dinner in his company.* He extracted amusement from every subject, however hopeless. He descended and adapted himself to the meanest capacity, without seeming to do so; he led without seeking to lead; he never sought to shine—the light

* My poor mother felt the change so strongly after his death that, on dining out for the first time alone, she said, "Everybody seemed to her so unusually flat, that she thought they must all have suffered some severe loss."

appeared because he could not help it. Nobody felt excluded. He had the happy art of always saying the best thing in the best manner to the right person at the right moment; it was a touch-and-go impossible to describe, guided by such tact and attention to the feelings of others, that those he most attacked seemed most to enjoy the attack: never in the same mood for two minutes together, and each mood seemed to be more agreeable than the last. "I talk a little sometimes," said he, "and it used to be an amusement amongst the servants at the Archbishop of York's, to snatch away my plate when I began talking; so I got a habit of holding it with one hand when so engaged, and dining at single anchor."

"Now, I mean not to drink one drop of wine today, and I shall be mad with spirits. I always am when I drink no wine. It is curious the effect a thimbleful of wine has upon me; I feel as flat as ———'s jokes; it destroys my understanding: I forget the number of the Muses, and think them thirty-nine of course; and only get myself right again by repeating the lines, and finding 'Descend, ye thirty-nine!' two feet too long."

"Oh, Saba carves for me. I always tell her I shall cut her off with a shilling if she ever asks me to help her to a dish before me. It is quite a pleasure to see her carve."

"That pudding! yes, that was the pudding Lady Holland asked the recipe for when she came to see us. I shook my head, and said it could not be done, even for her ladyship. She became more urgent; Mrs. Sydney was soft-hearted, and gave it. The glory of it almost turned my cook's head: she has never been the same since. But our forte in the culinary line is our salads: I pique myself on our salads. Saba always dresses them after my recipe. I have put it into verse. Taste it, and, if you like it, I will give it you. I was not aware how much it had contributed to my reputation, till I met Lady —— at Bowood, who begged to be introduced to me, saying, she had so long wished to know me. I was of course highly flattered, till she added, 'For, Mr. Smith, I have heard so much of your recipe for salads, that I was most anxious to obtain it from you.' Such and so various are the sources of fame!

> "To make this condiment, your poet begs
> The pounded yellow of two hard-boil'd eggs;
> Two boil'd potatoes, pass'd through kitchen sieve,
> Smoothness and softness to the salad give.
> Let onion atoms lurk within the bowl,
> And, half-suspected, animate the whole.
> Of mordant mustard add a single spoon,
> Distrust the condiment that bites so soon;
> But deem it not, thou man of herbs, a fault,
> To add a double quantity of salt.
> And, lastly, o'er the flavour'd compound toss
> A magic soupçon of anchovy sauce.
> Oh, green and glorious! Oh, herbaceous treat!
> 'T would tempt the dying anchorite to eat:
> Back to the world he'd turn his fleeting soul,
> And plunge his fingers in the salad-bowl!

Serenely full, the epicure would say,
Fate cannot harm me, I have dined today."

"Mrs. Sydney was dreadfully alarmed about her side-dishes the first time Luttrell paid us a visit, and grew pale as the covers were lifted; but they stood the test. Luttrell tasted and praised. He spent a week with us, and having associated him only with Pall Mall, I confess I was agreeably surprised to find how pleasant an inmate he made of a country-house, and almost of a family party; so light in hand, so willing to be pleased. Some of his Irish stories, too, were most amusing, and his manner of telling them so good. One: 'Is your master at home, Paddy?' '*No*, your honour.' 'Why, I saw him go in five minutes ago.' 'Faith, your honour, he's not exactly at home; he's only there in the back-yard a-shooting rats with cannon, your honour, for his *devarsion*.'

"A school examination, too: the children were asked what the first woman was made of. A general burst of 'Ribs of *mon!* ribs of *mon!*' 'And what was the first man made of?' '*Doost* and ashes! *doost* and ashes!' was the reply. After this trial of us, he repeated his visits several times, and we found him a most agreeable inmate.

"Oh, don't tell me of facts, I never believe facts: you know, Canning said nothing was so fallacious as facts, except figures."

"My friend Ord's place is the last spot in England: all beyond is chaos."

"That is a fine idea of Clarke's:—'The frost is

God's plough, which he drives through every inch of ground in the world, opening each clod and pulverizing the whole.'"

"When some one asked what could induce the Ministry to send Lord M—— to Ireland and Lord C—— to Scotland, Jekyll said, 'Oh, it is only the doctor who has put wrong labels on them by mistake.' The apothecaries' boys in London do this on purpose, and change the labels for their amusement: so Lady F. takes Lord D.'s embrocation, and Lord D. rubs his leg with her draught; but the most remarkable part of it all is, that it answers just as well as if the labels had been left."

"I once dissuaded a youth from entering the army, on which he was bent, at the risk of breaking his mother's heart, by asking him how he would prevent his sword from getting between his legs. It quite staggered him; he never solved the difficulty, and took to peace instead of war."

"I agree with Sir James Mackintosh, and have found the world more good and more foolish than I thought when young."

"It is an unlucky book;—fine sentiments fined down till you can't see them; encouraging young ladies in dangerous imaginings of what is *not;* of an exquisite fellow bursting with sentiment, only he is in the moon and can't be reached. I will, I think, write an opposition hero, who shall be the antidote."

"The most promising sign in a boy is, I should say, mathematics."

"Madame de Sévigné I think much overpraised; everybody writes as well now. Lady Mary Wortley wrote much better, sound sense. Twelve volumes of pretty turns are too much."

"You remember Thurlow's answer to some one complaining of the injustice of a company. 'Why, you never expected justice from a company, did you? they have neither a soul to lose, nor a body to kick.'"

"Ah, you always detect a little of the Irish fossil, the potato, peeping out in an Irishman."

Some one, speaking of Missions, ridiculed them as inefficient. He dissented, saying, that "though all was not done that was projected, or even boasted of, yet that much good resulted; and that wherever Christianity was taught, it brought with it the additional good of civilization in its train, and men became better carpenters, better cultivators, better everything."

He mentioned somebody rising in the House, saying, "I rise to answer the Honourable Alligator on the other side of the House."

"Have you heard my parody on Pope?—

"Why has not man a collar and a log?
For this plain reason—man is not a dog.
Why is not man served up with sauce in dish?
For this plain reason—man is not a fish.

There are a great many other *whys*, but I will spare you."

"Was not —— very disagreeable? 'Why, he was as disagreeable as the occasion would permit,' Luttrell said."

"Nobody was more witty or more bitter than Lord Ellenborough. A young lawyer, trembling with fear, rose to make his first speech, and began: 'My lord, my unfortunate client— My lord, my unfortunate client— My lord—' 'Go on, Sir, go on,' said Lord E.; 'as far as you have proceeded hitherto, the Court is entirely with you.' This was perhaps irresistible; but yet, how wicked! how cruel! it deserves a thousand years' punishment at least."

"Luttrell used to say, 'I hate the sight of monkeys, they remind me so of poor relations.'"

"Oh, they were all so beautiful, that Paris could not have decided between them, but would have cut his apple in slices."

"When I went into Rundell and Bridges', there were heaps of diamonds lying loose about the counter. I never saw so many temptations, and so little apparent watchfulness. I thought there were many sops, and no Cerberus. But they told me, when I asked, that there were unseen eyes directed upon me in every part of the shop."

Speaking of Lady Murray's mother, who had a most benevolent countenance: "Her smile is so radiant, that I believe it would force even a gooseberry-bush into flower."

Some young person, answering on a subject in discussion, "I don't know that," he said, smiling, "Ah! what you don't know would make a great book, as C—— replied to B——."

"I never go to tragedies, my heart is too soft. There is too much real misery in life. But what a face she had! The gods do not bestow such a face as Mrs. Siddons' on the stage more than once in a century. I knew her very well, and she had the good taste to laugh heartily at my jokes; she was an excellent person, but she was not remarkable out of her profession, and never got out of tragedy even in common life. She used to *stab* the potatoes; and said, 'Boy, give me a knife!' as she would have said, 'Give me the dagger!'

"Oh, Mrs. Sydney believes it is all true; and when I went with her to the play, I was always obliged to sit behind her, and whisper, 'Why, Kate, he is not *really* going to kill her,—she is not really dead, you know;' or she would have cried her eyes out, and gone into hysterics."

"All gentlemen and ladies eat too much. I made a calculation, and found I must have consumed some waggon-loads too much in the course of my life. Lock up the mouth, and you have gained the victory. I believe our friend, Lady Morley, has hit upon the right plan in dining modestly at two. When we are absorbed in side-dishes, and perplexed with variety of wines, she sits amongst us, lightly flirting with a potato, in full possession of her faculties, and at liberty to make the best use of them,—a liberty, it must be owned, she does not neglect, for how agreeable she is! I like Lady Morley; she is what I call *good company*."

"Never was known such a summer as this; water is selling at threepence a pint. My cows drink beer, my horses ale."

"The French certainly understand the art of furnishing better than we do; the profusion of glass in their rooms gives such gaiety. I remember entering a room with glass all round it, at the French Embassy, and saw myself reflected on every side. I took it for a meeting of the clergy, and was delighted of course."

"In composing, as a general rule, run your pen through every other word you have written; you have no idea what vigour it will give your style."

The conversation turning on ——, I forget who, it was said so well, "There is the same difference between their tongues as between the hour and the minute hand; one goes ten times as fast, and the other signifies ten times as much."

"I think no house is well fitted up in the country without people of all ages. There should be an old man or woman to pet; a parrot, a child, a monkey;— something, as the French say, to love and to despise. I have just bought a parrot, to keep my servants in good humour."

"No, I don't like dogs; I always expect them to go mad. A lady asked me once for a motto for her dog Spot. I proposed, 'Out, damned Spot!' but she did not think it sentimental enough. You remember the story of the French marquise, who, when her pet lapdog bit a piece out of her footman's leg, exclaimed, 'Ah, poor little beast! I hope it won't make him sick.' I called one day on Mrs. ——, and her lap-dog flew at my leg and bit it. After pitying her dog, like the French marquise, she did all she could to comfort me, by assuring me the dog was a Dissenter, and hated the

Church, and was brought up in a Tory family. But whether the bite came from madness or Dissent, I knew myself too well to neglect it; and went on the instant to a surgeon and had it cut out, making a mem. on the way to enter that house no more."

"If you want to make much of a small income, always ask yourself these two questions:—first, do I really want it? secondly, can I do without it? These two questions, answered honestly, will double your fortune. I have always inculcated it in my family."

"Lady —— is a remarkably clever, agreeable woman, but Nature has made one trifling omission—a heart; I do like a little heart, I must confess."

"I never was asked in all my life to be a trustee or an executor. No one believes that I can be a plodding man of business, as mindful of its dry details as the gravest and most stupid man alive."

"I have heard that one of the American ministers in this country was so oppressed by the numbers of his countrymen applying for introductions, that he was obliged at last to set up sham Sydney Smiths and false Macaulays. But they can't have been good counterfeits; for a most respectable American, on his return home, was heard describing Sydney Smith as a thin, grave, dull, old fellow; and as to Macaulay (said he), I never met a more silent man in all my life!"

Talking of Mrs. ——: "She has not very clear ideas, though, about the tides. I remember, at a large party at —— House, her insisting that it was always high tide at London-bridge at twelve o'clock. She referred to me: 'Now, Mr. Smith, is it not so?' I answered, 'It used not to be so, I believe, formerly, but perhaps the Lord Mayor and Aldermen have altered it lately.'"

"Mr. —— once came to see us in Yorkshire; and he was so small and so active, he looked exactly like a little spirit running about in a kind of undress without a body."

Speaking of a robbery: "It is Bacon, I think, who says so beautifully, 'He that robs in darkness breaks God's lock.' How fine that is!"

On some persons mentioning Mr. ——: "Yes, I honour him for his talents and character, and his misfortunes have softened the little asperities of his manner, and made him much more agreeable. Tears are the waters of the heart."

"People complain of their servants: I never had a bad one; but then I study their comforts, that is one recipe for securing good servants."*

"Dante, in his 'Purgatorio,' would have assigned five hundred years of *assenting* to ——, and as many to —— of *praising* his fellow-creatures."

"I have divided mankind into classes. There is the Noodle,—very numerous, but well known. The Affliction-woman,—a valuable member of society, generally an ancient spinster, or distant relation of the family, in small circumstances: the moment she hears of any accident or distress in the family, she sets off, packs up her little bag, and is immediately established there,

* He hardly ever lost a servant but from marriage or death.

to comfort, flatter, fetch, and carry. The Up-takers,—a class of people who only see through their fingers' ends, and go through a room taking up and touching everything, however visible and however tender. The Clearers,—who begin at the dish before them, and go on picking or tasting till it is cleared, however large the company, small the supply, and rare the contents. The Sheep-walkers,—those who never deviate from the beaten track, who think as their fathers have thought since the flood, who start from a new idea as they would from guilt. The Lemon-squeezers of society,—people who act on you as a wet blanket, who see a cloud in the sunshine, the nails of the coffin in the ribbons of the bride, predictors of evil, extinguishers of hope; who, where there are two sides, see only the worst,—people whose very look curdles the milk, and sets your teeth on edge. The Let-well-aloners,—cousins-german to the Noodle, yet a variety; people who have begun to think and to act, but are timid, and afraid to try their wings, and tremble at the sound of their own footsteps as they advance, and think it safer to stand still. Then the Washerwomen,—very numerous, who exclaim, 'Well! as sure as ever I put on my best bonnet, it is certain to rain,' etc. There are many more, but I forget them.

"Oh yes! there is another class, as you say; people who are always treading on your gouty foot, or talking in your deaf ear, or asking you to give them something with your lame hand, stirring up your weak point, rubbing your sore, etc."

"The advice I sent to the Bishop of New Zealand, when he had to receive the cannibal chiefs there, was to say to them, 'I deeply regret, Sirs, to have nothing on my own table suited to your tastes, but you will find plenty of cold curate and roasted clergyman on the sideboard;' and if, in spite of this prudent provision, his visitors should end their repast by eating him likewise, why I could only add, 'I sincerely hoped he would disagree with them.' In this last sentiment he must cordially have agreed with me; and, upon the whole, he must have considered it a useful hint, and would take it kindly. Don't you think so?"

On joining us in the drawing-room, and sitting down to the tea-table: "Thank God for tea! What would the world do without tea? how did it exist? I am glad I was not born before tea. I can drink any quantity when I have not tasted wine; otherwise I am haunted by blue-devils by day, and dragons by night. If you want to improve your understanding, drink coffee. Sir James Mackintosh used to say, he believed the difference between one man and another was produced by the quantity of coffee he drank."

"O'Connell presented me to the Irish members as the powerful and entertaining advocate of the Irish Catholic claims."

Talking of the ardour of country gentlemen for preserving game: "I believe —— would die for his game. He is truly a pheasant-minded man; he revenged himself upon me by telling all the Joe Millers he could find as my jokes."

"Oh, the Dean of —— deserves to be preached to death by wild curates."

"I am old, but I certainly have not that sign of old-age, extolling the past at the expense of the present. On the contrary, the progress of the world in the last fifty years almost takes my breath away. Steam and electricity have advanced it beyond the dreams of the wildest visionary two hundred years ago. By the bye, on the subject of steam, I have a most curious letter, which I extracted from a periodical, and will show you; it struck me as so interesting, that I made inquiries about it from the author of the publication, and have some reason to believe it is authentic.

Letter of Marion de Lorme to the Marquis de Cinq-Mars.

"*Paris, February*, 1641.

"My dear Effiart,

"While you are forgetting me at Narbonne, and giving yourself up to the pleasures of the Court and the delight of thwarting M. le Cardinal de Richelieu, I, according to your express desire, am doing the honours of Paris to your English lord the Marquis of Worcester; and I carry him about, or rather he carries me, from curiosity to curiosity, choosing always the most grave and serious, speaking little, listening with extreme attention, and fixing on those whom he interrogates two large blue eyes, which seem to pierce to the very centre of their thoughts. He is remarkable for never being satisfied with any explanations which are given him, and he never sees things in the light in which they are shown to him; you may judge of this by a visit we made together to Bicêtre, where he imagined he had discovered a genius in a madman.

"If this madman had not been actually raving, I verily believe your Marquis would have entreated his liberty, and have carried him off to London, in order to hear his extravagances from morning till night, at his ease. We were crossing the court of the madhouse, and I, more dead than alive with fright, kept close to my companion's side, when a frightful face appeared behind some immense bars, and a hoarse voice exclaimed, 'I am not mad! I am not mad! I have made a discovery which would enrich the country that adopted it.' 'What has he discovered?' asked our guide. 'Oh!' he answered, shrugging his shoulders, 'something trifling enough: you would never guess it; it is the use of the steam of boiling water.' I began to laugh. 'This man,' continued the keeper, 'is named Salomon de Caus; he came from Normandy four years ago, to present to the King a statement of the wonderful effects that might be produced from his invention. To listen to him, you would imagine that with steam you could navigate ships, move carriages; in fact, there is no end to the miracles which, he insists upon it, could be performed. The Cardinal sent the madman away without listening to him. Salomon de Caus, far from being discouraged, followed the Cardinal wherever he went with the most determined perseverance, who, tired of finding him for ever in his path, and annoyed at his folly, shut him up in Bicêtre, where he has now been for three years and a half, and where, as you hear, he calls out to every visitor that he is not mad, but that he has made a valuable discovery. He has even written a book on the subject, which I have here.'*

"Lord Worcester, who had listened to this account with much interest, after reflecting a time, asked for the book, of which, after having read several pages, he said, 'This man is not mad; in my country, instead of shutting him up, he would have been rewarded. Take me to him, for I should like to ask him some questions.' He was accordingly conducted to his cell; but, after a time, he came back sad and thoughtful. 'He is *indeed* mad now,' said he.; 'misfortune and captivity have alienated his reason; but it is you who have to answer for his madness; when you cast him into that cell, you confined the greatest genius of the age.' After this we went away, and since that time he has done nothing but talk of Salomon de Caus."

"I destroy, on principle, all letters to me, but I have no secrets myself. I should not care if almost every word I have written were published at Charing Cross. I live with open windows."

"This is a noble description of God's omnipresence (turning over the leaves of a book), 'His centre is everywhere, his circumference is nowhere.'"

Talking of New Year's Day and Christmas: "No, the returns of those fixed periods always make me

---

* This book is entitled, 'Les Raisons des Forces mouvantes, avec diverses machines tant utiles que puissantes.' (Pub. 1615, in folio.)

melancholy. I am glad when we have fairly turned the corner, and started afresh. I feel, like my friend Mackintosh, 'there is another child of Time lost,' as the year departs.

"What a loss you had in not knowing Mackintosh! how was it? .... Yes, his manner was cold; his shake of the hand came under the genus 'mortmain;' but his heart was overflowing with benevolence. I like that simile I made on him in my letter, of 'a great ship cutting its cable;'—it is fine, and it well described Mackintosh. His chief foible was indiscriminate praise. I amused myself the other day," said he, laughing, "in writing a termination of a speech for him; would you like to hear it? I will read it to you:—

"'It is impossible to conclude these observations without expressing the obligations I am under to a person in a much more humble scene of life,—I mean, Sir, the hackney-coachman by whom I have been driven to this meeting. To pass safely through the streets of a crowded metropolis must require, on the part of the driver, no common assemblage of qualities. He must have caution without timidity, activity without precipitation, and courage without rashness; he must have a clear perception of his object, and a dexterous use of his means. I can safely say of the individual in question, that, for a moderate reward, he has displayed unwearied skill; and to him I shall never forget that I owe unfractured integrity of limb, exemption from pain, and perhaps prolongation of existence.

"'Nor can I pass over the encouraging cheerfulness with which I was received by the waiter, nor the useful blaze of light communicated by the link-boys, as I descended from the carriage. It was with no common pleasure that I remarked in these men, not the mercenary bustle of venal service, but the genuine effusions of untutored benevolence; not the rapacity of subordinate agency, but the alacrity of humble friendship. What may not be said of a country where all the little accidents of life bring forth the hidden qualities of the heart,—where her vehicles are driven, her streets illumined, and her bells answered, by men teeming with all the refinements of civilized life?

"'I cannot conclude, Sir, without thanking you for the very clear and distinct manner in which you have announced the proposition on which we are to vote. It is but common justice to add, that public assemblies rarely witness articulation so perfect, language so select, and a manner so eminently remarkable for everything that is kind, impartial, and just.'"*

At ten we always went downstairs to prayers, in the library. Immediately after, if we were alone, appeared the 'farmer' at the door, lantern in hand. "David,

* This trifling critique on his old friend, good-humoured as it is, I should not have given without the permission of his family, who knew that Sir James, had he seen it, would have been the first to smile at it. I ought to add, that the same kind indulgence has been granted me wherever I have ventured on any anecdote that I feared might give pain.

bring me my coat and stick;" and off he set with
him, summer and winter, to visit his horses, and see
that they were all well fed, and comfortable in their
regions for the night. He kept up this custom all his
life.

On returning to the drawing-room, he usually asked
for a little music. "If I were to begin life again, I
would devote much time to music. All musical people
seem to me happy; it is the most engrossing pursuit;
almost the only innocent and unpunished passion.

"Never give way to melancholy: nothing encroaches
more; I fight against it vigorously.* One great remedy is, to take short views of life. Are you happy
now? Are you likely to remain so till this evening?
or next week? or next month? or next year? Then
why destroy present happiness by a distant misery,
which may never come at all, or you may never live to
see it? for every substantial grief has twenty shadows,
and most of them shadows of your own making."

Speaking of ——: "It was a beautiful old-age;
how fine those lines of Waller are—

'The soul's dark cottage, batter'd and decay'd,
Let in new lights through chinks that Time has made!'"

"Yes; —— was merry, not wise. You know, a
man of small understanding is merry where he can,
not where he should. Lightning must, I think, be
the wit of heaven."

Mr. P—— said to him, "I always write best with

* Yet I see, in his note-book,—"I wish I were of a more sanguine
temperament; I always anticipate the worst."

an amanuensis." "Oh! but are you quite sure he puts down what you dictate, my dear P. ?"

Speaking of a Revolutionist: "No man, I fear, can effect great benefits for his country without some sacrifice of the minor virtues."

"I often think what a different man I might have been if, like my friend Lord Holland, and others, I had passed my life with all that is most worth seeing and hearing in Europe, instead of being confined through the greater part of it to the society of the parish-clerk. I always feel it is combating with unequal weapons; but I have made a tolerable fight of it, nevertheless. I am rather an admirer of O'Connell: he, it cannot be denied, has done a great deal for Ireland, and, on the whole, I believe he meant well; but 'hell,' as Johnson says, 'is paved with good intentions.'"

A little more of such talk, intermixed with those brilliant and amusing bursts of humour and attack,— which I see prettily compared, in one of the printed sketches of him, to "summer lightning, that never harmed the object illumined by its flash,"—and then to bed; and all was quiet, and at peace, in the little parsonage.

I have endeavoured here,—partly from recollection, partly from my own and my friends' notes,—to give some faint idea of the style of my father's conversation and his manner of living with his family and friends. I flatter myself, by those who knew him intimately, it will not be thought an unfaithful copy. But, alas! without the look, the voice, the manner, the laugh, the thousand little delicate touches, the quick repartee, the connecting links from which these observations sprang,—without the master-spirit's voice to animate the whole,—without all this, I feel it is but a body without a soul. Yet, body as it is, to me it is most precious, as all that now remains to me of my father; and I would fain believe there are a few still alive who will accept this relic of a great man gone, with gratitude,—will live with him again in these pages,—will be reminded, by them, of him as he *was*, and not as I have here imperfectly attempted to describe him.

CHAPTER XII.

EXTRACT FROM LADY ——'S JOURNAL.—LAST ILLNESS.—COMES TO TOWN.—DR. CHAMBERS CALLED IN.—ANXIETY OF FRIENDS FOR HIS RECOVERY.—MEETING OF BROTHERS.—LIVING TO POOR CLERGYMAN.— DEATH OF SYDNEY SMITH.— DEATH OF HIS ELDEST BROTHER.

I HAVE but little more to add; my (to me) sad tale is nearly told; but I will here insert some extracts from a journal of a dear Scotch friend, who spent a month in his house, which, though never meant to see the light, have most kindly been given to me at my request; and which I feel to be valuable, not only because they are nearly the last notes I have of him (being taken the year before his death), but because they also, on many points, confirm, from notes taken at the moment, the traits I have given of him from mere recollection.

"'Do you not like the country?' 'I like London a great deal better; the study of men and women, better than trees and grass.'

"'Oh! some men are born happy. I often think, what a fortunate circumstance it was for me, in going to Edinburgh (quite a stranger), to fall at once into intimacy with such remarkable men as Jeffrey and the rest.' 'How was it?' 'I went to Edinburgh with a pupil,—I had nothing else. Then the Edinburgh Review,—what a machine that has been!'

"'I love Jeffrey very dearly;' and, speaking of his knowledge of all subjects, and his review of Madame de Staël: 'I used to say then that the nearest thing Jeffrey had ever seen to a fine Parisian lady was John Playfair.' How we laughed at this!

"'Miss Edgeworth was delightful,—so clever and sensible! She does not say witty things, but there is such a perfume of wit runs through all her conversation as makes it very brilliant.'

"We walked home after church; he paid visits to the cottagers, speaking to them frankly and cheerily, or scolding them for not coming to tell him they were better, or that they wanted more medicine.

"'Nobody' (says a sketch in the 'Spectator,' written by some friend) 'too obscure for Sydney to put in good-humour with themselves.' Nay, I have seen him brighten the countenance of his poor parishioners for the day, by a captivating phrase or two, when he met them, or visited their cottages. On one occasion, his parish-clerk being laid up with a broken shin, Sydney called to inquire. 'I'm getting round, your honour, but I sha'n't be fit for duty on Sunday.' 'Sorry for that, Lovelace; indeed, we shall miss you at the singing.' Then, turning to me,—'You can't think what a good hand Lovelace is at a psalm; you should hear him lead off the Old Hundredth.' At which the old clerk's eyes fairly glistened, and he stammered out, 'Oh! your honour's only saying that to cheer me up a bit.'

"Sometimes he had a good report to give of an absent son or daughter, whom he had seen in London, and obtained a place for. He employed many old people about the garden, and was anxious that everybody near him should be comfortable. 'Have you seen my doctor's shop? Come, I'll show it you.' I expressed my wonder. 'Yes, life is a difficult thing; here's everything prepared,—stomach-warmers, sore-throat collars, etc. I studied medicine, and went through the hospitals at Edinburgh; I know a good deal. I often regret that medical men will not talk more of their profession. It is a very interesting subject to every one, at least a little of it; but I never can get any of them to speak,—they look quite offended.'

"The poor people and the servants are very fond of him; he does them so much good, and gives them clothes, books, medicines. They look to him for everything, and they like his free speaking to them; he is so merry and frank: so my maid tells me.

"He sometimes read aloud to Mrs. Sydney and me in the evening, when anything struck him,—such as parts of Liebig,—so clearly and distinctly, observing shortly on parts as he read, and listening good-naturedly to our observations. We had each our arm-chair, lamp, and book in the evening, and not much conversation when alone. Occasionally he would sit with an air of profound meditation, and would begin as thus :—'Forgive us our trespasses, as we forgive them that trespass against us. That is new; that is peculiar to the Christian religion.' Or he would repeat the sublime prayers for the Queen, in his grand tones, to mark their fine composition.

"'I dine sometimes at ——, and the head of the bank sits at the foot of the table, looking so attentive, and bowing so obsequiously; and when I talk, *à tort et à travers*, as I am apt to do, I see by his expression that he says to himself, "There is a man I would not lend money to at fifteen per cent.; he's a rash man; he would buy bad Exchequer bills; he is not to be trusted." He little knows me.' 'That is very true,' said Mrs. Sydney; 'people are not aware that Sydney, with all his mirth, is one of the most cautious, prudent men that ever existed; he is always looking forward, and providing against what may happen.' 'Yes, I always expect the worst; but it has a good effect, for it makes me cautious.'

"'When I went to Edinburgh I had two introductions, to Sir William Forbes and Professor ——. He was clerk to the General Assembly of the Kirk. He said to me one day after dinner, "D—n the solemn league and covenant! it has spoiled the longs and shorts in Scotland."'

"'I like Dr. Fergusson much. William Clerk is an original man; how rare it is to meet an original man!'

"'I wish sometimes that I were a Scotchman, to have people care about me so much.'

"'The Americans, I see, call me a Minor Canon. They are abusing me dreadfully today: they call me Xantippe; they might at least have known my sex: and they say I am eighty-four. I don't know how it is,' said he, laughing, 'but everybody who behaves ill to me is sure to come to mischief before the year's out. I am not angry with them; I only say, I pity you, you are sure to suffer.'

"'Were you remarkable as a boy, Mr. Smith?' 'Yes, Madam, I was a remarkably fat boy. I was at one time to have been a supercargo to China, to Hongkong.'

"'Here is a hymn-book that an old man of eighty-four sends me, he says, because of his pleasure in hearing of my giving the living of Edmonton to Tate's son. I should have been better pleased if it had not cost me a shilling.' 'Oh!' said Mrs. Sydney, 'I would willingly have given a guinea for it.'

"'Here is an anonymous letter from some one who has a quantity of Mississippi bonds, asking me what he should do with them? How can I tell? they are not worth sixpence.'

"That month every post brought letters to him, either of complaint of the Americans, of the income-tax, or of some evil, which the writers (strangers) entreated Mr. Smith to write against, and to help them to remedy. There were also many feeling letters on the subject of his generosity to the family of Canon Tate. He could not conceive why the world praised him so much for that; he always spoke so simply about it, that it showed me how natural it was to his disposition to be kind and generous. He was evidently pleased by some of the newspapers' clever notices of his Letters to America. 'Well, they lay it on pretty thick today; where is Mrs. Sydney?' He was perpetually coming to her with something for her sympathy or consultation; and richly did she deserve that happiness, from her devoted love and admiration. One day I pointed out an article in the 'Times,' of one who was reckoned the Sydney Smith of Spain: it amused him.

"'I had once a mind to write a letter to young bishops; bishops I have known speak to their inferior clergy worse than they do to their footmen.' 'Why do you not, Mr. Smith?' 'Oh, it would be a life of contention; I am too old to bear a life of contention now.'

"'There is a specimen of national honesty! read that marked with red ink.' 'Do you mean a joke?' 'No, no.' 'Do give me a sign.' 'Well, I'll sometimes give you a sign when there is no joke, and you'll be sure to laugh. Frere used to tread on a man's toes to make him think he said something wrong. . . . When I was in Edinburgh, I said to a lady, speaking of the Dean of Faculty, that we thought our Deans in England had no faculties. She said, "Well, I call that a very good joke!"'

"'I hope somebody will tell me when I grow old and prosy; though I am not likely to get very prosy, I'm in general so short.' 'Yes, too short, Mr. Smith.'

"Christmas-day was one rich in recollections. The weather was fine. I looked out, and saw the maid Maria gravely and busily tying on oranges to the branches of the bay-trees, that were planted in large green tubs round the lawn. The effect was gay and sunny, and pleased him mightily. The sermon that day was a glorious one;—on Christmas, the contrast of the world before the blessed era, and the sudden effect after,—gratitude, immortal life, etc. I hope the sermon is preserved. I cannot give a good account of all that was interesting at that time,—of the children's feast, the schools, the prizes, the charities, etc.; but I remember my admiration of the variety of character which Mr. Smith displayed that day. From the sublime duties of the morning, he became, with the large family-party assembled at dinner, the Sydney Smith of London society; and in the evening he was delightful. 'I crave for music, Mrs. Smith; music! music!' He sang, with his sweet, rich voice, 'A few gay soarings yet.' He imitated an orchestra preluding, talking French, telling stories, and laughing so infectiously. Next morning he was merrier than ever; I found the party all at breakfast, waiting till I came, before he would allow a *Scotch cake* to be touched, which my maid had prepared (bad enough). He had often asked me to suggest some improvement to his house, something new—(poor I could think of nothing new, but cakes made with soda and buttermilk!); it was this cake we were all to take the same chance of suffering from, by eating it together. 'Let us make a tontine for the survivor,' said he, laughing. It was wonderful how he played upon this cake, on me, and on Scottish luxuries; he fancied that I feared to be too comfortable. 'Oh, that easy couch! you'll suffer for that a thousand years hence, depend upon it.'

"'Want of money is a great evil: I declare, every guinea I have gained I have been the happier. I was very poor till I was appointed to St. Paul's; that made me easy, and then my brother Courtenay's death made me rich.' An old friend congratulating him on his appointment to St. Pauls: 'Why, I think it makes me most happy to feel I can now keep a carriage and horses for her, in her old-age (pointing to Mrs. Sydney), which I could not have done before.'

"'I once rode on a turtle five feet along, supported by two people: piety trampling luxury underfoot! Do you take it?'

"The first sermon I heard in Combe Florey church was certainly meant for my good: 'Cast your care upon God, for he careth for you.' It was so comforting and encouraging! With what delight did I look and listen, in that church, to the grand form and powerful countenance, noble and melodious voice! In reading the Lessons and Psalms, he read so as almost to make a commentary on every word, and the meaning came out so rich and deep. His sermons were not given in St. Paul's with more interest and effect; and yet they were adapted to the congregation, from their plain and practical sense. Remembering him in St. Paul's crowded cathedral, and looking at him in the little village church, filled with peasantry, I was pleased to see him always the same.

"I wish I could convey the idea of his appearance as he sat in the bay-window of the library, writing. I used sometimes, in walking past, to venture near, to look at him. There was power, profundity, and meaning in his countenance; and he would often take up his papers with an amused expression. I was convinced that he was a very happy man. I often regretted that I had no spirits or courage to speak to him, or to join him in his walks in the garden, but I have much respect for the silence of a great man.

"These memorandums seem very simple, but I wished to be able to recall to myself the looks and tones of one whom I had been accustomed to admire through much of my life; and I feel, when writing for *myself*, that my impressions are conveyed.

"On New Year's Day, we were walking in the garden; he discovered a crocus, which had burst through the frozen earth; he stopped suddenly, gazed at it silently for a few seconds, and, touching it with his staff, pronounced solemnly, 'The resurrection of the world!'"

To this pretty, simple journal I have little to add. Yet how different are the minds of men! An apple fell to the ground, and Sir Isaac Newton saw in it one of the great laws of nature. How many men would have passed that little crocus, and seen in it only a flower: whilst to my father's mind (not quite unworthy of this great ancestor) it brought at one glance to his thoughts all the wonderful effects the breath of life, which had gone forth, was producing in every portion of the world, for man's benefit now, and was to produce on man himself in a world to come.

He saw but one resurrection upon earth more. In the spring he went up to London, as usual, for a short time; and whilst there, met, at the house of Mr. Van de Weyer, a literary man of some eminence who afterwards published a sketch of him in the 'Revue des Deux Mondes;' in which he introduced a short and humorous answer of my father's to him, not however intended for publication. My mother wishing to know some particulars of this from Mr. Van de Weyer, after my father's death, he had the kindness, amidst all the hurry of a sudden departure for Germany, to write out the following account of the transaction for her, which he has given me permission to insert.

"*June* 1852.

"My dear Mrs. Sydney Smith,

"I hasten, before our departure for Germany, to enclose, according to your wishes, several extracts from the letters which my poor friend Eugène Robin wrote to me on the subject of the article published by him in the 'Revue des Deux Mondes.'

"In 1844, Eugène Robin, who had left Brussels, where he had been educated, and had, at a very early age, distinguished himself, both as a poet and a critic, spent a few days with us in London; and, as he was anxious to know the best and most original writers of England, we had long conversations together on the works of Mr. Sydney Smith, which I lent him, and for which he soon felt and expressed a great admiration. On the 22nd of April, I received from him the following letter:—

"'Vous vous souvenez peut-être de m'avoir parlé de la collection des écrits de Jeffrey et de Sydney Smith sur lesquels il y avait de bons articles à faire pour la 'Revue des Deux Mondes.' Le 'Jeffrey' a été traité par M. Forcade, dans la dernière livraison ; mais le 'Sydney Smith' vient de m'échoir en partage. J'ai demandé le livre à Londres : mais je voudrais bien, comme vous connaissez intimement l'auteur, que vous eussiez la bonté, si vos loisirs vous le permettent, de me dire si ce sont là réellement tous ses ouvrages ; de me donner (c'est bien indiscret de vous demander ces choses-là) sur l'homme et sur l'écrivain de ces détails qu'avec votre esprit d'observation, vous seul pouvez bien connaître. Ils ajouteraient singulièrement de prix à un travail fait avec conscience. J'ai le *pain* de mon article; j'attends de vous le *sel*. Pourquoi m'avez-vous encouragé à ne voir en vous que l'homme de lettres bienveillant pour ses jeunes confrères ? Je ne vous importunerais pas de la sorte.'

"I immediately answered that I very much regretted not to be able to comply with his request, my very intimacy with Mr. Sydney Smith preventing me, without his consent, from sending for a Review any biographical anecdotes or critical observations on his life and writings; but I advised M. Robin to write himself to Mr. S. Smith, and I offered to deliver his letter, and to explain both *his* reasons for doing so, and *my* reasons for not acceding to his demand, and to obtain an answer for him. M. Robin sent me a charming letter (I regret that I have not kept a copy of it) for Mr. Sydney Smith, who kindly approved of what I had said and done, and entrusted to my care an answer to Eugène Robin's letter.*

" More than two months elapsed before Eugène Robin acknowledged the receipt of this letter to me in the following words:—

"'*Paris, le* 3 *Sept.*, 1844.

"' Vous avez bien voulu m'envoyer la lettre amicale et toujours spirituelle de votre ami le Révérend Sydney Smith. Elle m'a grandement encouragé à faire l'article dont je vous avais parlé; maintenant, ce travail est fini depuis plus de quinze jours; il n'y manque plus que quelques petits détails biographiques, qui, transmis par vous, selon le désir exprimé par M. Sydney Smith, relèveraient singulièrement mon récit et ma critique. Si vous vouliez faire un effort en faveur de l'aimable Chanoine de Saint-Paul, que ne vous devrais-je pas?'

"I have not kept a copy of my answer to him, the substance of which was communicated to Mr. Sydney Smith. The article appeared soon after, and Mr. Sydney Smith was informed of its publication by M.

* The letter, having been already published, is not given here.

Robin. This letter was not sent through me: I heard of it by the two following notes from Mr. Sydney Smith:—

"'*October* 21, 1844.

"'You may remember I wrote through you to Eugène Robin, giving, at his request, some account of myself. I have received a letter from him, stating that the Review is published, and that he has quoted a part of my letter. I confess this rather alarms me. Will it be putting you to an inconvenience if I beg the loan of the Review for two or three hours? I will deviate from my usual custom, and return it punctually.'

"'*October* 24.

"'I have received the Review by post, so I will not trouble you for yours.

"'Eugène has said more about me than I deserve. He is of himself a little long; but I am very much pleased and flattered by the approbation of so clever a man.

"'He had better not have quoted my letter; but there is no great harm. Yours,
"'SYDNEY SMITH.'

"We leave tomorrow. Believe me, my dear Mrs. Sydney Smith,
"Yours very faithfully,
"SYLVAIN VAN DE WEYER."

Here, though slightly anticipating events, I shall

insert two most touching letters from his friend Lord Jeffrey,—the one on the occasion of his long, last illness, and the other on receiving the fragment on the Irish Church, after my father's death. And I give them with the more pleasure, as they not only furnish fresh proof of the tenderness and kindness of Lord Jeffrey's nature, but afford ample testimony to the devotion and admiration he bore my father, and which my father's deep love for him so fully deserved. To my regret, this has been almost passed over, or barely alluded to, in the Life lately published of Lord Jeffrey.

"*Edinburgh, Feb.* 10*th*, 1845.

"My dear Saba,

" I do not know when I have felt more moved and delighted, than when Professor Pillans came into my room yesterday with a short letter from our beloved Sydney (but in his wife's handwriting), cheerfully written ; and saying, among other things, and in substance, that he 'looked forward to his recovery, and at all events was making very valuable progress:' I think those were the words. I need not tell you how sad we have all been about him, nor what a gloom the accounts we have lately received have thrown over the circle of his ancient friends. While that lasted, I for one at least had not courage to distress you by any inquiry; but this letter has excited a less painful anxiety, and I hope you will forgive me for the trouble it leads me to give you. You cannot over-estimate the interest I take in the oldest and truest of my remaining friends; and I believe I may say the same of Murray. Do then, my dear child, let us know whether we may not hope again.

"And believe me always affectionately yours,

"F. JEFFREY."

"*Haileybury College, Hertford, April* 21, 1845.

"My very dear Saba,

"I have felt several times in the last six weeks that I ought to have written to some of you; but in truth, my dear child, I had not the courage; and today it is not so much because I have the courage, as because I cannot help it.

"That startling and matchless Fragment was laid upon my table this morning; and before I had read out the first sentence, the real presence of my beloved and incomparable friend was so brought before me, in all his brilliancy, benevolence, and flashing decision, that I seemed again to hear his voice and read in his eye, and burst into an agony of crying. I went through the whole in the same state of feeling: my fancy kindled, and my intellect illumined, but my heart struck through with the sense of our loss, so suddenly and so deeply impressed by this seeming restoration.

"I do not think he ever wrote anything so good, and I feel mournfully that there is no one man alive who could have so written. The effect, I am persuaded, will be greater than from any of his other publications: it is a voice from the grave. And it may truly be said that those who will not listen to it, would not be persuaded though one were to rise from the dead.

"It relieves me to say all this, and you must forgive it. Heaven bless you, my dear child! With kind remembrances from all here,

"Ever very affectionately yours,
"F. JEFFREY."

During the summer of this year, he received many of his old friends; and, amongst others, his eldest and now only brother, Robert, Mr. Hallam, and Mr. Everett, the American minister. Of this visit I find this touching notice in a letter of Mr. Everett's to my mother, on receiving the volume of posthumous sermons she published:—

"One of them I heard him preach in his little village church at Combe Florey. The reading of it brings back to me, in the freshest recollection, that delightful visit,—one of the brightest spots in my English residence—though I am painfully affected by considering that the two great men whose society I then enjoyed are gone; men who, in their peculiar paths of eminence, have not left their equals behind them." On another occasion Mr. Everett says:—"The first remark that I made to myself, after listening to Mr. Sydney Smith's conversation, was, that if he had not been known as the wittiest man of his day, he would have been accounted one of the wisest."

My father opened his house for a month to that poor, interesting family for whom he had interceded with so much success with Sir Robert Peel, and who were pining for a little fresh air. Amongst these was a clever, imaginative little boy, by whom he was much interested. Every evening he examined into his conduct during the day; and, if blameless, sent him to bed with a large red wafer stuck in the middle of his forehead as a reward. The Order of the Garter could not have made the child more proud. Once only, during his visit, did he forfeit the red wafer, and went sobbing and broken-hearted to bed; having been convicted, first, of cutting off the whiskers of Muff, Annie Kay's favourite cat; and last, though not least, meddling with the poetical salad when dressed. Such crimes could not, of course, be pardoned!

My father went, for a short time, in the autumn, to the sea-side, complaining much of languor. He said, "I feel so weak, both in body and mind, that I verily believe, if the knife were put into my hand, I should not have strength or energy enough to stick it into a Dissenter."

In October my father was taken seriously ill; and Dr. Holland went down immediately to Combe Florey, and advised his coming up to town, where he might be constantly under his care. He bore the journey well; and for the first two months, though very weak, went out in his carriage every day, saw his friends, broke out into moments of his natural gaiety, saying one day, with his bright smile, to General Fox (when they were keeping him on very low diet), and not allowing him any meat, "Ah, Charles! I wish I were allowed even the wing of a roasted butterfly;" and was at times so like his former self, that, though Dr. Holland was uneasy about him, we could not give up hope.

But other and more urgent symptoms coming on, Dr. Holland became so anxious, that he begged that Dr. Chambers might be called in. My father most unwillingly consented,—not from any dislike of Dr. Chambers, but from having the most perfect confidence in Dr. Holland's care and skill.

That evening he, for the first time, told his old maid and nurse, Annie Kay, that he knew his danger; said where and how he should wish to be buried;— then spoke of us all, but told her we must cheer him, and keep up his spirits, if he lingered long.

But he had such a dread of sorrowful faces around him, and of inflicting pain, that to us he always spoke calmly and cheerfully, and as if unaware of his danger.

He now never left his bed. Though suffering much, he was gentle, calm, and patient; and sometimes even cheerful. He spoke but little. Once he said to me, taking my hand, "I should like to get well, if it were only to please Dr. Holland; it would, I know, make him so happy; this illness has endeared him so much to me."

Speaking once of the extraordinary interest that had been evinced by his friends for his recovery (for the inquiries at his door were incessant),—"It gives me pleasure, I own," he said, "as it shows I have not misused the powers entrusted to me." But he was most touched by the following letter from Lady Grey to my mother, expressing the feelings towards him, of one of the friends he most loved and honoured,—one who was, like himself, lying on that bed from which he was never to rise, and who was speaking as it were his farewell before entering on eternity.

"Lord Grey is intensely anxious about him. There is nobody of whom he so constantly thinks; nobody whom, in the course of his own long illness, he so ardently wished to see. Need I add, dear Mrs. Sydney, that, excepting only our children, there is nobody for whom we both feel so sincere an affection. God knows how truly I feel for your anxiety. Who is so sadly entitled to do so as I am? But I will hope the best, and that we may both be blessed by seeing the person most dear to us restored to health."

One evening, when the room was half-darkened, and he had been resting long in silence, and I thought him asleep, he suddenly burst forth, in a voice so strong and full that it startled us,—

"We talk of human life as a journey, but how variously is that journey performed! There are some who come forth girt, and shod, and mantled, to walk on velvet lawns and smooth terraces, where every gale is arrested, and every beam is tempered. There are others who walk on the Alpine paths of life, against driving misery, and through stormy sorrows, over sharp afflictions; walk with bare feet, and naked breast, jaded, mangled, and chilled."

And then he sank into perfect silence again. In

quoting this beautiful passage from his sermon on Riches, his mind seems to have turned to the long and hard struggles of his own early life.

The present painful struggle did not last many days longer. He often lay silent and lost in thought, then spoke a few words of kindness to those around. He seemed to meet death with that calmness which the memory of a well-spent life, and trust in the mercy of God, can alone give.

Almost the last person he saw was his favourite and now only-surviving brother, Bobus; and nothing could be more affecting than to see these two brothers thus parting on the brink of the grave; for my dear uncle only left my father's deathbed to lie down on his own, —literally fulfilling the petition my father so touchingly made to him in one of his early letters, on hearing of his illness, "to take care of himself, and wait for him,"—and before the end of a fortnight had followed him to the grave.

"*Heslington*, 1813.

"Dear Bobus,

"Pray take care of yourself. We shall both be a brown infragrant powder in thirty or forty years. Let us contrive to last out for the same, or nearly the same time. Weary will the latter half of my pilgrimage be, if you leave me in the lurch.

"Ever your affectionate brother,
"Sydney Smith."

Of the genius, learning, and virtue that were lost

to the world in that grave, I dare not attempt to speak; it belongs to other and abler pens than mine to tell; but to me my uncle's death was as the death of a second father,—the extinction of all I have ever known or conceived that was brightest and best in the world.

A very eminent man, who had the rare privilege of associating intimately with my uncle, writes of him to Sir Henry Holland:—"I never knew a mind with so gigantic a grasp. Our talk when alone was always most serious."

These beautiful and characteristic lines were found in my uncle's desk, supposed to have been composed by him shortly before his death:—

"'Hîc jacet!'—O humanarum meta ultima rerum!
Ultra quam labor et luctus curæque quiescunt,
Ultra quam penduntur opes et gloria flocci;
Et redit ad nihilum vana hæc et turbida vita:
Ut te respicerent homines! Quæ bella per orbem,
Qui motus animorum et quanta pericula nostra
Acciperent facilem sine cæde et sanguine finem!
Tu mihi versare ante oculos, non tristis imago,
Sed monitrix, ut me ipse regam, domus hæc mihi cum sit
Vestibulum tumuli, et senii penultima sedes."

"'Hîc jacet!'—O last goal of human things, beyond which labour and mourning and cares are at rest,—beyond which riches and glory are weighed as nothing, and this vain and turbid life returns to nought! Oh that men would thus regard thee! What wars throughout the world, what passions of the soul, how many dangers besetting us, might so obtain an easy termination without slaughter or blood! Mayest thou be present before my eyes, not a mournful image, but an admonisher, that I should regulate myself; since this house is to me the vestibule of the tomb, and the *next to closing* seat of my old-age!"

My father died at peace with himself and with all the world; anxious, to the last, to promote the comfort and happiness of others. He sent messages of kindness and forgiveness to the few he thought had injured him. Almost his last act was, bestowing a small living of £120 per annum on a poor, worthy, and friendless clergyman, who had lived a long life of struggle with poverty on £40 per annum.* Full of happiness and gratitude, he entreated he might be allowed to see my father; but the latter so dreaded any agitation that he most unwillingly consented, saying, "Then he must not thank me; I am too weak to bear it." He entered,—my father gave him a few words of advice,—the clergyman silently pressed his hand, and blessed his death-bed. Surely such blessings are not given in vain!

My father expired on the 22nd of February, 1845,

* In dictating a few words in his favour (for he was too weak to write) to the Bishop of Llandaff, he says:—"In addition to his other merits, I am sure he will have one in your eyes, for he is an out-and-out Tory." So little did party-feelings influence my father in bestowing preferment!

—his death caused by hydrothorax, or water on the chest, consequent upon disease of the heart, which had probably existed for a considerable time, but rapidly increased during the few months preceding his death. His son closed his eyes. He was buried, by his own desire, as privately as possible, in the cemetery of Kensal Green; where his eldest son, Douglas, and now my mother, repose by his side.

And if true greatness consists, as my dear and valued old friend Mr. Rogers once quoted here from an ancient Greek writer, "in doing what deserves to be written, and writing what deserves to be read, and in making mankind happier and better for your life," my father was a truly great and good man.

My mother's anxiety to have a Memoir written of my father had induced her to apply very soon after his death to Mr. Moore, for his able assistance; but upon further consideration it was thought the event was then too recent; and before sufficient materials could be collected, Mr. Moore's health rendered the task impossible. The following letter refers to my mother's request to Lord Jeffrey to contribute his recollections of my father.

"*June* 14, 1845.
"My dear Mrs. Smith,
"I do not systematically destroy my letters, but I

take no care of them, and very few, I fear, have been preserved. I shall make a search, however, and send you all I can. I was very glad to hear some time ago, that Moore had agreed to assist in preparing the memorial, about which you are naturally so much interested. He will do it, I am sure, in a right spirit, and with the feeling which we are all anxious to see brought to its execution. Then he writes gracefully, is so great a favourite with the public, that the addition of his name cannot fail to be a great recommendation. If it occurs to me, on reflection, that there is anything I can contribute in the way you suggest, I shall be most happy to have my name once more associated with his on such an occasion. You know it must always be a pleasure to me to comply with any request of yours; and the form in which you wish this to be done, is certainly that which I should prefer to any other. Yet the models to which you refer, might *well* deter me from attempting anything that might lead to comparison.*

"I am glad to think of you at Munden,† rather than in Green-street, in this charming weather; and beg to be most kindly remembered there to my beloved Emily and all her belongings.

"I have not had much to boast of in the way of health since my return, but have still been well enough hitherto to get through with my work. We are fixed

---

* Sydney's Letters to the Editors of Sir J. Mackintosh and Mr. Horner's Memoirs.

† Mr. Hibbert's house in Hertfordshire.

here now, I think, pretty much till winter, and expect to be joined by Charley and her infant, in a fortnight.

"With kindest regards,
"Ever very affectionately yours,
"F. JEFFREY."

"*Craigcrook.*"

"*Derby.*

"My dear Mrs. Sydney,

"Your kind note of the 12th came to me at the Euston Hotel this morning, when I was in the act of sallying forth to join the train which brought me here two hours ago. So you see I could not possibly thank you any earlier, for your kind inquiries; nor gratify myself by the interesting pilgrimage to Green-street, which I should otherwise have undertaken with such a deep devotion of feeling. I hope yet to live, however, to commune with my heart at that shrine.* I am glad that Eddis has been so successful. For calm and true expression, and the rendering of what is moral, rather than passionate, in our natures, I think he is the first of our living artists. I have indeed been very ill and recover but slowly, though I have little actual suffering, and hope to be a little less feeble and shabby yet before I die. Notwithstanding, I have no anxiety, nor low spirits, though the animal vitality is at times low enough, God knows. My affections and the enjoyment of beautiful nature, I thank

---

* A portrait of my father, which Mr. Eddis had just painted for my mother.

heaven, are as fresh and lively as in the first poetical days of my youth, and with these there is nothing very miserable in the infirmity of age. We are taking two of our grandchildren down with us, and I hope to have the whole household reunited at Craigcrook, on the first days of July. They are all (except the poor patriarch who tells you so) in the full flush of health and gaiety, and would make a brightness in a darker home than mine.

"Give my true and tender love to my dear Emily. I often think of her in her early home at Foston, and in that still earlier Yorkshire home, where she tempted me to expose myself on the jackass.*

"With kind remembrances to Hibbert and all his descendants, God bless you all, and always.

"Very affectionately yours,

"F. JEFFREY."

Hints on Female Education.

Though the subject of education is now much more generally studied and understood than it was formerly, yet the following slight hints, written at the request of a very young mother, when my father was a very young man, may not be entirely without value

* See Narrative, p. 153.

and interest to some young mother now; and at least show how early he felt the value and importance of education to women. I received them too late to insert them in their proper place.

"I am afraid, my dear Madam, you will find in these few hints little which you have not already anticipated, and that their only merit will be, that intention of being useful to your children by which they are dictated. Your daughters will have a great deal to do, and you will have a great deal to superintend; and exertion on their part, and inspection on yours, will lose very much of their effects without a systematic distribution of time. I cannot compliment you with having been a great economist of life. In your own instance indeed it is not of much importance; but the education of your daughters ought to (and I am sure will) impose upon you a restraint of natural propensities. If you wish to be useful to them, you must be active, persevering, and systematic; you must lay out the day in regular plots and parterres; and toil and relax at intervals, fixed as much as your other affairs will permit. The consideration of religion may perhaps be brought too frequently before the minds of young people. Pleasure and consolation through life may be derived from a judicious religious education; a mistaken zeal may embitter the future days of a child with superstition, melancholy, and terror. Short prayers at rising and going to bed; a regular attendance at church; the precepts of a mother as a friend, sparingly and opportunely applied, appear to me to be the best kind of foundation for the superstructure of religion. It will be wise perhaps to teach them very early, that Sunday is a day on which their ordinary studies should be laid aside, and others of a more serious nature attended to. What the religious books are which are to be put into the hands of children, you know best; but there are some which, when their understandings become more enlarged, your daughters should certainly read, such as* . . .

"God has made us with strong passions and little wisdom. To inspire the notion that infallible vengeance will be the consequence of every little deviation from our duty is to encourage melancholy and despair. Women have often ill health and irritable nerves; they want moreover that strong coercion over the fancy which judgment exercises in the minds of men; hence they are apt to cloud their minds with secret fears and superstitious presentiments. Check, my dear Madam, as you value their future comfort, every appearance of this in your daughters; dispel that prophetic gloom which dives into futurity, to extract sorrow from days and years to come, and which considers its own unhappy visions as the decrees of Providence. We know nothing of tomorrow; our business is to be good and happy today.

"One of the great practical goods which Christi-

---

* Omitted, because, since this period, works fitted for the young have become so numerous and are so improved, that the list is of little use.

anity is every day producing to society is that extreme attention to the necessities of the poor, for which this country is so remarkable. I hope you will give your daughters a taste for active interference of this kind; nothing makes a woman so amiable and respectable.

"I would keep from my daughters immoral books, sceptical books, and novels; from which last I except Sir C. Grandison. I confess I have a very great dread of novels; the general moral may be good, but they dwell on subjects and scenes which it appears to me it is the great object of female education to exclude. A woman's heart does not want softening; it is a strange composition of tears, sighs, sorrows, ecstasies, fears, smiles, etc. etc.;—a man is all flesh and blood.

"I hope at the proper time you will take your children into the world. It will please them, relieve them from that painful shyness and embarrassment inseparable from a retired life, and give them the fair chance they ought to have of settling to advantage.

"The accomplishments are of use, as they embellish and occupy the mind; but after all, they are subordinate points of education, and too much time may very easily be given to them. It is very agreeable to look at good drawings; it is very delightful to hear good music; but good sense, sound judgment, and cultivated understanding, are superior to everything else;—they make the good wife, the enlightened mother, the interesting companion. Do not suppose I am decrying accomplishments. I am only giving them their just rank, and guarding against that exclusive care and absorbent eagerness with which it is at present the fashion to cultivate them.

"You mean to give your girls a taste for reading. Nothing else can so well enable them to pass their lives with dignity, with innocence, and with interest. Let us go into detail, and see if we can chalk out a convenient plan for them. They must learn French; do you know enough of this language to instruct them, or must they have a master? If the latter, the grammar, pronunciation, etc., will be his affair. In the choice of books it will be very much in your power to direct them; the first will be easy, and suitable to children in point of language; such books abound,—you cannot mistake them; then the whole field of French literature is open for you to select from. For example, when you think them old enough, and sufficiently acquainted with the language, let them read Bourdaloue and Massillon's Sermons, Bossuet's Oraisons Funèbres, Sermons of Father Elisée, as specimens of the sacred eloquence of the French; let them read some of the best plays of Pierre Corneille, Racine, Molière, Voltaire's tragedies, some of Boileau, particularly the Lutrin, the Henriade of Voltaire. Supposing they wish to read French history, always take care to make geography and chronology go hand in hand with history, without which it is nothing but a confused jumble of places and events. When they have read the history of Greece and Rome, they should not fail to read Plutarch's Lives; one of the most delightful books antiquity has left us. They will of course pay an early attention to the history of their own country, which they will find curiously detailed in Henry, philosophically in Hume, drily and accurately in Rapin. With the poets and dramatic writers of our own country you are as well acquainted as myself. I hope they will learn Italian. In arithmetic it does not appear to be of consequence that they should go far, not further perhaps than compound division; but I would certainly endeavour, by much practice, to make them very dexterous in the common operations of subtracting, multiplying, and adding. It is of great importance to give them correct notions in the common elements of geography and astronomy, and to make them quite at their ease in the use of maps;—this will be done in very little time. In the order of study, the acquirement of what is preparatory to general literature will first require your attention, as well as those which are of indispensable necessity; I mean writing, ciphering, French, geography, spelling, etc. When these first dificulties are got over, put them boldly on the Greek and Roman history in the mornings, and poetry or *belles lettres*—English or French—in the afternoons. Remark to them, encourage them to make their remarks to you; applaud, blame, encourage, and use every little pious artifice in your power to give them that sure, best, and happiest of all worldly attainments—a taste for literary improvement.

"I have recommended a division of studies into those of the morning and evening, because I think it can be very easily done without producing confusion, and it is tedious to dwell upon one subject for a whole day. If you can get them to read in a connected method, you will have gained a point of great importance. For example, Spenser precedes Dryden, Pope, etc.; and by following this order of precedence, you see the improvement of language, and remark how each poet is indebted to those who went before him. Voyages and travels, and the history of modern Europe, would exhaust the longest life. Botany they will be delighted with.

"I have given a list of some few books in the principal departments of knowledge, in case they should strike into any one of them. The truth is, it is not important what part of knowledge they love best. A woman who loves history, is not more respectable than a woman who loves natural philosophy; either will afford innocent, dignified, improving occupation. If they show no predilection, then give them one: if they do, follow it. We move most quickly to that point where we wish to go.

"Let your children see that you are sorry to restrain them, happy to indulge them. Confess your ignorance when they put questions to you which you cannot answer, and refer them elsewhere; and relax from your instruction and authority in proportion as your children want them less. I write positively, my dear Madam, to avoid the long and circuitous language of diffidence, not because I attach any value to my opinions.

"I have contented myself with general hints, because in writing on these subjects it is no very difficult thing to slip into a folio volume. I have omitted the mention of many things which I know you will do well, and have purposely introduced that of others where I have some apprehensions of you. If it were not to make you an offer unworthy of acceptance, I should say that my serious and most zealous advice is always at your command.

"Adieu, my dear Madam; take courage, exert yourself. If there be one sight on earth which commands interest, respect, and assistance from men, it is that of a good mother, who, under the providence of God, exerts her whole strength for the advantage and improvement of her children.

"Your most sincere well-wisher,

"SYDNEY SMITH."

Epitaph.

TO

SYDNEY SMITH,

ONE OF THE BEST OF MEN.

HIS TALENTS, THOUGH ADMITTED BY HIS CONTEMPORARIES TO BE GREAT,

WERE SURPASSED BY

HIS UNOSTENTATIOUS BENEVOLENCE, HIS FEARLESS LOVE OF TRUTH,

AND HIS ENDEAVOUR TO PROMOTE THE HAPPINESS OF MANKIND

BY RELIGIOUS TOLERATION

AND

BY RATIONAL FREEDOM.

HE WAS BORN THE 3RD OF JUNE, 1771; HE BECAME CANON RESIDENTIARY

OF ST. PAUL'S CATHEDRAL, 1831; HE DIED FEBRUARY THE 22ND, 1845.

[On the opposite side of the Tomb.]

DOUGLAS SMITH,

THE ELDEST SON OF THE REV. SYDNEY SMITH,

AND OF

CATHARINE AMELIA, HIS WIFE.

HE WAS BORN FEBRUARY 27, 1805; HE DIED APRIL 15, 1829.

HIS LIFE WAS BLAMELESS.

HIS DEATH WAS THE FIRST SORROW

HE EVER OCCASIONED HIS PARENTS,

BUT IT WAS DEEP AND LASTING.

List of the Rev. Sydney Smith's Articles in the Edinburgh Review.

Vol.	Art.	Page.	Vol.	Art.	Page.	Vol.	Art.	Page.
1	2	18	12	9	151	32	6	389
1	3	24	13	2	25	33	3	68
1	9	83	13	5	77	33	5	91
1	12	94	13	4	333	34	5	109
1	16	113	14	3	40	34	2	320
1	18	122	14	11	145	34	8	422
1	20	128	14	5	353	35	5	92
1	6	314	14	13	490	35	7	123
1	10	382	15	3	40	35	2	286
2	2	30	15	3	299	36	6	110
2	4	53	16	7	158	36	3	353
2	6	86	16	3	326	37	2	325
2	14	136	16	7	399	37	7	432
2	17	172	17	4	330	38	4	85
2	22	202	17	8	393	39	2	43
2	2	287	18	3	325	39	2	299
2	4	330	21	4	93	40	2	31
2	10	398	22	4	67	40	7	427
3	12	146	23	8	189	41	7	143
3	7	334	31	2	44	42	4	367
3	9	355	31	6	132	43	2	299
9	12	177	31	2	295	43	7	395
10	4	299	32	2	28	44	2	47
10	6	329	32	3	309	45	3	74
11	5	341	32	6	111	45	7	423
12	5	82						

INDEX.

Absence of mind, 363, 364.
Abstraction, power of, 115.
Allen, Mr., recommendation of, to Lord Holland, 21.
Amalgams, moral, 215.
America, reported visit to, 303.
Animals, interest in, 118, 174; medicine administered to, 117; scratcher for, 118.
Apologue on Toleration, 218; letter of Mr. Everett relating to, 219.
Apothecary's shop, 356, 394.
Arms of the Smith family, 243.
Austin's (Mrs.) account of sermon at St. Paul's, 307.

Ballot, pamphlet on the, 322.
Banker, dining with a, 395.
Belgium, visit to, 253, 254; interview with the King, 253.
Benevolence, fragment on, 133.
Berkeley Chapel, morning preachership at, 79.
Berry, Miss, Ode by, 84; visit to, 264.
Bible names, 349.
Birth and ancestry, 1, 2.
Bishop, duties of a, 237; marriage of a, 258.
Bishopric, views with regard to a, 233, 235, 236; probability of elevation to, 244.
Bishopthorpe, visit to, 177.
Blind, sermon for the, 58.
Blinds, coloured patchwork, 178.
Bobus. *See* Smith, Robert.
Body, the, a fragment on, 125.
Books, love of, 180, 239.

Bristol, becomes Canon of, 216; sermon at the Cathedral, 216; popularity at, 230; riots at, 230.
Bunch, 159, 178, 186, 194.
Business habits, 114, 395.

Calamity, horse so named, 174.
Carlisle, Lady, lines by, 329.
Carlisle, Lord, commencement of friendship of, 167; frequent visits of, 168.
Catholic Emancipation, petition for, 201; speech in favour of, 203.
Cheerfulness, remarks on, 131.
Chess, 214.
Children, fondness for, 113, 119, 353; interest in the pursuits of, 114, 280.
Chimneys, smoky, 118.
Cholera, spread of the, 240.
Christianity, evidences of, 53; tolerant spirit of, 54.
Christmas Day at Combe Florey, 398.
Church, state of the, 24.
Classes of society, 381.
Clergyman, poor, living obtained for a, 413.
Club, the, 91.
Cockerell, Mr., letter from, on performance of duties as Canon of St. Paul's, 249.
Combe Florey, removal to, 225; rebuilds parsonage-house, 228; visit of Lord Jeffrey, 228; library at, 239; visit of Lord John Russell, 240; mode of

428   INDEX.

life at, 331; Christmas Day at, 398; sermon at, 399; last return to, 408.
Composition, rapid, habit of, 112.
Court, presentation at, 222.
Courtenay Smith, death of, 280.
Curacy on Salisbury Plain, 10; the squire, 12.

Dandy, thawing a, 181.
Dante, tortures described by, 266.
Davy, Lady, visit of, 154.
Deer, parsonic, 345.
Delinquents, juvenile, 165.
Denman, Lord, 355.
Diary, portions of, 120–125.
Dining out in the country, 147.
Dogs, dislike of, 200, 379.
Donkey, a favourite, 152.
Douglas Smith, birth of, 65; sent to Westminster School, 182; goes to Oxford, 197; death, 224; letter to Lady Wenlock relating to his death, 225.
Dryden's house, 265.
Dudley, Lord, anecdotes of, 364, 365.

Ecclesiastical Commission, contest with the, 271.
Ecclesiastical Duties and Revenues Bill, petition against, 274.
Economy practised, 204.
Edgeworth, Miss, visit of, to London, 309; letter from, 309; conversation of, 393.
Edinburgh, society at, 13; residence at, 13, 60, 393.
Edinburgh Review, origin of, 22; state of society at the establishment of, 23; moral courage in contributing to, 24; character of writings in, 30–37; Sydney Smith ceases to write for, 229; publication of his contributions to, 229.
Edmonton, the living of, 289; address of parishioners, 292; letter to the Bishop of London relating to, 294.
Education, 31; importance of religious, 55; views on, 319, 335, 359; female, hints on, 417.

Ellenborough, Lord, anecdote of, 377.
Erasmus, life of, 316.
Everett, Mr., visit of, 407.
Exchange of living, efforts to obtain, 109, 154.

Fallacies, 360.
Farmers, annual dinner to, 116.
Female education, hints on, 417.
Filial affection, instance of, 187.
Fireplaces, importance of, 261.
Fishmongers' Hall, invitation to dine at, 105.
Flowers, love of, 257.
Foundling Hospital, appointed to the preachership of the, 68; anecdote, 92.
Foston-le-Clay, obtains the living of, 100; induction, 100; conversation at the Archbishop's, 100; compelled to reside on living, 107; resolves to build, 108; commences building, 156; house completed, 161; the household, 163, 164, 180; account of a visit, by a clergyman, 209; Mr. Loch's opinion of the parsonage-house, 227; revisited, 281.
Fox, Miss, 247.
Franklin, admiration of, 353.
Friendship, remarks on, 130.
Fry, Mrs., a visit with, to Newgate, 165.

Game Laws, 33, 165.
Garden chair, 365; lines on receiving, 328.
Gardens for the poor, 119.
Grattan, Mr., death of, 189; character of, 190.
Grenville, Mr., old-age of, 263, 368; letter from, 286.
Grey, Lord, first visit to, 105; fall of his administration, 244; proposed inscription for monument to, 278.

Handwriting, badness of, 192.
Happiness, recipe for, 295.
Hardness of character, 296.
Harvest, failure of, in 1816, 171.

INDEX. 429

Hatherton, Lord, letter to, 216.
Heslington, residence at, 110; mode of life at, 111; visits of friends, 143.
Hints, historical, 139.
Holland, Lord, friendship of, 78, 95; letter from, relating to Plymley's Letters, 104; visits Foston, 172; offers the living of Ampthill, 176; letter to, relative to a bishopric, 236; death of, 281; portrait of, 282.
Holland House, first visit to, 77; society at, 77.
Holland, Dr., attendance of, in last illness, 403.
Holland, tour in, 253, 254.
Horner, L., first acquaintance with, 17; character of, 18, 169; removal to London, 90; declining health and death, 169; letter of Sydney Smith to his brother, 170.
Humour, instances of want of perception of, 267, 367.
Hunt, trial of, 188.

Immortal, the, 160, 166, 211, 212.
Immortality, evidence of, 52.
Impertinence, official, 193.
Innocence vindicated, 244.
Ireland, condition of, 103; sketch of English misrule in, 141.
Irreligion, abhorrence of, 205.
Italian refugee, marriage of an, 176.

Jeffrey, Lord, visit of, at Heslington, 149, 153; lines on, 153; visit to, at Edinburgh, 192; letters to, on the principles of the Edinburgh Review, 206; visit to Combe Florey, 228; Sydney Smith's regard for, 393; letters from, during last illness, 405; letters relating to Memoir, 414.
Johnson, Dr., anecdote of, 115.
Journal of a Lady, 315; of a Scotch friend, 392.
Justice, love of, 29, 234.
Justice of the Peace, Sydney Smith becomes a, 164.

Kay, Annie, 163, 180, 355, 409.

Labels, doctors', 375.
Lectures, extracts from, 39, 40; delivery of, at the Royal Institution, 81; public interest excited by, 81–83.
Legacy, 191.
Lemons, store of, 357.
Leyden, Mr., 21.
Liberal opinions, advocacy of, 27; penalties attending, 28.
Liberty, views respecting, 26.
License for a chapel, efforts to obtain, 69; correspondence relating to, 69–76.
Life, how usually spent, 318.
Londesborough, obtains the living of, 204.
London, removal to, 65; society in, 66, 77, 88, 257, 259.
Longevity, 316.
Lucan, a copy of, sent to Mr. Grenville, 286.
Luttrell, Mr., visit of, 374.
Lyndhurst, Lord, visit of, 188; promotion by, 216; renewed kindness of, 225.

Macaulay, Mr., letter from, on English misrule in Ireland, 142; opinion of, 363.
Mackintosh, Sir J., anecdote of, 89; return of, from India, 150; visit of, at Heslington, 150; at Foston, 194; Sydney Smith's regard for, 195, 241; death of, 241; character, 242; correspondence with, 242; remarks on, 383, 387; imitation of a speech of, 387.
Manners, on the neglect of, as a part of education, 359.
Marcet, Dr. and Mrs., visit of, 183; incidents related by Mrs. Marcet, 183, 186, 330; letter from, 293.
Marion de Lorme, letter of, 384.
Marriage, 19; office for, 351; definition of, 363.
Maxims and rules of life, 120.
Medicine, study and practice of, 61–63, 117, 246, 355.

430   INDEX.

Melancholy, remedy for, 389.
Mind, the, a fragment on, 137.
Missions, opinion of, 376.
Moore, T., visit of, 287; letters from, 287-289; requested to write Memoir, 414.
Moral philosophy, study of, 63; lectures on, 81.
Murray's (Lord) sketch of Sydney Smith, 326.
Music, remark on, 389.

Netherhaven, curacy of, 10; life at, 11; intimacy with the squire, 12.
New Zealand, advice to a Bishop of, 383.
Newton, Sir Isaac, an ancestor, 3.
Nice person, definition of a, 196.
North Pole, Jeffrey and the, 17.

Occupation, incessant, 111; essay on, 127.
Olier, Miss, character of, 2-4.
Opinions, moderation of, 25, 26.

Paris, visit to, 205.
Parish-clerk at Foston, 107.
Parishioners, advice to, 337.
Parsonage-house at Foston, account of building the, 158; removal to, 161.
Partington, Mrs., 241.
Paul's, St., becomes Canon of, 241; letter from Mr. Cockerell relating to Canonry, 248; remarks of the Dean, 252.
Peasantry, significance of words used by the, 344.
Peel, Sir Robert, correspondence with, 312.
Peter the Cruel, 110, 117.
Philips, Sir G., visit to, 166.
Pictures, purchase of, 96; appreciation of, 269, 270.
Plymley's Letters, appearance of, 102; public interest in, 102; letter from Lord Holland relating to, 104.
Poor, sympathy with the, 352, 393, 394.
Pope, parody on, 376.
Preaching at St. Paul's, impression produced by, 306; at Combe Florey, 399.
Preferment, letters on, 233-236.
Promotion, hopes of, 207; letter on, 208; becomes Canon of Bristol, 215, and of St. Paul's, 241.
Pybus, Miss, marriage to, 19.

Quaker, roasting a, 146.
Quakers, heroic conduct of, 172.

Raven, anecdote of a, 317.
Reading, rapid, habit of, 111.
Religious views, 51.
Repudiation, American, 297; Mr. Ticknor's letter on, 298.
Residence Bill, passing of the, 106.
Riding, unskilful, 172, 177.
Robin, M., article by, in the 'Revue des Deux Mondes,' 401; correspondence relating to, 402-404.
Rogers, Mr., visits Foston, 172; illness of, 195.
Romilly, Sir S., visit of, at Heslington, 144; sermon on the death of, 144.
Royal Institution, lectures at the, on Moral Philosophy, 81.
Russell, Lord John, letter to, 235; reply of, 236.

Salad, recipe for, 373.
Scotch, regard for the, 14; peculiarities of the, 15, 16.
Scratcher, the universal, 118.
Screaming gate, the, 350.
Sermons, preface to, 41-51; characteristics of, 56-60; effect produced by, 80; publishes two volumes of, 108; preached at York, 198.
Sévigné, Madame de, 376.
Shaking hands, lesson on, 350.
Sheridan, dining with, 368.
Shooting, objections to, 144.
Shopping, 177.
Shyness, 262, 367.
Siddons, Mrs., 95, 378.
Singing, fondness for, 214.
Sister, death of, 168.

INDEX. 431

Sketches, a few unfinished, 125.
Smith, Robert, return of, from India, 149; remarkable conversational powers of, 150; Indian fame of, 151; visit of, at Heslington, 151; illness, 151; visit to his brother during last illness, 411; death, 411; character, 412; lines written by, 414.
Smith, Robert, sen., singular character of, 1, 2; visit to, 189.
Smith, Sydney: birth and ancestry, 1, 2; early character, 5; school days at Winchester, 7; goes to Oxford, 8; residence in France, 8; college life, 9; choice of a profession, 10; becomes a curate on Salisbury Plain, 10; engaged as tutor by Mr. Beach, 12, 60; arrival at Edinburgh, 13; marriage, 18; his fortune, 19; early housekeeping, 20; generosity, 20, 21; birth of daughter, 22; moral courage, 24; freedom from crude opinions, 25, 26; illness of daughter, 61; studies medicine, 63; quits Edinburgh, 64; birth of son, 65; removal to London, 65; cheerfulness, 95, 224; obtains the rectory of Foston, 100; removes to Sunning, 101; compelled to reside on living, 107; leaves London, 109; removes to Heslington, 110; visits London, 150; generosity of character, 149, 151, 179; commences building, 156; birth of second son, 160; removal to Foston, 161; the living of Ampthill offered, 176; visits Edinburgh, 182, 192; visit to his brother in London, 192; improved circumstances, 204; visits Paris, 205; hopes of promotion, 207; marriage of youngest daughter, 215; becomes Canon of Bristol, 215; resigns Foston, and removes to Combe Florey, 225; ceases writing for the Edinburgh Review, 229; publishes his contributions, 230; marriage of eldest daughter, 243; christens granddaughter, 246; takes a house in London, 247; revisits Paris, 247; fragments of conversation, 258–270; return to Combe Florey, 279; unexpected wealth, 280; revisits Foston, 281; mode of life at Combe Florey, 330, 388, 394; habits of study, 370; last return to London, 401; goes to the seaside, 408; last illness, 408; anxiety of friends, 409; visit of his brother Robert, 411.
Somersetshire, climate of, 346.
Squire, a country, 157.
Staël, Madame de, visits England, 150; becomes acquainted with Mr. Robert Smith, 150.
Stewart, Dugald, death of, 269.
Stomach-pump, 357.
Stowell, Lord, 104.
Study, plans of, 113.
Style, beauty of, 335.
Suppers, weekly, 88; the country cousin, 89.
Swing, Letters to, 237.

Talleyrand, anecdote of, 4; acquaintance with, 205; conversation of, 255; opinion of his wit, 255.
Taunton, speech at county meeting held at, 231; effect produced by, 232.
Taylor, Jeremy, apologue by, on Toleration, 218.
Thomson, Mrs., letter to, relating to the death of his son, 225.
Ticknor, Mr., letter of, on repudiation, 298.
Toleration, 54; sermon on, in the Temple Church, 93, and in the Cathedral at Bristol, 216, 217; Taylor's apologue in illustration of, 218.
Travelling, amusing incidents of, 182.
Turtle, stroking a, 269; riding on a, 399.

Utilitarians, 334.

Van de Weyer, M., 254; letters to, 305, 323, 324; visit of, 323; letter from, relating to M. Robin, 401.
Visitation sermon, 177.
Vulgarity, freedom from, 37.
Volunteers, sermon to, 67.

Wainwright, Rev. J. M., of New York, letter from, 303.
Wealth, views of, 399.

Webster, Mr. Daniel, correspondence with, 283.
Wenlock, Lady, letter to, 225.
Whishaw, Mr., letter to, on the death of Horner, 170.
Winchester School, 6.
Writings, character and subjects of his, 30–37.

York, residence near, 109; streets of, 111; the assizes at, 188, 198; sermons preached at the Cathedral, 198.

END OF VOLUME I.

www.ingramcontent.com/pod-product-compliance
Lightning Source LLC
Chambersburg PA
CBHW031323230426
43670CB00006B/224